Toward an Integrative Medicine

Toward an Integrative Medicine

Merging Alternative Therapies with Biomedicine

HANS BAER

ALTAMIRA
PRESS

A Division of
ROWMAN & LITTLEFIELD PUBLISHERS, INC.
Walnut Creek • Lanham • New York • Toronto • Oxford

AltaMira Press
A division of Rowman & Littlefield Publishers, Inc.
1630 North Main Street, #367
Walnut Creek, CA 94596
www.altamirapress.com

Rowman & Littlefield Publishers, Inc.
A wholly owned subsidiary of The Rowman & Littlefield Publishing Group, Inc.
4501 Forbes Boulevard, Suite 200
Lanham, MD 20706

PO Box 317
Oxford
OX2 9RU, UK

British Library Cataloguing in Publication Information Available

Library of Congress Cataloging-in-Publication Data

Baer, Hans A., 1944-
  Toward an integrative medicine : merging alternative therapies with biomedicine / Hans Baer.
    p. ; cm.
  Includes bibliographical references and index.
  ISBN 0-7591-0301-1 (hardcover : alk. paper) — ISBN 0-7591-0302-X (pbk. : alk. paper)
  1. Integrative medicine. 2. Holistic medicine. 3. Alternative medicine.
[DNLM: 1. Holistic Health. 2. Complementary Therapies. W 61 B1412t 2004]
  I. Title.

R733.B225 2004
613—dc22

2004010638

Printed in the United States of America

∞™ The paper used in this publication meets the minimum requirements of American National Standard for Information Sciences—Permanence of Paper for Printed Library Materials, ANSI/NISO Z39.48-1992.

613
Ba

Contents

Acknowledgments

Numerous institutions, organizations, and individuals contributed to my understanding of the holistic health and complementary and alternative medicine/integrative medicines movements in the United States. Students in my class on medical pluralism in North America and Europe at the University of California, Berkeley, in spring 1994 provided me with important insights into the holistic health movement and acupuncture and Oriental medicine in the San Francisco Bay Area through both their miniethnographies and their conversations with me on alternative therapeutic systems. While I was a visiting professor at Arizona State University in 1997–1998, certain students provided me with insights on alternative medicine through various ethnographic projects that they did in my classes. Furthermore, the students in my seminar on comparative health systems at George Washington University in spring 2003 provided me with insights into various complementary and alternative medicine or integrative medicine sites in the Washington, D.C., area based on the ethnographic projects that they conducted for my class.

The following people in particular have contributed to my insights on alternative medical systems in the United States: Alan Adams, Robert Anderson, Ian Coulter, Joe Keating, Caroline Peterson, and Walter Wardwell on chiropractic; Damien Brandeis, Robert Broadwell, Michael Cronin, Louise Edwards, Joanna Hagan, Ron Hobbs, Joe Pizzorno, Jim Sensenig, David Sleich, Stephen Sporn, Karen Vandeveer, Susan Williams, and JoAnn Ynez on naturopathic medicine; Dana Ullman on homeopathy; Janneli Miller on herbalism; Kathy Sanders on massage therapy; and Jill Crewes and Robbie Davis-Floyd on "direct-entry" or lay midwifery. I also gleaned many insights about alternative medicine in the course of giving lectures at the Canadian Memorial College of Chiropractic in Toronto, the Palmer College of Chiropractic in Davenport (Iowa), and the Los Angeles Chiropractic College and at American Association of Naturopathic Physicians meetings, the Northwest Naturopathic Conference, and an Arizona Naturopathic Medical Association conference, as well as while attending numerous classes at the Southwest College of Naturopathic Medicine in Tempe, Arizona.

I am highly indebted to David J. Hess at Rensselaer Polytechnic Institute and an anonymous reader for having read an early draft of this book in its entirety and to Janneli Miller for her input in the section on herbalism. I also appreciate the willingness of the *Medical Anthropology Quarterly* to incorporate into this book material from my article titled "The Work of Andrew Weil and Deepak Chopra—Two Holistic Health/New Age Gurus: A Critique of the Holistic Health/New Age Movements," which appeared in the June 2003 issue of that journal. Last but not least, I appreciate the assistance that Rosalie Robertson has provided me, not only with the publication of this book but with two others, namely, *Recreating Utopia in the Desert: A Sectarian Challenge to Modern Mormonism* while she was an editor at the State University of New York Press and *Biomedicine and Alternative Healing Systems in America* while she was an editor at the University of Wisconsin Press.

Introduction

In contrast to tribal or indigenous societies, each of which has a more or less coherent medical system that is an integral part of the larger sociocultural system, complex or state societies manifest the coexistence of an array of medical systems or a pattern of medical pluralism that is part and parcel of their socially stratified and culturally diverse nature. From this perspective, the medical system of a society consists of the totality of medical subsystems that coexist in a cooperative or, more often, competitive relationship with one another. In modern industrial or postindustrial societies, in addition to biomedicine, the dominant medical subsystem, one finds other medical subsystems, such as homeopathy, osteopathy, chiropractic, naturopathy, religious healing systems, and folk medical systems. Patterns of medical pluralism tend to reflect hierarchical relations in the larger society. Patterns of hierarchy may be based on class, caste, racial, ethnic, regional, religious, and gender divisions.

This book represents a sequel to a previous book titled *Biomedicine and Alternative Healing Systems in America* (2001). That book chronicles the evolution of U.S. medicine from a pluralistic system—one in which regular medicine (also known as biomedicine) was the predominant but not clearly dominant system in an array of alternative healing modalities—in the nineteenth century to a dominative system—one in which biomedicine became clearly dominant over alternative approaches—in the twentieth century.

In state societies, alternative medical systems or health movements often exhibit counterhegemonic elements that resist, often in subtle forms, the elitist, hierarchical, bureaucratic, and iatrogenic aspects of biomedicine. Alternative or heterodox medical systems often are initiated by individuals or people who reject some important aspect of biomedicine. Although their theories of disease causation may be more naturalistic than personalistic, many scholars have likened them to religious sects. Indeed, healing often is part and parcel of certain religious movements, such as Spiritualism, Christian Science, Unity, Religious Science, Pentecostalism, the charismatic movement, and Scientology. Furthermore, religion and healing almost always are intertwined in both indigenous medical systems and folk medical systems in complex societies. Just as churches or denominations castigate unconventional religious groups as "cults" or "sects," historically there has been a strong tendency for biomedicine to refer to heterodox medical systems in the same manner (Fishbein 1932; Reed 1932).

Wardwell, however, questions the utility of comparing the model of medical orthodoxy and medical sects with the sect–denomination model in the sociology of religion:

> Since there can be a number of different religious denominations at one time, any religious sect has the potential for evolving into a denomination, although it normally has to modify its theology in order to accommodate to the established social order. Medical sects, however, do not evolve into denominations. As they evolve, they tend to merge into the medical mainstream. (Wardwell 1972:763)

New medical systems or synthetic ensembles of therapies, such as the popular health movement in the nineteenth century or the holistic health movement in the twentieth century, may be viewed as health movements. According to Roth, as a new health movement grows, particularly in capitalist societies, it accumulates

> more and more members who are interested in making a good living and raising their status in the outer world. In the health sphere, this means they become more concerned with obtaining respectable (or at least respectable-looking) credentials, providing services that more closely follow the medical model, and eventually even developing working relationships with the orthodox medical world. (Roth 1976:40–41)

Roth (1976:120–22) maintains that a health movement that goes beyond this middle stage may follow one of four paths: (1) evolution into the dominant form of medicine (e.g., biomedicine); (2) merger with the dominant medical system (e.g., homeopathy and eclecticism in the early twentieth century); (3) steady decline and perhaps eventual extinction (e.g., hydropathy); and (4) absorption by the dominant medical system as an auxiliary practice (e.g., pharmacy and physical therapy). In addition to these possible outcomes, an alternative medical system may evolve into a parallel form of medicine (e.g., osteopathic medicine in the United States) that has the same legal rights and closely resembles both philosophically and therapeutically the dominant medical system. Finally, a heterodox or alternative medical system may develop into a semilegitimate or even fully legitimate "limited form of medicine." Some health practitioners, such as dentists, podiatrists, optometrists, and psychologists, function independently of biomedicine but "limit the range of procedures, instruments, or techniques they use in treatment" (Wardwell 1992:43–44). In their drive for legitimation, emerging health groups generally must appeal to certain strategic elites in the larger society (Larkin 1983).

In my discussion of various partially professionalized or lay heterodox medical systems in the United States in chapter 6 of *Biomedicine and Alternative Healing Systems in America*, I situate them in the context of the holistic health movement that emerged in the early 1970s and came to encompass an extremely varied assortment of alternative medical therapies and practices. Although a wide variety of alternatives to biomedicine have existed around the globe, many alternative medical systems underwent either a growth spurt or even a comeback under the umbrella of this popular movement, particularly in Western societies such as the United States, Canada, Britain, Germany, the Netherlands, the Scandinavian countries, and Australia (Goldstein 1999; Sharma 1992; Cant and Sharma 1996; Schepers and Hermans 1998; Kelner and Wellman 2000). The holistic health movement is by no means a monolithic phenomenon and varies considerably from society to society. It encompasses an extremely variegated assortment of alternative medical systems, such as homeopathy, herbalism, naturopathy, and bodywork, with divergent philosophical premises. Although it appears to have its strongest expression in Western societies, it draws heavily upon various Eastern healing systems, such as Chinese medicine and Ayurveda. To a large extent, the holistic health movement overlaps with the New Age movement, which has also become very popular in Western societies and varies in its expression depending on the national context. Like the holistic health movement, New Ageism focuses on a balance in the interaction of mind, body, and spirit in its attempts to achieve experiential health and well-being. New Ageism also incorporates many therapeutic techniques and practices, including meditation, guided visualization, channeling, rebirthing, psychic healing, and neoshamanism.

This book focuses on the social transformation of the holistic health and New Age movement over the course of the past three decades within the context of the United States. Just as various alternative healing approaches, including hydropathy, vegetarianism, and Grahamanism, emerged in the early nineteenth century under the umbrella of what medical historians have termed the popular health movement as a response to the inadequacies of regular or "heroic" medicine, the holistic health movement as a popular phenomenon began to appear on the West Coast in the early 1970s and quickly became intertwined with New Ageism as it expanded to other parts of the United States as well as to other countries, including Canada, Australia, Britain, and various northwestern European nations. Perhaps inspired by the experimental ethos of the time, various biomedical and osteopathic physicians and particularly nurses as well as biomedical schools began also to take an interest in alternative therapies and discussed the development of an integrative medicine.

Although chiropractic had already achieved some semblance of legitimacy by the early 1970s as the result of hard-fought campaigns going back to its emergence in the late nineteenth century, the holistic health movement not only contributed to its ongoing legitimation but also provided the space that contributed to the rejuvenation of naturopathy (an alternative medical system that began to emerge around 1900) and the expansion of Oriental medicine and acupuncture (an alternative system that gained considerable legitimacy due to the new open-door policy that the Nixon administration extended to the People's Republic of China) as professionalized heterodox medical systems. In part emulating the success stories of the chiropractors, naturopaths, and acupuncturists, various other alternative practitioners, including homeopaths, bodyworkers, and lay midwives, began to seek legitimation by creating professional associations and training institutions as well as lobbying for licensing or certification.

By the late 1970s, an increasing number of biomedical and osteopathic physicians began to recognize both the limitations of their conventional approach to illness and the fact that they were losing many of their more affluent patients to alternative or heterodox practitioners. Gradually, these physicians began to incorporate alternative therapies into their practices, and some even became the directors of holistic health or integrative medicine centers where they coordinated the activities of an array of alternative therapists. A group of M.D.'s and D.O.'s established the American Holistic Medical Association in 1978. In time, more and more biomedical schools began to offer courses on alternative medicine—a process that still is in progress. Due to political pressure, Congress mandated the establishment of the Office of Alternative Medicine in 1992 (renamed the National Center for Complementary and Alternative Medicine in 1999) within the National Institutes of Health (NIH). The demise of the Clinton health plan in the early 1990s provided a shot in the arm to an already-expanding managed care industry. Health insurance, health maintenance organizations, and hospitals have become increasingly interested in alternative therapies as a way of satisfying patients' demands and curtailing costs.

THE SHIFT FROM HOLISTIC HEALTH TO COMPLEMENTARY AND ALTERNATIVE MEDICINE OR INTEGRATIVE MEDICINE

The basic premises of the holistic health movement are laid out in several resource guides that appeared in the late 1970s and early 1980s (Kaslof 1978; Otto and Knight 1979; Sobel 1979; Hastings, Fadiman, and Gordon 1980; Bauman et al. 1981; Bliss 1985). These sources include short essays on a wide variety of healing systems and therapeutic techniques by laypersons, alternative practitioners, and holistic M.D.'s and nurses and provide a baseline for a popular movement that has undergone major transformations in a matter of three decades or so.

While proponents of the holistic health movement vary in terms of what they regard to be the basic premises of the holistic health perspective, sociologist June S. Lowenberg (1989:15–50) presents a comprehensive overview of the core beliefs, meanings, and values exhibited by holistic health practitioners and patients. She delineates seven elements of the holistic health model: (1) holism, which entails the recognition of the uniqueness of each individual and the notion that the humanness entails the "interrelation of the physical, mental, emotional, spiritual, and social dimensions" (Lowenberg 1989:19); (2) an emphasis on health promotion; (3) the recognition that illness represents a state of imbalance or "dis-ease" in a person's life and provides an opportunity to alter one's lifestyle; (4) the belief that the patient's health ultimately is the patient's responsibility; (5) the notion that the health practitioner should mobilize the patient's innate healing capacity and act as an educator, consultant, and facilitator in an egalitarian and mutual relationship with the patient; (6) an openness to a variety of healing traditions and practices from many cultures, including Eastern and indigenous ones; and (7) a new consciousness that includes a present-time orientation and subjective and intuitive approaches to life. As will become more apparent in this book, these elements of holistic medicine are ideals, some of which are not fully adhered to in practice. For example, whereas the holistic health movement often subscribes to the assertion that the individual is part of a larger internal system that consists of a body, mind, and spirit and that this internal system is embedded in a larger sociocultural and natural environment, in most cases holistic practitioners give priority to mind–body–spirit connections over mind–body–spirit–society connections.

Ironically, holistic health as a popular movement is quickly being tamed and evolving into a professionalized entity increasingly referred to as *complementary and alternative medicine* (CAM) or *integrative medicine*. *Alternative medicine* generally refers to all medical systems or therapies lying outside the purview of biomedicine that are used *instead* of it. *Complementary medicine* refers to medical systems or therapies that are used *alongside* or as adjuncts to biomedicine. Finally, *integrative medicine* refers to efforts on the part of conventional physicians to blend biomedical and CAM therapies or the collaborative efforts between biomedical physicians and CAM practitioners to address health care needs of specific patients. The shift from a discussion of holistic health, holistic medicine, or simply alternative medicine to CAM or integrative medicine over the past decade or so is perhaps most apparent in the titles of various books and periodicals. During that time, numerous biomedical practitioners have written overviews of CAM (Rosenfeld 1996; Bratman 1997; Jonas and Levin 1999; Novey 2000; Diamond 2001; Micozzi 2001). The shift from holistic health to CAM is also exemplified by an article titled "The Evolution of Complementary and Alternative Medicine in the United States: The Push and Pull of Holistic Health Care into the Medical Mainstream" (Caplan, Harrison, and Galantiono 2003).

Defining CAM

Scholars have proposed various typologies of CAM therapies. Fulder (1996:107) delineates five "therapeutic modalities of complementary medicine": (1) ethnic medical systems, such as acupuncture and Chinese medicine and Ayurveda; (2) manual therapies, such as osteopathy, chiropractic, massage, Alexander technique, and reflexology; (3) therapies for "mind-body," such as hypnotherapy, psychic healing, radionics, and anthrosophical medicine; (4) nature-cure therapies, such as naturopathy and hygienic methods; and (5) nonallopathic medicinal systems, such as homeopathy and herbalism.

Kaptchuk and Eisenberg (2001) present a typology of "unconventional healing practices" based on the following CAM sectors: (1) professionalized or distinct medical systems; (2) popular health reform (alternative dietary and lifestyle practices); (3) New Age healing; (4) psychological interventions: mind cure and "mind–body" medicine; (5) nonnormative scientific enterprises; and (6) parochial unconventional medicine. Professionalized or distinct medical systems include chiropractic, acupuncture, homeopathy, naturopathy, massage, and dual-functioning (or holistic) M.D.'s. Popular health reform practices include health food stores, popular health books and journals, charismatic health leaders, alternative provider recommendations, and neighborly health advice. New Age healing draws a wide array of religions (e.g., Hinduism, Christianity, Buddhism, neopaganism) and energy healing therapies (e.g., crystals, qi gong, Reiki). Psychological interventions draw from either Mind Cure or New Thought (e.g., visualizations, affirmations, meditations), psychotherapy, or cognitive-behavioral psychology. Nonnormative scientific enterprises tend to appeal to patients with highly dangerous diseases, such as cancer, and include therapies such as Livingston-Wheeler pleomorphis bacteria cancer vaccine and hair analysis, which purportedly detects many diseases and nutrient imbalances. Parochial unconventional medicine includes three main categories: (1) ethnomedicine (e.g., *curanderismo* among Mexican Americans and Native American healing systems); (2) folk medicine practices (e.g., wearing of copper bracelets for arthritis); and (3) religious healing (e.g., faith healing, Christian Science, Mind Cure).

Tataryn (2002) presents an elaborate typology based on four broad categories of paradigms of health and disease: (1) body-based paradigms, (2) mind–body paradigms, (3) body–energy paradigms, and (4) body–spirit paradigms. Body therapies focus on physical substances, including diets and supplements (e.g., herbal remedies, macrobiotics), extracts and concentrates (e.g., laetrile, ozone therapy), or chemicals/synthetics (e.g., chemotherapy, chelation therapy); and physical manipulation (e.g., massage, chiropractic, colonic irrigation, surgery). Body–mind therapies include affirmations/ suggestion, counseling, hypnosis, imagery/visualization, meditation, psy-chotherapy, stress reduction, and support groups. Body–energy therapies include acupressure, acupuncture, Chinese medicine, homeopathy, polarity therapy, reflexology, Reiki, therapeutic touch, and yoga. Body–spirit thera-pies include ceremonies, exorcism, faith healing, indigenous or "First Na-tions" healing, prayer, psychic healing, and shamanism.

Based on these typologies, what has come to be termed *complementary and alternative medicine* is an amorphous category that encompasses many med-ical systems and therapies. As in any typology, categories of CAM in the three schemes discussed overlap with each. Also, all of the schemes tend to privilege Western and Asian therapies over indigenous, folk, and religious therapies. Furthermore, the distinction between conventional and alternative medicine is a matter of historical circumstances and sociocultural setting (Frohock 2002). For example, whereas osteopathy emerged as a distinct alternative medicine system in the late nineteenth century, in the United States it has evolved into osteopathic medicine and surgery or a parallel medical system to biomedicine and can for the most part be included within the rubric of con-ventional medicine. Conversely, in other Anglophile countries—namely, Canada, Britain, and Australia—osteopathy, like chiropractic, continues to function primarily as a manual medical system and can be still categorized as complementary or alternative.

Cassidy (2002) correctly argues that biomedical hegemony pervades the notion of CAM:

> This issue of the dominant practice versus "all others" lies behind the whole concept of CAM, which is surely a misperception that we should be just about ready to give up. For, if we are agreed that there are many medicines and that they can be sorted in terms of their philosophical underpinnings, then we must come to see that *all* are alternatives, and *all* can complement others. In short, biomedicine ought not to be treated as the standard against which all others are compared (which remains all too common) but as one among many, itself a complementary and alternative practice. (894)

Indeed, Wolpe (2002:165) argues that CAM is "what sociologists refer to as a residual category" in that it is "defined not by its internal coherence but by its exclusion from other categories of medicine."

In contrast to the aforementioned schemes, which preclude biomedicine, Nienstedt (1998) presents a "model of complementary medicine and practice," which includes it. Her typology delineates four categories or quadrants: (1) biomedicine (e.g., M.D.'s, D.O.'s, dentists, optometrists, podiatrists, psychologists, pharmacists, nurses, physician assistants, medical technologists, physical therapists, dietitians); (2) body healing alternatives (e.g., chiropractors, homeopaths, medical herbalists, naturopaths, colonic therapists, massage therapists, nutrition counselors, reflexologists, iridologists, and aromatherapists); (3) mind–spirit alternatives (e.g., Christian Scientists, Edgar Cayce healers, charismatic Catholic healers, hypnotherapists, psychic healers, transcendental meditation); and (4) cross-cultural alternatives (e.g., yoga, shamanism, Ayurveda, folk medicine, Reiki therapists, shiatsu, Chinese acupuncture, Native American healers). Although Nienstedt's scheme includes biomedicine, it does not make any reference to the power difference that exists between biomedicine and other medical and therapeutic systems. In passing, it should be noted that Kelner and Wellman (2000:6) recognize that a pecking order does exist with plural medical systems by noting that one "useful way to classify CAM therapies is based on the extent of legitimacy and public acceptance: (1) top of the hierarchy (osteopathy, chiropractic, and acupuncture); (2) middle range (naturopathy and homeopathy); (3) bottom of the hierarchy (rebirthing and Reiki)."

I developed a model of medical pluralism in the United States that recognizes biomedical hegemony and recognizes such power differences within plural medical systems. I refer to this model as the *dominative medical system* because of the fact that biomedicine exerts dominance over other medical or therapeutic systems (Baer 1989, 2001). I based my scheme on the thesis that the principal practitioners of each medical subsystem tend to be drawn from specific classes, racial and ethnic categories, and genders depending on their status in the larger society. Thus, the U.S. dominative medical system consists of the levels depicted in figure A.1. With some modification, I believe that the model of the dominative medical system can be applied to other societies. For the most part, the therapeutic systems that fall under the rubric of CAM tend to follow under the categories of professionalized, partially professionalized, and lay heterodox medical systems. Within this framework, for example, whereas M.D.'s tend to be white, upper- and upper-middle-class males, folk healers tend to be working-class women of color.

Defining Integrative Medicine

Integrative medicine or integrative health care has come to refer to a "system of medicine that integrates conventional care with CAM" (Cohen 1998:2). Diamond (2001:14) argues that the terms *alternative* and *complementary* are divisive and should be discarded by integrative or integrated medicine. In many cases, however, the terms *CAM* and *integrative medicine* are used interchangeably (see Milton and Benjamin 1999). In *Integrative Health Care: Complementary and Alternative Therapies for the Whole Person*,

---

Biomedicine
Osteopathic Medicine (a parallel medical system focusing on primary care)
Professionalized Heterodox Medical Systems
   Chiropractic
   Naturopathy
   Oriental medicine and acupuncture
Partially Professionalized or Lay Heterodox Medical Systems
   Homeopathy
   Herbalism
   Bodywork
   Body–Mind Medicine
   Midwifery
Anglo-American Religious Healing Systems
   Spiritualism
   Seventh-Day Adventism
   New Thought Healing Systems (Christian Science, Unity, Religious Science, etc.)
   Pentecostalism
   Scientology
Folk Medical Systems
   European American Folk Medicine
   African American Folk Medicine
   Vodun
   Curanderismo
   Espiritismo
   Santería
   Chinese American Folk Medicine
   Japanese American Folk Medicine
   Hmong American Folk Medicine
   Native American Healing Traditions

FIGURE A.1.
The U.S. Dominative Medical System

as brown rice, whole grain bread, herbal teas, and soy products, all of which could be purchased in bulk. As sources of health information and moral support, the co-ops were indispensable. (89)

Food cooperatives and the large chains, such as Wild Oats, that grew out of them evolved into important purveyors of botanicals, vitamin and nutritional supplements, and natural foods as well as books and magazines on alternative therapies (Cox 1994). They also offer important venues for alternative practitioners to advertise their services and even offer classes and workshops. As Miller (1991:135) observes, "many a suburban family now has food concerns that were once the province of far-out hippies." In keeping with their hang-loose attitude, the hippies also explored Eastern mysticism, Sufism, Native American traditions, the Jewish Kabbalah, astrology, and various Western occult traditions.

The Human Potential Movement

Alster (1989:36) maintains that the holistic health movement has a "clear but indirect link" with humanistic psychology. The human potential movement emerged from a number of sources in the United States during the mid-1960s and spread throughout the English-speaking world and Europe (Wallis 1985:23). It claimed to be concerned with the quality of both personal and social life in the modern world and emerged out of social skills training or t-groups. It drew heavily from humanistic psychology, particularly from the work of Abraham Maslow, Carl Rogers, and Fritz Perls (Plumb 1993:4). The human potential movement eventually splintered into three parts: transpersonal psychology, experiential encounter, and radical therapy. It also drew on therapeutic approaches such as vegetarianism, natural birthing, transcendental meditation, yoga, Arica, psychosynthesis, Silva mind control, transactional analysis, biofeedback, est, bioenergetics, and psychic healing (Stone 1976). According to Westley (1983:185), "most human potential movements, despite the temptations of tax shelters, overtly refute the religious label and claim to be therapies."

Given the liberal and radical political leanings of many of its participants, the human potential movement also incorporated aspects of participatory democracy, environmentalism, and feminism. David Harris, the founder of the Association of Holistic Health and Mandala Society in San Diego, was active in the human potential movement and cofounded the National Center for the Exploration of Human Potential (Lowenberg 1989:73). The Association for Humanistic Psychology, headquartered in San Francisco, served as the professional and research arm of the human potential movement. It grew out of the *Journal of Humanistic Psychology* started by Abraham Maslow and Anthony Sutich. Other founders included Eric Fromm, Carl Rogers, Viktor Frankl, Rollo May, and Charlotte Buhler.

An assortment of encounter groups put human potential philosophy in action. Several hundred human potential groups ran the continuum from the more conservative t-groups, such as the National Training Laboratories (founded in 1947) in Bethel, Maine, to the more avant-garde growth centers, such as the Esalen Institute on the West Coast, to various self-help groups. Synanon consisted of various self-help communities (primarily in California) oriented to recovering alcohol and drug addicts (Ofshe 1976). Esalen, founded by Michael Murphy and Richard Price in 1961 and based in Big Sur and San Francisco, was the oldest and best known of the growth or encounter centers and attracted some twenty-five thousand people per year. Speakers during its peak included luminaries such as Alan Watts, Arnold Toynbee, Ken Kesey, Paul Tillich, Norman O. Brown, Rollo May, Carl Rogers, and Carlos Castaneda (Moskowitz 2001:230). Abraham Maslow also made frequent appearances at Esalen that focused on self-awareness and overcoming inhibitions. Taylor (1999:238) maintains that the Esalen Institute "became known as the modern temple of the body, the growth center of the new millennium, and a mecca for the American counterculture movement." While it officially had a no-drugs policy, it informally experimented with psychedelic drugs and also drew on massage, Rolfing, shiatsu, polarity therapy, Feldenkreis, Gestalt therapy, tai chi, meditation, psychosynthesis, Sufism, prayer, art, music, poetry, and Gestalt therapy. Fritz Perls became therapist-in-residence at Esalen in 1964. Werner Erhard became another human potential guru when he established est (Erhard training) in 1971. He had attended seminars in sensitivity training and group awareness at Esalen in 1962 and 1964 (Taylor 1999:251) and drew on Zen Buddhism, Scientology, and various therapeutic systems (Chryssides 1999:279). Est reportedly provided training for some eighty-three thousand people in twelve cities during its first year of operation (Moskowitz 2001:236). Encounter groups provided Americans with a "dignified setting for the exploration of sexual and sensual feeling" (Stone 1976:109). They began to wane in popularity in the late 1970s.

Reichian Psychotherapy

Freund (1982:22–23) argues that much of holistic medicine is neo-Reichian or post-Reichian in that, like Wilhelm Reich, who sought to synthesize Freudianism and Marxism, it acknowledges a relationship between repressive social structures and muscular armor or tension. Grossinger (1990:305) argues that what he terms "post-Reichian bodywork" has incorporated elements from Zen Buddhism, yoga, chiropractic, Alexander technique, and Feldenkreis. Alexander Lowen is a prominent neo-Reichian therapist who has furthered the bioenergetic approach that emphasizes emotions rather than performance as traditional Reichian therapy does.

Psychosomatic Medicine, the Wellness Movement, and Humanistic Medicine

Psychiatrist Franz Alexander and his colleagues at the Chicago Institute for Psychoanalysis discovered organic ailments could be related to patients' emotional states, thus paving the way for psychosomatic medicine and the formation of the Academy of Psychoanalytic Medicine in 1954 (Otto and Knight 1979:6–7). Flanders Dunbar, M.D., also played an instrumental role in the development of psychosomatic medicine by authoring *Mind and Body: Introduction to Psychosomatic Medicine* (1955). Halpert Dunn first addressed the concept of wellness in the early 1960s in his book *High Level Wellness* (1961). John Travis established the first wellness center in California in the 1970s (Bright 2002:11). Engel (1977) introduced the concept of biopsychosocial medicine as an effort to further overcome biological reductionism in biomedicine and to integrate biological, psychological, and social domains in the study of health and disease (see Armstrong [1987] for a sociological critique of the limitations of this model). Kenneth R. Pelletier has served as a key proponent of initially humanistic medicine and later the holistic health movement. He authored *Mind as Healer, Mind as Slayer* (1977), *Toward a Science of Consciousness* (1978), and *Holistic Medicine* (1979) and presently serves as a clinical professor at the University of Maryland and the University of Arizona and as the director of the Corporate Health Improvement Program (Horrigan 2002).

Western Heterodox Medical Systems

Various heterodox medical systems, which were either relatively well established or struggling for survival, were able to capitalize on the rhetoric of the holistic health movement. As Porter so astutely observes, "Marginal medicine actually appealed to a sense of the whole person—the unity of mental and physical experience—and sometimes also to two other unities: the oneness of the person with the world, and the cooperation of patient and doctor" (Porter 1999:79–80).

Although chiropractic had already achieved some legitimacy by the early 1970s, it often sought to present itself as a drugless and comprehensive health care system that viewed the patient in a broad biopsychosocial context. Although naturopathy, unlike chiropractic, found itself in a desperate struggle for survival in the early 1970s, its theoretical vagueness and predilection for therapeutic eclecticism made it preadapted to the holistic health movement. As Rosch and Kearney (1985:1407) observe, "holistic medicine relies upon the utilization of naturopathic modalities of therapy rather than upon pharmacological agents or other artificial interventions." While various U.S. biomedical physicians had expressed an interest in acupuncture prior to the emergence of the holistic health movement, its Chinese roots and emphasis on the flow of energy also made it amendable to the holistic health movement. At the founding convention of the American Association of Acupuncturists and Oriental Medicine in Los Angeles in 1981, R. A. Dale proclaimed:

> Acupuncture is a part of a larger struggle going on today between the old and new, between dying and rebirthing, between the very decay and death of our species and our fullest liberation. Acupuncture is part of a New Age which facilitates integral health and flowering of our humanity. (quoted in Skrabanek 1985:191)

Eastern Philosophy, Religion, and Medical Systems

The 1960s and the 1970s witnessed the advent of a "new religious consciousness" or what various sociologists have termed "new religious movements" (NRMs), which either were Asian imports or drew on Eastern metaphysical systems. As Fuller (1989:96) observes, "what Eastern philosophies provide adherents of sundry American healing systems is legitimation of their belief in the existence of 'subtle energies' and the efficacy of certain meditational states of consciousness in opening individuals to wide ranges of experience unattainable through reason or sensory awareness alone." The Hart-Celler Immigration Law of 1965 paved the way for a new wave of Asian immigrants who exposed European Americans to traditional forms of Buddhism (particularly Zen and Tibetan Buddhism) and Hinduism, both of which stressed meditation and detachment from the world. Indeed, the beatniks of the 1950s, inspired particularly by the likes of Alan Watts, Alan Ginsburg, and Jack Kerouac, expressed an even earlier interest in Zen Buddhism.

Transcendental meditation (TM) was introduced into the United States by Maharishi Mehesh Yogi (born 1911), who visited the United States first in 1959 and many times during the 1960s. TM, which consists of yogic meditation techniques designed to reduce stress and enhance self-awareness, proclaimed that it could serve as the portal to joy and ecstasy. Bainbridge (1997:187) describes it as a "highly simplified form of Hinduism, adapted for Westerners who did not possess the cultural background to accept the full panoply of Hindu beliefs, symbols, and practices." It overlapped with the human potential movement (Williams 2002:476) and found widespread appeal in the hippie counterculture. The maharishi established the Students International Meditation Society, which had branches at over a thousand U.S. campuses during the 1970s (Eck 2001:109). In 1974, he purchased the campus of the bankrupt Parsons College in Fairfield, Iowa, and established Maharishi International University (D'Antonio 1992:242–88). He played an instrumental role in exposing the U.S. public to Ayurveda (Reddy 2002).

Hatha yoga, the practice of physical control and accompanying meditation, also became very popular during the 1960s and 1970s. New Eastern religions, such as Soka Gakkai from Japan, ISKCON (the Hare Krishna sect), and Reverend Moon's Unification from South Korea, were also imported during the 1960s and probably raised the receptiveness of Americans to Eastern healing techniques. Dawson delineates the following attributes of the new religious consciousness: (1) a marked individualism focusing on what religious commitment can do for the individual rather than society or the group, (2) an emphasis on religious experience as opposed to belief or dogma, (3) the fostering of ecstasy that in turn leads to enlightenment on the part of the believer, (4) a syncretism that entails a tolerant incorporation of elements from different religious traditions, (5) an emphasis on holism and rejection of dualism, and (6) flexible organizational structures.

The Feminist Movement and Its Associated Natural Birthing Movement

As part of the feminist or women's liberation movement that began to emerge in the late 1960s, women began to take control of their bodies and established self-help gynecology clinics (Morgen 2002). The California Feminist Women's Health Centers offered participatory gynecology clinics where women met in a relaxed atmosphere with self-help workers and a female M.D. or nurse practitioner (Ruzek 1981:566). The Boston Women's Health Book Collective's *Our Bodies, Ourselves* (1998)—a volume that has gone through several editions—emphasized the need for women to assume responsibility for their bodies and to recognize mind–body–spirit connections in addressing health problems. The feminist movement challenged male domination in the physician–patient relationship, questioned the competency of biomedical physicians, and pointed out the existence of various iatrogenic practices, such as the negative side effects of oral contraceptives (Lowenberg 1989:67–68). Many women became interested in natural therapies as a gentler and kinder form of health care. The natural birthing movement and the lay midwifery movement among white middle-class women derived from the desire both to engage in "natural" health practices and to empower themselves.

The Environmental Movement

The environmental movement drew inspiration from the civil rights movement, the anti–Vietnam War movement, the farm workers' movement, the hippie movement, the women's liberation movement, and the New Left (Gordon 1980; Bright 2002:10). As Grossinger (1995a:483) observes, "the medical crisis parallels an ecological one: short-sighted, goal-oriented, and materialistic responses to intricate and subtle organic processes lead to iatrogenic diseases, a degraded biosphere, and, of course, addiction to more of the same in increasingly simplified loops of diagnosis and treatment." On the whole, the holistic health movement came to draw more on deep ecology than either the social ecology associated with anarchist Murray Bookchin and ecosocialism or eco-Marxism. Deep ecology views humans as an integral part of the natural environment and thus maintains that they should try to live in harmony with it. It draws on Eastern philosophies or religions such as Taoism, Buddhism, and Hinduism because they regard nature passively and stresses the need for "each individual to change attitudes, values and lifestyles to emphasise respect for and peaceful cooperation with nature" (Pepper 1996:21). Deep ecology tends to equate cosmic holism with holistic health. In this view, "[p]olluting the body with drugs, alcohol, and white bread is the personal version of polluting the planet with nuclear waste, toxic chemicals, and pesticides" (Zimmerman 1994:83).

THE NEW AGE MOVEMENT AND ITS INTEREST IN HEALING

The holistic health movement overlaps considerably with the New Age movement. Alice Bailey, the founder of the Arcane School, reportedly coined the phrase "New Age" in the 1920s and prophesized the coming of the Age of Aquarius as a period of peace, harmony, and tranquility (Raschke 1988:333; Hess 1993:21). During the 1950s, various UFO groups in the United States viewed the purported appearance of alien aircraft from outer space as signs of an imminent "New Age" (Sutcliffe 2003:84). The New Age movement per se appears to have emerged in the late 1960s and early 1970s, particularly in the United States and Great Britain, but also in other parts of the world (Prince and Riches 2000). York (1995:42) characterizes the New Age movement as "especially an American-Canadian-British-Dutch-West German-Australian-New Zealand phenomenon." Sutcliffe (2003) reports:

> entries for "New Age: faiths and practices:" Eight countries were represented: In a search I conducted on the worldwide web on 17 August 2001, Yahoo! found 228 US, UK, Canada, Australia, New Zealand, Denmark, Sweden, and—curiously— Turkey. The vast majority (171) were in the US (California alone amounting to one-third of this total) followed by Australia (20) and the UK (14). (226–27)

Despite a strong niche in particularly the Anglo-American world, the New Age movement seeks to bridge East–West connections, as is evidenced by the title of an important promulgator of its ideas, the *East–West Journal*.

According to Melton, Clark, and Kelly (1991:169), the "New Age and Holistic Health movements in theory exist independently, but are united philosophically by one central concept: that the individual person is responsible for his or her own life and for seeking out the means of transformation needed to achieve a better quality of life." New Agers are staunch romantics and critics of the technological and depersonalized nature of Western society. Sebald (1984) delineates the following characteristics of the New Age movement: (1) skepticism of science and technology, (2) an emphasis on natural healing, (3) an emphasis on small-scale economics, (4) a desire of a religious-spiritual reorientation, and (5) the creation of new reality and undoing of conventional norms. Like the holistic health movement, the New Age movement appears to have its most immediate roots in the human potential movement and the counterculture of the 1960s.

Although it has a "comparatively strong American flavour" (Hanegraaff 1998:97), it has spread to other parts of the world, particularly Anglophone countries as well as Western European countries, including Germany and Scandinavia. It also has drawn on (1) Western metaphysics, particularly Gnosticism, Swedenborgianism, spiritualism, Christian Science, New Thought, and theosophy; (2) Eastern religions, particularly Hinduism and Buddhism; (3) Jungianism; (4) neopaganism and particularly neoshamanism; and (5) an adaptation of new scientific paradigms, such as chaos theory and ones that emphasize the importance of energy in healing. In this regard, Hess (1993:37) asserts that New Agers "incorporate and rework the research of anthropologists, physicists, philosophers, and other scientists and scholars to legitimate a discourse that also sanctions crystal healing, channeling, astral bodies, goddess religion, and other beliefs and practices generally associated with popular culture." The New Age movement also stresses a this-worldly rather than other-worldly orientation, a holistic view of the interrelationship between the self and the cosmos, the evolution of consciousness, and the psychologization of religion or sacralization of psychology (Hanegraaff 1998:365–66).

New Agers seek to create a "new planetary culture" characterized by inner peace, wellness, unity, self-actualization, and attainment of higher consciousness. They believe that most, if not all, religions contain a hidden core of authentic spirituality (Hanegraaff 1998:327). Many New Agers view Christ as a personification of spiritual enlightenment and Buddha as having manifested the Christ Energy. Like other metaphysical movements, including New Thought, New Agers also tend to seek God within themselves (Bloom 1992:32). While some scholars have emphasized the significance of Eastern religious concepts in the New Age movement, others view it as the most recent expression of American metaphysical religion that historically has drawn on mesmerism, Swedenborgianism, Spiritualism, New England Transcendentalism, New Thought, and Theosophy (Albanese 1999a:353–56).

Prominent New Age spokespersons include David Spangler, Marilyn Ferguson, Jean Houston, Ram Dass, Fritof Capra, Shirley MacLaine, Michael Harner, and Matthew Fox. While residing in a New Age community called Findhorn in Scotland, David Spangler, an American, began channeling a supernatural entity calling itself "Limitless Love and Truth" on July 31, 1970 (Hanegraaff 1998:38). He became the theologian of the New Age movement by authoring *Revelation: The Birth of a New Age* (1976). Upon returning to the United States, Spangler discovered that his book had become essential reading in the emerging New Age movement. Since his initial fascination with channeling, he has disassociated himself from the channeling subculture and has come to speak "in tones of quiet authority about the need to create a better world" (Hanegraaff 1998:104).

Marilyn Ferguson authored an early manifesto titled *The Aquarian Conspiracy: Personal and Social Transformation* (1980) of the New Age movement. She argues that the world has embarked on an evolutionary process that begins with an accumulation of individual transformations that would lead to social networks that bring about more macroscopic changes.

Matthew Fox has emerged as an important link between mainstream Christianity and New Ageism. He is a former Dominican priest and now Episcopal priest who authored *The Coming of the Cosmic Christ* (1989) and *Creation Spirituality* (1990). He views creation spirituality as a synthesis of indigenous religions, Western mysticism, world religions, and cosmology and draws also from feminism, the social justice movement, and environmentalism.

Some New Agers define themselves as neopagans. According to Orion (1995:182), "almost every Neopagan thinks of him- or herself as a healer." Of the 189 neopagans in Orion's survey, 75.6 percent reported meditating; 73.0 percent, visualizing; 53.9 percent, using massage therapy; 53.9 percent, using herbs; 50.8 percent, using vitamin therapy; and 40.7 percent, using crystal healing. York (1995:146) argues that while there is some overlap between the New Age movement and neopaganism, the latter attempts to experience the supernatural more actively by engaging in collective ceremonies, and the former relies on meditation and other more passive rituals. Nevertheless, both movements emphasize attaining salvation in this life, particularly in the form of good health and tranquility. York (1995:146) contends that neoshamanism has been serving as a link between New Ageism and neopaganism. Neoshamanism is a movement that idealizes the shamanistic practices of Native Americans and other indigenous peoples around the world (Jakobsen 1999:147–206; Johnston 2002). Some Native Americans, however, regard New Age dabbling into shamanism as an illegitimate appropriation of their sacred traditions (Deloria 1998).

Healing, including the notion of holistic health, pervades the New Age movement (English-Lueck 1990:4; Hanegraaff 1998:119). Albanese (1993) describes New Age healing as follows:

> Healing . . . is a work of reconciliation predicated on communication. As such, healing in the new spirituality assumes a harmony of forces, a homeostasis that represents the balancing of physiological, emotional, and spiritual powers. But healing also means the power and freedom to act in decisive and effective ways. So healing, besides being harmonial, is also about having the vital force to take control of self and to leave one's imprint on a larger environment. (138)

New Age healing includes a seemingly endless proliferation of therapeutic techniques and practices, such as centering, channeling, astral projection, guided visualization, iridiology, reflexology, chromotherapy, rebirthing, and healing with the power of pyramids and crystals. New Agers tend to see matter and energy as intricately intertwined and believe that the latter is a vital component in efforts to reach self-actualization and transcendence over the mundane nature of everyday life. Levin and Coreil (1986) delineate three types of New Age healing approaches: (1) body-centered groups that stress secular and Western therapies, such as Silva mind control, that aim at psychosomatic health; (2) mind-oriented groups that draw on Western metaphysical or religious therapies, such as those associated with theosophy and Edgar Cayce's Association for Research and Enlightenment; and (3) soul-oriented groups that stress Buddhist and Hindu mystical practices, such as meditation.

Psychotherapists have been particularly prominent in New Age circles and have authored numerous New Age materials (Torgovnick 1996:180). Helen Cohn Schucman (1909–1981), a psychologist at Presbyterian Hospital in New York and an associate professor of medical psychology at Columbia University's medical school, became a central figure in the New Age movement when she published *A Course in Miracles* (1973)—a compilation consisting of a textbook, workbook, and teachers' manual. The contents of this work are based on dream images and symbols that the author received from a channel from 1965 to 1973. The text calls on humans to eradicate impediments to love and to nurture forgiveness of self and others. Albanese (1999a:351) asserts that *A Course in Miracles* blends Christian concepts of "forgiveness and reconciliation, with themes of the illusoriness of the world and the unreality of appearances." James Hillman, a renowned Jungian psychotherapist, along with his protégé Thomas More, the author of *Care of the Soul* (1997), have emerged as central figures in the New Age movement (Tacey 2001:118–30).

Although some observers have asserted that New Ageism has begun to go into decline, Sutcliffe (2003:113) maintains that in reality, it has evolved into a discourse of spirituality that "has become fairly comfortably established across the cultural spectrum as a symbolic repudiation of 'organised religion.'"

INSTITUTIONS PROPAGATING THE HOLISTIC HEALTH/NEW AGE MOVEMENT

Health food stores, many of which emerged as a result of the counterculture, have played a central role in disseminating information about holistic health and alternative therapies to a wider public. Bookstores constitute important gathering sites for New Agers. "There are little shrines in which one can meditate (sans shoes) in some bookstores. The shops are often staffed by people in the know—whose role falls somewhere between Waldenbooks clerks and clergy—people who can recommend holistic healers or hook readers up with New Age organizations" (Simonds 1992:73).

Holistic health centers also emerged as part and parcel of the holistic health movement (Mattson 1982:92–104). These included the Wholistic Health Centers, a "network of low cost, primary care clinics in suburbs, cities, and rural areas on the East Coast and West Coast," which was established as a free clinic in Springfield, Ohio, by Granger Westberg, a Christian minister (Gordon 1984:233). The Berkeley Holistic Health Center started in 1975 in a chiropractic office and grew into a collective consisting of workers and volunteers (Dosch 1980:378). It published a newsletter titled the *Holistic Health Quarterly*, *The Holistic Health Handbook* in 1978, and two holistic health guides in 1980 and 1985. The Berkeley Holistic Health Center offered classes on alternative medicine and created a referral file to acupuncturists, naturopaths, midwives, nutritional counselors, herbalists, and other alternative practitioners as well as holistic M.D.'s and dentists. Gordon (1984:243) contends that by the early 1980s, several hundred holistic health centers were scattered around the country. David Edelberg established the American Holistic Centers, three of which are located in the Chicago area, one in Denver, and one in Boston (Patel 1998:68). Holistic Approaches to Cancer Care (established in 1998) based in New York City is a nonprofit project of the Tides Center, "a public charity organization whose purpose is to promote positive social change through innovative programs emphasizing social justice, economic opportunity, democracy, and environmental awareness" (flyer). It is interested in providing education about cancer prevention and treatment to low-income people and people of color and stresses therapeutic modalities such as meditation, visualizations, herbal medicine, qi gong, reflexology, and nutritional eating.

Other major institutions associated with the holistic health/New Age movement include the Holistic Health and Nutrition Institute in Mill Valley, California; the Open Education Exchange in Oakland; the East West Academy of Healing Arts, the Holistic Life University, and the California Institute of Integral Studies, all in San Francisco; the Himalayan Institute (established in 1971) in the Pocono Mountains of northeastern Pennsylvania; the Yes Educational Society in Washington, D.C.; the Omega Institute in the Catskill Mountains; the New York Open Center; and the Naropa Institute in Boulder, Colorado. In 1989, the American Holistic Health Association was established to encourage biomedical physicians and other health practitioners to adopt holistic principles. Numerous holistic health centers employing teams consisting of biomedical physicians, osteopathic physicians, chiropractors, naturopathic physicians, acupuncturists, clinical psychologists and social workers, herbalists, homeopaths, massage therapists and other body workers have sprung up in many parts of the United States (Gordon 1984). Organizations and schools emphasizing holistic health have included or include the Holistic Health Practitioners' Association in the San Francisco Bay Area; the Association of Holistic Health/Mandala Society based in San Diego; the Alternative Medical Association; the National Council on Wholistic Therapeutics; the American Holistic Medical Association; the American Holistic Health Association; the American Holistic Nurses' Association; the John F. Kennedy University Graduate School for Holistic Studies in Orinda, California; and Columbia Pacific University in the Bay Area (Markell 1981).

In many ways, the holistic health/New Age movement functions as what Rodney Stark and William Bainbridge (1985) characterize as an "audience cult" in which participants communicate with each other not so much by meeting in specific places but by reading certain books and magazines and visiting certain websites. *Open Mind Magazine* based in Sedona, Arizona, is a quarterly magazine with a circulation of some forty-five thousand people scattered around the United States and elsewhere. Although the New Ageism continues by and large to function as a client and audience movement, a few New Age congregations have emerged in various cities around the country, particularly in the West. In addition to functioning as clients or members of an audience, New Agers sometimes act as ecotourists or pilgrims to special sacred locales, such as Sedona, Arizona, and Glastonbury, England. As Ivakhiv (2001:51) observes, "[a]s they become popular travel destinations, these sites are marketed and packaged, turned into spectacle and display, and a particular type of New Age 'tourist gaze' is given shape through guidebooks, postcards, and sacred site tours led by recognized or self-proclaimed spiritual authorities." Probably prompted by the spectacular beauty of the Red Rock country of Sedona and nearby Oak Creek Canyon, New Agers have identified "vortexes" or underground energy sources that have sparked a brisk business to which pilgrims or curiosity-seekers are transported in brightly painted Jeeps.

While most New Agers remain relatively dispersed rather than concentrated in congregations or communities, some New Agers have established "ceremonial circles" that stress group spirituality over the teacher–disciple relationship (Cimino and Lattin 1998:78). Sedona is one place where a New Age community, although a highly eclectic one, has emerged. Ivakhiv (2001:174–75) estimates that out of a population of some sixteen thousand in greater Sedona, a couple thousand belong to the area's New Age community. In the late 1950s, various spiritualists, including Mary Lou Keller, who is known as Sedona's "matriarch of metaphysics," moved to the area. In addition to teaching yoga and selling real estate, Keller provided space for lectures, seminars, and workshops in the Keller Building and facilitated the establishment of several metaphysical groups in the area, including ECKankar, Rainbow Ray Focus, the Unity School of Christianity, and her own Sedona Church of Light (established in 1973).

In the late 1970s, Page Bryant, a protégé of the neoshaman guru Sun Bear, identified seven vortexes based on channeled information. He reportedly came to lament the commercialism that accompanied the fascination with vortexes, noting that "a lot of innocent people, old ladies and such, are being ripped off" (quoted in D'Antonio 1992:61). Some New Agers constructed a medicine wheel in the late 1980s on Schnebly Hill that emerged into an important ceremonial site. The Center in Sedona (established in 1988), most recently called the Hub of the New Age Community, served as an important gathering spot and established connections with other New Age groups, including the Healing Center of Arizona, the Crystal Sanctuary, and the Center for Advanced Energy Healing (Ivakhiv 2001:175). New Agers in Sedona coexist in a rather tenuous relationship with employees of the National Forest Service, which has repeatedly contested the former's use of public land, traditional Christians (particularly those affiliated with evangelical churches), and affluent retirees or owners of second homes who have flooded the area.

SOCIAL PROFILES OF HOLISTIC HEALTH/NEW AGE HEALERS AND PATIENTS

English-Lueck presents the following characterization of alternative healers in Paraiso:

> Holistic health practitioners are not a monolithic block. Besides diverse personalities and practices, there is a variety of functional roles. A few visiting and local practitioners are renowned catalysts, founders of well-known therapies. Most holistic healers who are visible to the public are practitioners who are also teachers. Some rarely or never teach and prefer just to practice. Among this category are those who choose to work in informal, confidential networks. They may, or may not, choose to practice with the blessing of the law. Novice practitioners, not yet through their rites of passage, may also have informal networks of clients. (English-Lueck 1990:27)

The qualifications of holistic healers in Paraiso vary widely, with some being M.D.'s, dentists, optometrists, psychologists, chiropractors, and licensed acupuncturists and others lacking any licensing or extensive training, such as spiritual healers and various genres of bodyworkers (English-Lueck 1990:29). Other types of alternative practitioners operating in the community include naturopaths, herbalists, yoga instructors, and reflexologists. Many alternative practitioners, particularly bodyworkers, employ a variety of therapeutic techniques depending on the needs and desires of their clients. Out of the estimated 790 to 830 alternative practitioners in Paraiso, only 253 practice publicly. Alternative practitioners include naturopaths, herbalists, massage therapists, yoga instructors, reflexologists, and psychic healers. Many alternative practitioners, particularly bodyworkers, employ a variety of therapeutic techniques depending on the needs and desires of their clients.

The holistic health/New Age movement tends to cater to two clienteles: (1) upper- and upper-middle-class people with disposable incomes and (2) members of the counterculture who have chosen to funnel their limited financial resources into alternative therapies. Mattson (1982) conducted a survey of clients at the San Andreas Health Council, a holistic health center with both a clinic and classes. She obtained completed questionnaires from 166 clients, with some 400 clients not having completed the questionnaire. One hundred thirteen (68 percent) of her informants were female; 107 (65 percent) had baccalaureate degrees or higher; 58 (35 percent) were professionals and 29 (17 percent) worked in "helping occupations"; and 55 (33 percent) had family incomes over $20,000 a year, with 42 (25 percent) with family incomes of $10,000 to $19,999 (Mattson 1982:117). Mattson observes that her findings, "while not a random sampling of holistic health advocates, bear out the general impression that they are a well-educated, well-off group, and nearly all white" (118).

The ability of alternative practitioners to attract clients is limited by the fact that most health insurance companies do not cover their services. According to Bratman (1997:211), "[w]hile the insurance coverage for alternative medicine is gradually increasing, the process is much slower than advocates would prefer." Therapies such as acupuncture, homeopathy, and naturopathy are often labor-intensive and time-consuming. In that holistic or alternative health services are often not covered by insurance policies, Medicare, and Medicaid, they by default tend to cater to more affluent people. As Salmon (1984:257) observes, "the 'worried well' of middle-age and middle class . . . has the discretionary income to buy these services from entrepreneurs who have turned a cosmic ecological concern into a sales package marketed to aid coping with a stressful social existence." Alster (1989:186) delineates three categories of people who become attracted to holistic health: (1) "true believers," (2) "recruits after a period of initial skepticism," and (3) "outsiders influenced by the movement."

Anthropologist Mary Douglas (1999) emphasizes the countercultural orientation of many adherents of holistic health:

> The choice of holistic medicine will not be an isolated preference uncoordinated with other values upheld by the patient. Even labeling it more spiritual and claiming it preferable for that reason implies a latent protest against an

established culture labeled materialist. . . . It is not necessarily an overtly political protest, nor does the person who holds these views need to articulate them in a more clearly political way. It is enough that they are saying that they believe that all bodies need a gentle therapy. (36)

In contrast to Individualists, who value rugged competition, and Hierarchists, who argue for a need for authoritative structures, Douglas suggests that holistic health enthusiasts tend to be either Isolates, who tend to live on the margins of society, or Enclavists, who form ethnic, religious, or therapeutic communities. She asserts that "where Enclavists and Isolates flourish, the spiritual critique will continue to challenge the definitions of reality given by traditional Western medicine" (Douglas 1999:40).

Providing a social profile of New Agers is difficult in that, as Fuller observes: Very few people ever use the term when describing their own religious beliefs; even the 14 percent of Baby Boomers who describe themselves as metaphysical seekers rarely identify themselves as New Agers. There is, after all, no such thing as an organized New Age movement. Those interested in one alternative spiritual topic may have absolutely no interest at all in other topics that usually get lumped together as New Age. Yet it is probably fair to say that those who describe themselves as "spiritual, but not religious" are in general agreement with the broad principles of these alternative philosophies. (Fuller 2001:99)

Despite the tendency on the part of some people to make a distinction between spirituality and religiosity—the latter being much more defined as behavior associated with organized or "explicit" religion—various surveys indicate that most Americans tend to view themselves as both "religious and spiritual" (Marler and Hadaway 2002).

At any rate, Danforth (1989) maintains that New Agers are generally white, well-educated, upper-middle-class urbanites, many of whom grew up during the 1960s but were trying to adjust to the more conservative ethos of the following era. She argues that New Agers often suffer from an existential malaise and find a sense of emotional intimacy in the small groups associated with the movement. When Torgovnick (1996:177) attended a New Age conference sponsored by Common Boundary, she surmised that the attendees were "overwhelmingly white (perhaps 99 percent), mostly female (perhaps 85 percent), and well-educated."

While recognizing the existence of high-priced workshops and conferences, Albanese (1999a:367) asserts that "there is a strong working-class component within the New Age movement, although its presence is quiet and less noticeable." In a survey of consumption patterns of New Age materials in Texas, Mears and Ellison (2000) report the following:

> The wealthier and better educated are not more likely to purchase New Age materials. Indeed, the likelihood of New Age consumption is somewhat higher among persons lacking high school degrees and among those who have been unemployed, disabled, or laid off. Women are no more likely than men to purchase such materials. Persons in their 20s—not baby boomers (i.e., individuals in their 40s and 50s)—are more likely to be New Age consumers, suggesting a cohort (Generation X) or age effect. Similarly, never married persons—not their married counterparts—are much more likely to be New Age consumers. In contrast to popular conceptions, Hispanics and African Americans are more likely than non-Hispanic whites to purchase New Age materials. And, finally, contrary to previous suggestions, urban residents are no more likely than rural or suburban residents to purchase New Age materials. (301–2)

It may be that whereas New Age seminars and workshops tend to be attended primarily by upper- and upper-middle-class individuals, the articles of mass consumption, such as self-help books, magazines, and audio- and video-tapes, are within the purchasing power of lower-middle- and working-class people. At any rate, it is virtually impossible to determine the numbers of Americans who participate in the New Age movement in some way or another. The New Age section in most bookstores, however, strongly suggests that the New Age movement is a mass phenomenon.

THE HOLISTIC HEALTH/NEW AGE MOVEMENT: COUNTERHEGEMONIC OR HEGEMONIC?

Various scholars have suggested that the holistic health movement contains the potential to serve as a counterhegemonic vehicle for challenging the status quo. During the early stages of the movement, Berliner and Salmon (1979) argued that it contained the potential to pick up the banner of social medicine and to function as a critique of capitalist institutions, despite its apolitical, entrepreneurial, elitist, and authoritarian tendencies. In a similar vein, Freund (1982:37) stated that holistic medicine "can offer some of the tools and the politically radicalizing consciousness that are needed for initiating revolution; it can sensitize us to new levels and nuances of social oppression." More recently, Lyng (1990) describes the holistic health movement as a "countersystem" that challenges biomedical hegemony. Conversely, other scholars have asserted that it plays a contradictory role in contemporary U.S. capitalist society (McKee 1988).

The holistic health movement exhibits contradictory tendencies in that it has simultaneously been undergoing processes of professionalization as an increasing number of heterodox practitioners seek licensure and certification, resistance to professionalization on the part of some lay therapists who seek to maintain their autonomy, and even co-optation by organized biomedicine, which has come to recognize that many of its more affluent patients have been turning to alternative therapies. These are processes that I discuss in subsequent chapters.

By and large, the holistic health movement engages in a rather limited holism in that it focuses on the individual rather than society (Alster 1989; Goldstein 1992). According to Beckford (1984:269), the "holistic imagery" constitutes an "invisible religion of privatism." While indeed it makes mind–body–spirit connections, it tends to leave out political, economic, and social structural factors in its search for the etiology of disease. The holistic health movement exhorts its adherents to make lifestyle changes, such as dieting, exercising, avoiding smoking and heavy drinking, and managing stress, but it tends to downplay the role of poverty, unemployment and underemployment, low wages, stress in the workplace, environmental pollution, occupational hazards, the culture of consumption, and the alienation of modern life in disease etiology. As Montgomery (1993) so astutely observes:

> Never in this [holistic health] discourse are there allotments made for such things as class, race, age or the like. No social context for the personal is ever admitted. There is nothing that approaches a true social criticism, no examination of institutional structures, whether dealing with food production and distribution or with the development of preferences, tastes and so forth. (83)

In a similar vein, Antonovsky (1994:11) asserts that the holistic health movement has failed to "confront the social structural sources of the forces that make for well-being." Freund (1982) argues that while theoretically holistic approaches recognize the impact of environmental factors in disease etiology, both holistic M.D.'s and D.O.'s and alternative practitioners do little to alter the environment. He states:

> Many of the solutions advocated by holistic medicine have been appropriately described as "Buddhist solutions" by Eyer—ones that advocate withdrawal and are more suited to professional and managerial classes who possess control over their environment that make such solutions possible. (32)

New Agers also often express a deep concern for the environment and may even regard "environmental action as being an explicitly spiritual activity" (Bloch 1998:66). Conversely, in his overview of the New Age community in Sedona, Ivakhiv (1997:379) notes that "for all its mythologizing of the Sedona–Red Rock landscape, it is a rare event when the *Sedona Journal of Emergence* actually urges its readers to do something (in the 'third dimension' of physical and social reality) about some environmental issue."

Although some New Agers subscribe to a loose notion of socialism, most of them might be characterized as liberal, some are libertarian, and many appear to be apolitical (Kyle 1995:114–31). As Hanegraaff (1998) observes:

> The left-wing political beliefs of the counterculture and its commitment to radical action are no longer characteristic of the New Age movement of the 1980s. The writings of Marx, Che Guevara or Mao Tse-Tung are completely absent in the modern New Age bookshop, and New Age spokesmen do not usually call on their audiences to take political action in the streets (they may, however, organize group meditations for world healing). (11)

For the most part, the New Age movement has made its peace with capitalism. Although Bruce (1996:221) asserts that most New Agers tend to view themselves at odds with capitalism, they generally represent the epitome of individualism and consumerism—values that are part and parcel of capitalism. Danforth (1989) asserts that the New Age movement seeks to juxtapose two contradictory ideologies: (1) mainstream U.S. culture and (2) the counterculture. In doing so, it permits its adherents to achieve material success while doing their own thing. She asserts that the New Age movement has allowed many countercultural types, such as Jerry Rubin, to reintegrate into the larger society. In a similar vein, while recognizing that New Age consciousness contains some positive elements, such as an emphasis on exercise and organic and natural foods, Parenti (1994:17–18) argues that it exhibits a form of self-centeredness that "resembles the hyper-individualism of the free-market society in which it flourishes" and neglects the "common struggle for collective empowerment and social betterment."

The holistic health/New Age movement early on began to exhibit signs of increasing entrepreneurialization. Rosch and Kearney (1985:1405) note that it has "witnessed the appearance of a number of entrepreneurs and even charlatans who seek to exploit the appeal of 'holism' or naturopathic principles." I detected a pronounced ethos of entrepreneurialization at the San Francisco Whole Life Expo in spring 1994 where chiropractors, Rolfers, health food proponents, New Age psychic healers, and many other alternative practitioners hawked their wares to what appeared to be a predominantly white, middle-class clientele. Goldstein (1992) suggests that the holistic health movement has been evolving into a "marketed social movement":

> Marketed social movements are characterized by sophisticated promotional and recruitment strategies, a membership that is sharply distinguished from the leadership, participation as a product package and the growth of membership as a primary goal. . . . Particularly those sectors of the health movement that have been most enmeshed in proprietary organizations rely on professional administrators and exclude most members from decision-making. The social movement becomes a product to be sold to people, regardless of whether they need it. (151)

Albanese (1999b:320) observes that "commercialization has become the hall-mark of the New Age." Simonds (1992:73) describes the New Age movement as a "strong manifestation of the psychologification of religion, offering an odd mix of commercialism and spirituality."

Alster (1989:148) argues that the holistic health movement functions as an "ersatz religion" that promises its adherents that they may attain salvation through their own individual efforts. It serves as a "distorted response to the problems of loss of community and loss of values" (154). She also maintains that the holistic health movement may contribute to a "certain hypochondria" and a preoccupation with health that may draw "attention on minor discomforts that otherwise might have gone unnoticed" (89). Grossinger (1990:350) argues that the holistic health movement has created "holistic health junkies" who go from treatment to treatment in order to find an ill-defined biopsychosocial salvation.

Despite the growing presence of hegemonic elements within the holistic health/New Age movement, various scholars have argued that it provides patients disenchanted with biomedicine, some of whom become alternative practitioners, with a space to resist biomedical dominance. Based on their ethnographic research on the Committee for Freedom of Choice in Cancer Therapy, a largely conservative Christian organization, and the Natural Living Group, a New Age healing organization, Schneirov and Geczik (1998) argue that such alternative health-support groups provide their members with a mechanism for resisting biomedical bureaucratic supervision. More recently, by drawing on interviews with two female patients, one European American and the other African American, who have turned to a constellation of alternative therapies to treat chronic illnesses that biomedical physicians had dismissed, Thompson (2003:103) suggest that the "consumption of holistic healing alternatives easily takes on a mix and match quality that avoids dependence upon (and hence confinement within) any one approach or single authoritarian definition of their bodies and identities."

CONCLUSION

The holistic health/New Age movement in its present form has not lived up to its potential. It engages in a rather limited holism, in that its focus is largely on the individual rather than on society and its institutions. In emphasizing individual responsibility for health, wellness, and spirituality, it provides an alternative form of medical hegemony by reinforcing individualizing patterns in U.S. society specifically and in the capitalist world system.

The Semilegitimation of Four Professionalized Heterodox Medical Systems

Harries-Jenkins (1970:57–58) asserts that professionalization has escaped definition due to the "concomitant failure to define 'professional' or to delineate 'profession.'" Professionals have been defined by a set of traits including specialized skills and training, esoteric knowledge, limited membership associations, codes of ethics, a service orientation, income by fees rather than wages, universalism, and recognition of their authority by the larger society (Goldstein and Donaldson 1979:322). Social scientists thus construct an ideal type that is used as a measure of the degree of professionalization achieved by different occupational groups.

Critics of this method assert that it "justifies the prerogatives and power of the leading professions" (Manning 1976:75). Other scholars view professionalization as the degree to which an occupational group has exclusive access to a particular type of work, and the power to delegate related work to subordinate occupations. Larson (1979:609) used this definition in asserting that professionalization "is aimed at monopoly: monopoly of opportunities in a market of services or labor, and, inseparably, monopoly of status and work privileges in an occupational hierarchy." Since this definition assumes that biomedicine has achieved dominance over subordinate occupations, such as nursing, physical therapy, and other allied health groups, it obscures the ongoing struggle for greater autonomy by these occupations and well as alternative or heterodox health practitioners.

A drive toward professionalization appears repeatedly within the context of the holistic health movement in the sense that schools of alternative medicine and organizations of alternative practitioners seek to obtain legitimacy, generally in the form of licensing, certification, or registration from the state or recognition from an accrediting agency, even one internal to a specific alternative medical system.

Van Hernal (2001) delineates three forms of professional licensure for health practitioners: mandatory licensure, title licensure or certification, and registration. In the case of licensure, "only those who are licensed may engage in the licensed activity and violators (unlicensed practitioners) may face criminal as well as civil penalties" (3). Under certification, the practitioner possessing certification "may use a professional title to describe his or her qualifications, while nonlicensed practitioners may perform the same service provided they do not use the licensed title" (3). Finally, under registration, "providers need only register their personal information and qualifications with the state agency, which is empowered to investigate complaints against such registered practitioners" (3).

Licensing laws have played a crucial role in the development of U.S. chiropractic, naturopathy, acupuncture, and Oriental medicine as well as partially professionalized heterodox therapeutic systems discussed in chapter 3. To protect themselves from prosecution against laws prohibiting the practice of medicine by anyone other than an M.D. or D.O., and to gain some degree of legitimacy, most heterodox practitioners have favored licensure, which generally was initially opposed by organized biomedicine.

Heterodox practitioners, particularly chiropractors, have conducted intense campaigns to obtain licensure and have often found support among sympathetic politicians, many of whom have utilized alternative medicine to address their own ailments or those of family members. Nevertheless, in the struggles between rival medical systems, the state, which holds the power to confer licensure, has tended to side with biomedicine. Licensure has played and continues to play a double-edged role in the development of heterodox therapeutic systems in the sense that it forces them to adopt aspects of biomedical theory so that their students and practitioners can pass licensing examinations. To avoid dramatic changes in the health care system, the legitimation granted to alternative medical systems extended by the state is generally only partial in that heterodox practitioners are forced to comply with the structures, standards, and processes that are dominated by biomedicine. Cohen (2000:17) argues that while licensure or other forms of state credentialing purportedly serve to protect the public from charlatans and incompetent practitioners, it often fails to achieve this and essentially creates barriers to entry into a particular health occupation.

This chapter focuses on four professionalized heterodox medical systems—chiropractic, naturopathy, Oriental medicine and acupuncture, and homeopathy—that have achieved at least semilegitimation, including mandatory licensure at least in some states. Chiropractic was the last of the heterodox medical systems that arose in the nineteenth century as popular protests against the perceived shortcomings of regular or allopathic medicine. Unlike many of the other systems, such as homeopathy, botanic medicine or eclecticism, and osteopathy, which disappeared, were absorbed by biomedicine, or adopted many of its premises and practices, chiropractic continues to function on the fringes of biomedicine. Despite a history of considerable internal factionalism, it had evolved into the most viable and successful example of alternative medicine in the United States by the time the holistic health movement emerged.

In contrast, naturopathy appeared to be on its last legs at this time. Indeed, Roth (1976:121) referred to naturopathy as an example of a dying health movement attempting "a last ditch struggle to survive." As this chapter indicates, naturopathy was able to capitalize on its predilection for therapeutic eclecticism and underwent a partial rejuvenation within the context of the holistic health movement. Grossinger (1990:473) maintains that early U.S. naturopathy became viewed in the public minds as a "medley of huckerism, quackery, and charismatic healing." On the surface, naturopathy appears to be the most holistic of the various heterodox medical systems in that it posits the interaction of all parts of the system—body, mind, spirit, environment, and society (McKee 1988:777). Theoretically, it does not require the individual to adjust to a "toxic environment," but in reality it adopts an individualistic perspective that is compatible with capitalist ideology in that it emphasizes internal personal changes rather than external social changes. Conversely, naturopathy does not facilitate capital accumulation and commodification of health care to nearly the same extent as biomedicine does (McKee 1988:779).

In a somewhat different vein than naturopathy, which emerged around 1900, Oriental medicine and acupuncture, while an ancient system in East Asia, were also able to arouse considerable interest in the United States by becoming part and parcel of the larger holistic health movement. They have obtained their greatest level of recognition in California, where about half of all licensed acupuncturists in the United States presently practice. Acupuncture and Oriental medicine have become popular in the treatment of a wide array of chronic conditions, such as back pain, as well as in the treatment of drug addiction and for countering the adverse effects, particularly neuropathy, of antiretroviral medications used in HIV/AIDS treatment.

Despite the fact that homeopathy as a heterodox medical system had more or less been fully co-opted by biomedicine in the early decades of the twentieth century, it found renewed appeal among some M.D.'s, professionalized heterodox practitioners, and clinical psychologists beginning in the 1970s. In the late 1970s, the San Francisco Bay area appears to have served as "the center of a new revival of homeopathy led largely by nonphysicians" (Gurin 1979:12). According to Rogers (1998:202), "when homeopathy was 'rediscovered' by American physicians and the lay public in the 1970s and 1980s, the flowering occurred not at Hahnemann or in Philadelphia but in California and Oregon." Various young radical biomedical physicians expressed their rebellion against organized biomedicine by turning to homeopathy as an alternative therapeutic modality (Grossinger 1990:344). Dana Ullman, an East Bay–based layperson with a master's degree in public health, has also served as a key player in the rejuvenation of homeopathy (Ullman 1991). He has written numerous articles and books about homeopathy, has served as the president of the Foundation of Homeopathic Education and Research, and is the director of Homeopathic Educational Services. A turf battle has developed within homeopathic circles between the professionalists and the counterculturalists that the former appears to be winning.

CHIROPRACTIC—FROM DRUGLESS GENERAL PRACTICE TO MUSCULOSKELETAL SPECIALTY

Daniel David Palmer, who claimed that divine inspiration was the source of his medical doctrine, was the charismatic prophet of chiropractic or its "Discoverer." He posited that disease emanates from "sublaxations" or spinal displacements that result in nerve transmission interference, which in turn trigger dysfunctions in various bodily organs. Spinal adjustment restores the normal "nerve force," and health follows. D.D.'s son, B.J., served as the principal promoter or "Developer" of the new faith. D.D. established the Palmer Infirmary and Chiropractic in 1897. Under the astute management of his flamboyant son, the Palmer school grew into the mecca or "Fountainhead" of chiropractic education and culture. In time, literally hundreds of other chiropractic schools appeared and, in most cases, disappeared.

In contrasting themselves to biomedical physicians, chiropractors often assert they practice a form of health care that focuses on the treatment of the whole person. In reality, however, the holism of chiropractic is limited in that it relies heavily, like biomedicine and osteopathy, on notions such as the machine analogy. As McQueen (1978:74) observes, "Chiropractic and osteopathic concern themselves with structure and function of the machine. Healing occurs by making structural corrections." Furthermore, biomedicine, osteopathy, and chiropractic, at least in their original forms, are based on the belief that healing involves the removal of a single cause: a pathogen in the case of biomedicine, a lesion in the case of osteopathy, and a subluxation in the case of chiropractic. All three medical systems downplay the role of political, economic, social structural, and environmental factors in disease etiology. At the therapeutic level, the development of U.S. chiropractic was shaped by the fierce battles between the "straights"—those who wished to focus on spinal adjustment—and the "mixers"—those who wished to incorporate other modalities, such as physiotherapy, hydrotherapy, electrotherapy, colonic irrigation, dietetics, exercise, and vitamin therapy, from what is loosely termed *naturopathy*. Due to its strong eclectic bent, naturopathy provided chiropractor mixers, at least until the 1950s, with a ready source from which to add a variety of therapeutic techniques.

Instead of employing the emic or insider terms of *straight* and *mixer*, historian J. Stuart Moore (1993) sees U.S. chiropractic as a division between the "harmonialists" and the "mechanical rationalists." The harmonialists, starting with D. D. Palmer himself, believed that Matter and Spirit are intricately intertwined. Like Andrew Taylor Still, the founder of osteopathy, Palmer drew on tenets of magnetic healing, Spiritualism, and bonesetting (although he apparently did not give the latter its due credit) in formulating his manual medical system. The harmonial chiropractors quickly assumed two "clearly distinguishable temperaments" (Moore 1993:99). Among the first group,

[c]hiropractic became a substitute religion, supplying a comprehensive examination of reality, complete in itself with claims of divine powers, suffering saints

and martyrs, and sacred writings and utterances from the prophets (the Palmers) who provided the ultimate source of authority—all wrapped in a millennial eschatology. (Moore 1993:99)

Among the second group, which Moore suggests perhaps characterized the majority of the harmonialists, chiropractic became transformed in the Christian approach to health.

Efforts to Legitimize Chiropractic

In their efforts to achieve legitimacy and improved status in the United States, chiropractors have adopted a wide variety of strategies, including establishing professional associations, colleges, patient support groups, and practice-building seminars and conducting lobbying campaigns and even a major antitrust suit against both organized biomedicine and osteopathic medicine. Chiropractic history has entailed the emergence as well as the demise of rival associations at both the state and national levels.

Solon M. Langsworthy established the short-lived American Chiropractic Association in 1905 as the first national chiropractic association. In response, B. J. Palmer established the United Chiropractors Association (UCA) a year later. Because the UCA began to admit mixers, he formed in 1926 the Chiropractic Health Bureau, renamed the International Chiropractors Association (ICA) in 1941. A group of mixers established a new American Chiropractic Association (ACA) in the early 1920s (Wardwell 1992:100). It merged in 1930 with remnants of the UCA to form the National Chiropractic Association (NCA). All of these associations pushed for licensing laws, defended arrested chiropractors accused of practicing medicine without a license, and engaged in public relations in order to create a more positive image of the profession.

After B.J.'s death in 1963, Alan A. Adams left the ICA to form yet another incarnation of the American Chiropractic Association that became primarily associated with mixer chiropractic. In reality, the distinction between the straights and mixers has always been somewhat fuzzy. After the federal government recognized the Council on Chiropractic Education (CCE) in 1974, which had been established by the ACA, the ICA accepted the authority of this body as well. Both the ICA and the ACA have their present headquarters in Washington, D.C. Thomas Gerlardi headed up a faction of chiropractors, often referred to as the "superstraights," who believed that the ICA had departed from the principles of straight chiropractic by forming the Federation of Straight Chiropractic Organizations.

Many of chiropractic's internal conflicts have expressed themselves in the creation of rival colleges. Wiese and Ferguson (1985) identified 392 different chiropractic colleges that have existed at one time or another. In the mid-1930s, John J. Nugent, a NCA member, spearheaded an educational reform effort that eventually resulted in the closing of many of what were regarded to be inferior institutions. Whereas the Palmer School of Chiropractic has historically functioned as the Mecca of straight chiropractic, the National School of Chiropractic in Illinois has been regarded as the premier institution of mixer chiropractic. The Association of Chiropractic Colleges represents seventeen U.S. chiropractic colleges, depicted in table 2.1, as well as the Canadian Memorial Chiropractic College in Toronto (www.chirocolleges.org/colleges .html, accessed June 15, 2003).

With the exception of the College of Chiropractic at the University of Bridgeport, which is owned by the Unification Movement, all other U.S. chiropractic colleges are free-standing operations. The Professors World Peace Group, a Unification Church front organization, infused $50 million into the institution in exchange for control of the board of trustees (Clarkson 1997:56–59). In 1995, the University of Bridgeport granted the Reverend Sun Myung Moon a honorary

Table 2.1.   U.S. Chiropractic Colleges

College	Established	Location
Palmer College of Chiropractic	1897	Davenport, Iowa
National University of Health Sciences	1906	Lombard, Ill.
Logan Chiropractic College	1906	Chesterfield, Mo.
Texas Chiropractic College	1908	Pasadena, Tex.
Southern California University of Health Sciences– Los Angeles College of Chiropractic	1911	Whittier, Calif.
Cleveland Chiropractic College–Los Angeles	1911	Los Angeles, Calif.
New York Chiropractic College	1919	Seneca Falls, N.Y.
Cleveland Chiropractic College	1922	Kansas City, Mo.
Western States Chiropractic College	1934	Portland, Ore.
Northwestern Health Sciences University	1941	Minneapolis, Minn.
Sherman College of Straight Chiropractic	1973	Spartanburg, S.C.
Life University	1975	Marietta, Ga.
Palmer College of Chiropractic West	1978	San Jose, Calif.
Life Chiropractic College West	1982	Hayward, Calif.
Parker College of Chiropractic	1982	Dallas, Tex.
University of Bridgeport College of Chiropractic	1990	Bridgeport, Conn.
Palmer College of Chiropractic Florida	2002	Port Orange, Fla.

doctorate. The University of Bridgeport also operates one of the four four-year naturopathic colleges. In contrast to the United States, where no chiropractic schools are affiliated with state universities, the chiropractic college at the Preston Institute of Technology in Melbourne is the only state-supported chiropractic school in the world. Of the nineteen U.S. osteopathic medical colleges, six of them are affiliated with state universities: those at Michigan State, the University of North Texas, Oklahoma State, Ohio University, the State University of New York at Old Westbury, and the University of Medicine and Dentistry of New Jersey. The West Virginia School of Osteopathic Medicine is a free-standing state-supported institution. Along with the fact that osteopathic physicians had obtained full practice rights in all fifty states and the District of Columbia by the early 1970s, this fact illustrates the greater legitimacy that osteopathic medicine enjoys compared to chiropractic in the United States. The Institute for Alternative Futures (1998:4–14) study reports that "[a]cupuncture is taught at some chiropractic colleges; the National College of Chiropractic is launching a training program in naturopathy and acupuncture."

Licensing laws played a crucial role in the legitimization of U.S. chiropractic. In 1913, Kansas became the first state to enact chiropractic legislation; by 1938, all but seven states had passed chiropractic licensing laws. The last states to license chiropractors were New York (1963), Massachusetts (1966), Mississippi (1973), and Louisiana (1974). As a way of broadening their scope of practice, many mixer chiropractors obtained licensure as naturopaths. Until the 1950s, many mixer colleges offered their students the doctor of naturopathy (N.D.) degree along with the doctor of chiropractic (D.C.) degree. Chiropractic licensing laws vary considerably in terms of scope of practice. Whereas Oregon permits chiropractors to practice obstetrics, perform minor surgery, and sign birth and death certificates, Washington state allows only spinal adjustment.

As a professionalized heterodox medical system, chiropractic has offered upward social mobility for thousands of lower-middle-class and working-class individuals (White and Skipper 1971; Wild 1978). Chiropractic has recruited a fair number of its practitioners from the ranks of satisfied patients (Moore 1993:94). Precise figures on the number of chiropractors in the country are difficult to obtain. An Institute for Alternative Futures (1998:2–5) study indicated that there were some 55,000 chiropractors in practice in 1995 and projected that there would be 68,160 in 2000 and 84,700 in 2005. These figures suggest that chiropractic continues to be a growing profession.

Despite vigorous opposition historically by biomedicine, chiropractic has undergone considerable legitimation since the early 1970s. Since then, government support for chiropractic has included (1) coverage under workers' compensation in all fifty states and the District of Columbia, (2) the allowance of sick leave based on a statement from a chiropractor for federal employees, (3) federal income tax deductions for chiropractic care, (4) coverage for chiropractic in all or nearly all states under Medicaid and Medicare, (5) grants to chiropractic students, and (6) some funding for chiropractic research. The U.S. Office of Education recognized the ACA's Council on Chiropractic Education as an official accrediting agency in 1974. In 1975, the National Institutes for Health (NIH) organized a Workshop on the Research Status of Spinal Manipulative Therapy that included M.D.'s, D.O.'s, and chiropractors.

Chiropractic won a major victory in the protracted *Wilk v. American Medical Association* (AMA) court case, which ended with a decision by U.S. District Court for the Northern District of Illinois in 1987 forbidding the American Medical Association, the American Osteopathic Association, and the American Hospital Association "from restricting, regulating or impeding" hospitals or M.D.'s from associating professionally with chiropractors (Whorton 2002:285). The AMA appealed the decision but was refused by the U.S. Supreme Court in 1990. In November 1992, president-elect Bill Clinton asked Stanley Heard, who had been the Clinton family chiropractor, to spearhead an effort to define chiropractic for his managed competition national health care plan (Smith-Cunnien 1998:117). This initiative led to the creation of the National Chiropractic Health Care Advisory Committee, which resulted in a 223-page report titled "Health Care for the 21st Century: Opportunities for Change—A Chiropractic Perspective."

Due to intensive efforts and support from the chiropractic profession, satisfied patients and patient support groups, labor unions, and supportive state legislators (many of whom have, like Clinton, been chiropractic patients), chiropractic has managed to achieve semilegitimacy within U.S. society. Indeed, some chiropractic enthusiasts have asserted that chiropractic has evolved into a "mainstream alternative" to biomedicine. Moore (1993:138) argues that chiropractic "has moved into position as the orthodox, nontraditional approach to health—a type of orthodox unorthodoxy . . . [that] . . . now occupies a unique, middle ground between regular medicine and the harmonial-type therapies of the holistic health movement that have blossomed in the past quarter century." It could be argued, however, that osteopathic medicine, which achieved full practice rights in all fifty states and the District of Columbia by the early 1970s, occupies a middle ground between biomedicine and chiropractic. On this matter, Robert Anderson (1997), a medical anthropologist/chiropractor/biomedical physician, astutely argues:

> There is no evidence to suggest that the medical establishment is inclined to grant mainstream status to chiropractic as a profession now or in the near future. Quite aside from economic incentives to maintain a mainstream monopoly, a mercenary but powerful fact of life, the power brokers of medicine are also disinclined on theoretical grounds to authorize chiropractic as an equal but different explanatory model for what causes diseases, for how diseases are diagnosed, and for the treatment of diseases because it is based on logical speculation rather than clinical science. (556)

Nevertheless, it is interesting to note that at least some M.D.'s are more prone to be open to chiropractic care. For example, a Time-Life Medical video titled "Back Pain" released in 1996, which notes that chiropractic plays a primary role in the treatment of back pain, is hosted by former U.S. surgeon general C. Everett Coop (Chapman-Smith 1997:596).

The Niche of Chiropractic in the U.S. Dominative Medical System

A study by the Stanford Research Institute (1960:30) concluded that in contrast to the straights who viewed themselves as drugless general practitioners, many mixers had come to regard themselves as specialists in not only manipulative therapy but also the treatment of a wide variety of other ailments. Roth (1976:74) maintains that many chiropractic mixers "want to capture as much of the health therapy market as they possibly can." At the same time, many chiropractors, particularly mixers, have come to view themselves as specialists. Wardwell (1982:217) contends that, for both straights and mixers, "the vast majority of chiropractic treatment is for neuromuscular-skeletal conditions with perhaps 10 to 15 percent for organization conditions." Based on questionnaires administered to forty-four chiropractors in the Los Angeles metropolitan area, Coulter, Hays, and Danielson (1996:75) report that "the most frequent recommendations are those most directly relevant to the complaints of back-related problems rather than general health and preventive care."

Some evidence suggests that in certain rural areas, some chiropractors, if not many, do indeed function as drugless general practitioners. In some underserved areas, as Krause (1977:44–45) observes, chiropractors play the dominant "physician" role in the community. Despite this, however, chiropractors have for the most part been relegated to serving as musculoskeletal specialists, despite the desire on the part of many to the contrary. In contrast to M.D.'s, who more and more have become employees of hospitals, medical schools, and HMOs, most D.C.'s continue to function as independent entrepreneurs, either working as solo practitioners or practicing in small groups (Smith-Cunnien 1998:128). A few chiropractors are on staff at a number of hospitals, particularly in terms of access to labs and imaging equipment (Whorton 2002:288). One chiropractor even has a faculty position at a biomedical school teaching radiology.

NATUROPATHIC MEDICINE: IRONIC SUCCESS WITHIN THE CONTEXT OF THE HOLISTIC HEALTH MOVEMENT

Despite its near demise by the early 1970s, U.S. naturopathic medicine has been part and parcel of the burgeoning holistic health movement. It emerged as a distinctive heterodox medical system a little over a century ago and shortly after the emergence of both osteopathy and chiropractic (Baer 1987). After purchasing the term *naturopathy* from John Scheel, who coined the term in 1895, to describe his vision of medicine (Wendel 1951:17), Benedict Lust, the father of American naturopathy, established the American School of Naturopathy in New York City in 1901 and the Naturopathic Society of America the following year. He established sanitaria in New York City, New Jersey, and Florida and offered naturopathic correspondence courses through his journal (Kirchfeld and Boyle 1994:194–201). Carl Schultz, who had studied regular medicine, homeopathy, and nature cure in Germany prior to immigrating to California in 1885, established the Association of Naturopathic Physicians of California in 1901, the Naturopathic Institute and Sanitarium of California in Los Angeles in 1905, and later the Naturopathic College of California (Kirchfeld and Boyle 1994:212). Henry Lindlahr, who first had been a successful businessman and mayor in Montana, obtained training in biomedicine and went on to become an icon within early U.S. naturopathy, despite the fact that he referred to his approach as nature cure or natural therapeutics (Kirchfeld and Boyle 1994:227–50). He established the Lindlahr Health Resort in Elmhurst, Illinois, in 1914 and the Lindlahr College of Nature Cure and Osteopathy. His textbook *Natural Therapeutics* (1981) remains a standard work within the naturopathic profession.

With the establishment of other sanitaria and colleges, U.S. naturopathy underwent a process of relatively rapid growth until around the 1930s, followed by a period of gradual decline, almost to the point of complete extinction, during the next three or four decades.

The Emergence, Decline, and Rejuvenation of Naturopathy

Weil (1995a:138) maintains that naturopathy

emerged slowly and without clear definition from an informal grouping of people who shared certain beliefs about health and medicine. . . . In some ways, the original naturopaths were glorified hygienists, who felt that clean living was the way to good health—hence the emphasis on fresh air, good diet, water, light, herbs, and other simple measures.

Naturopaths regard disease as a response to bodily toxins and imbalances in a person's social, psychic, and spiritual environment. Germs are not the cause of disease per se but rather are pathogens that take advantage of the body when it is in a weakened state. Naturopaths adhere to the notion of *vis mediatrix naturae*—the healing power of nature—and emphasize preventive health, education, and client responsibility. Their specific therapeutic approaches, however, have varied historically and cross-culturally (Pizzorno 1996). In the past, many naturopaths relied heavily on water treatments, colonic irrigation, dietetics, fasting, and exercise. While some naturopaths continue to advocate these modalities, others draw on acupuncture, spinal manipulation, homeopathy, herbalism, vitamin therapy, faith healing, and even Ayurvedic and Chinese medicine. According to Bloomfield (1983:116), "naturopathy for some people means all the forms of nonallopathic medicine which depend on 'natural' remedies and treatments." In essence, naturopathy more than any other alternative medical system can be viewed as a microcosm of the holistic health movement.

At any rate, in addition to the school established by Benedict Lust, various other naturopaths established schools during the first three decades of the twentieth century. A 1927 AMA study listed twelve naturopathic schools with fewer than two hundred students (Reed 1932:69–70). Zeff (1996:59) asserts that "by the 1930s there were but two dozen schools." Naturopaths at one point during the heyday of American naturopathy were licensed to practice under either naturopathic or drugless practitioner laws in twenty-five states (Finken 1986:41). Estimates of the number of naturopaths in the 1920s and 1930s vary considerably. Reed (1932:62) cited the existence of some 2,500 naturopaths and related practitioners in the United States during the early 1930s, but Whorton (1986:28) estimates the existence of some 400 "sanipractors"—a term that was used for naturopaths in the Pacific Northwest—in Washington State in 1925 alone.

In their efforts to become broad-spectrum practitioners, many chiropractors expanded their range of healing modalities by borrowing from naturopathy. Due to its extreme eclecticism, naturopathy provided chiropractic mixers with a ready vehicle by which to add a wide variety of techniques, such as hydropathy, physiotherapy, electrotherapy, dietetics, and colonic irrigation to their regimen of treatment. As opposed to chiropractic straights, who tend, at least theoretically, to restrict their regimen of treatment to spinal adjustment, the mixers have historically incorporated a wide variety of other modalities into their scope of practice. In reality, most chiropractors fall somewhere along the straight–mixer continuum, although in recent decades a faction of "superstraights" has emerged as a response to the mixing that many straights have adopted. At any rate, for many years, mixer schools offered their students the N.D. (doctor of naturopathy) diploma in addition to the D.C. (doctor of chiropractic) diploma. Furthermore, many naturopathic schools taught chiropractic techniques and granted D.C. diplomas.

The growing prestige of biomedicine and the advent of "miracle drugs" appears to have adversely affected naturopathy, but the details of this impact still need to be specified (Cody 1999:36–37). Biomedicine managed to convince the general public that its approach of therapeutic intervention constituted the most scientific and effective approach to health care. Perhaps more important, as Brown (1979:71) asserts, it "discovered an ideology that was compatible with the world view of, and politically and economically useful to, the capitalist class and the emerging managerial and professional stratum." The Flexner Report of 1910, which was sponsored by the corporate-sponsored Carnegie Foundation on a recommendation of the AMA that a comprehensive survey of medical education be made, also ensured the hegemony of the biomedical profession. The decision of the corporate-sponsored philanthropies, particularly the Rockefeller

Foundation, not to fund schools defined as inferior by the Flexner Report in part contributed to the demise of not only several black and women's biomedical colleges but also several homeopathic and eclectic ones.

By the 1940s, naturopathy found itself in a crisis. The leadership of the American Naturopathic Association attempted to upgrade the quality of naturopathic education by forming the National Board of Naturopathic Examiners, which required a high school diploma for admission to naturopathic schools and a full four years of study for graduation from them, but encountered resistance from the schools (Whorton 2002:234). At the same time that biomedicine was in the process of achieving prominence, following the death of Lust in 1945, the ANA splintered into six different organizations, in part due to regional divisions (Kirchfeld and Boyle 1994:202–3). Indeed, Lust reportedly in his last years had been "deeply troubled by all the dissension and dishonesty he saw within the ranks of so-called naturopaths" and "called out repeatedly to the pure of heart among his followers to beware of 'the internal enemies' of naturopathy" (Whorton 2002:234).

Several naturopathic physicians in Washington, Oregon, and British Columbia established a forum for sharing concerns by organizing the Northwest Naturopathic Convention in 1956, an organization that served to fill the gap created by the demise of the American Association of Naturopathic Physicians and Surgeons in the mid-1950s and the National Association of Naturopathic Physicians sometime afterward (Farnsworth 1999:1–2). During the 1940s and 1950s, the mixer chiropractic schools dropped their N.D. diplomas because more and more states had broadened the scope of practice defined under their chiropractic licensing laws. From 1940 to 1963, the AMA engaged in a systematic attack on various heterodox medical systems, particularly chiropractic but also naturopathy. Since many naturopaths practiced under chiropractic licenses, Lisa (1994:272) asserts "that the medical establishment treated naturopathy and chiropractic the same . . . [and thereby] the tactics used against each stemmed from strategies developed by the AMA to eliminate both from the health-care system."

After World War II, severe limitations were placed on naturopaths through court decisions. The Tennessee legislature declared the practice of naturopathy a gross misdemeanor (Miller 1985:57). In 1953, the attorney general in Texas ruled the licensure of naturopaths unconstitutional (*American Association of Naturopathic Physicians Quarterly Newsletter* 1986:4). Spurred on by lobbying from organized biomedicine, the Georgia legislature eliminated the naturopathic board of examiners in 1956 (Lisa 1994:268). Florida, which had first licensed naturopaths in the 1920s, ended licensure for them in 1959. California passed a "sunset" law in 1964 that permitted previously licensed naturopaths to practice but prohibited new naturopathic licenses (*American Association of Naturopathic Physicians Quarterly Newsletter* 1987:3). By 1958, only five states (Arizona, Colorado, Connecticut, Virginia, and Utah) provided separate licensure for naturopaths, although a few states licensed them under drugless practitioner laws (Homola 1963:75). Ultimately, the decline of naturopathy must be viewed as an outgrowth of the growing hegemonic influence of biomedicine and the absence of relatively national organizations and lobbying efforts—both of which chiropractic managed to attain.

Despite its weakened position by midcentury, naturopathy found a last-ditch stronghold of sorts in the Pacific Northwest, a region that has repeatedly provided a sanctuary for maverick social movements and alternative medical systems (Whorton 1986). Whereas most state governments either refused to grant legal recognition to naturopathy or dropped former licensing laws permitting it, Washington and Oregon continued to provide a relatively open environment for sanipractors or naturopaths. In responding to the plans of the Western States College of Chiropractic to drop its N.D. program, Charles Stone, Frank Spaulding, and W. Martin Bleything established the National College of Naturopathic Medicine (NCNM) in Portland, Oregon, in 1956. NCNM opened a branch campus in Seattle in 1969 that closed its doors after the 1976 graduation ceremony. During the 1970s, however, even the main campus of NCNM functioned for a while on the brink of collapse with only a handful of students.

While it appeared indeed that U.S. naturopathy was in its last days by the early 1970s, signs of reversal in the tide began to appear by the end of the decade. Because its emphasis on vitalism and therapeutic eclecticism had preadapted it for the holistic health movement—one that emphasizes holism and a wide array of natural therapies—that emerged in the 1970s, naturopathy was able to undergo a process of organizational rejuvenation and moderate growth during the last two decades of the twentieth century (Baer 1992). The rejuvenation of U.S. naturopathy has manifested itself in the existence of licensure for naturopathic physicians in twelve states, the growth of the American Association of Naturopathic Physicians (established in 1986), and the presence of four-year naturopathic colleges in Portland, Oregon; the Seattle area; Tempe, Arizona; and Bridgeport, Connecticut. Despite these successes, U.S. naturopathy as a professionalized heterodox system faces several dilemmas as it enters the new millennium. These include (1) the fact that it has only succeeded in obtaining licensure in two sections of the country—namely, the Far West (Washington, Oregon, Idaho, Montana, Arizona, Alaska, Hawaii, and, most recently, California) and New England (Connecticut, Vermont, New Hampshire, and Maine); (2) increasing competition from partially professionalized naturopaths, many of whom are graduates of short-term or correspondence schools and at least some of whom are M.D.'s or D.O.'s; and (3) the danger of being co-opted by biomedicine as the latter increasingly adopts natural healing modalities.

In 1978, three NCNM graduates and an administrative person established the John Bastyr College of Naturopathic Medicine (JBCNM), now Bastyr University, in Seattle. Under the presidency of Joseph Pizzorno Jr., one of the school's founders, JBCNM graduated its first class in 1982, and in 1983 it received Candidacy for Accreditation by the Northwest Association—a first for the naturopathic profession. In the fall of 1979, another new four-year naturopathic school, the Pacific College of Naturopathic Medicine (PCNM), opened its doors in Monte Rio, California. Mismanagement and the lack of licensure for naturopaths in California appear to have contributed to the rapid demise of the school. In 1993, the Southwest College of Naturopathic Medicine (SCNM) opened its doors in Scottsdale, Arizona, and joined JBCNM and NCNM as the third of the current four-year naturopathic colleges. The school later relocated its campus to Tempe and opened a clinic in Scottsdale. A fourth four-year naturopathic college was launched in 1997 at the University of Bridgeport.

In contrast to the ultraconservative orientation of the Unification movement, many younger naturopathic physicians are politically liberal. In an interview that I had in early November 1999 with Ron Hobbs, a former dean of the university's naturopathic college, he stated that the Unification political and religious agenda had not to date had an obvious impact upon the operation of the naturopathic college. At any rate, ecclesiastical and heterodox medical politics sometimes makes for strange bedfellows. Table 2.2 lists the four-year naturopathic colleges in the United States.

The curriculum at naturopathic colleges in the first two years has come to bear much resemblance with that at biomedical colleges. In a comparative

Table 2.2.   U.S. Naturopathic Colleges

College	Established	Location
National College of Naturopathic Medicine	1956	Portland, Ore.
Bastyr University	1978	Bothell, Wash.
Southwest College of Naturopathic Medicine	1993	Tempe, Ariz.
Bridgeport University College of Naturopathic Medicine	1997	Bridgeport, Conn.

study, Jensen (1997:277) reports that whereas biomedical schools offer 380 hours of basic science instruction in anatomy, 125 in physiology, 109 in biochemistry, 114 in pharmacology, 166 in pathology, and 185 in microbiology/immunology, naturopathic colleges offer 350 hours in anatomy, 250 in physiology, 125 in biochemistry, 100 in pharmacology, 125 in pathology, and 175 in microbiology/immunology. Naturopathic colleges have a minimum of 75 hours in physical diagnosis, 100 in clinical diagnosis, 50 in radiological diagnosis, 150 in herbal medicine, 125 in nutritional medicine, 150 in physical medicine, 25 in acupuncture, 50 in minor surgery, and 144 in homeopathy (Jensen 1997:278).

Whorton (2002:289) identifies the emergence of two factions of naturopathic physicians by the 1960s: (1) the nature cure advocates who emphasized a vitalistic philosophy and (2) the "liberal practitioners belonging to the so-called western group" that wanted to incorporate biomedicine into naturopathy. This schism continues both within the naturopathic profession and at naturopathic colleges. Whereas National College tends to be associated with the vitalist tradition, Bastyr University tends to be associated with the more biomedically oriented scientific one. Indeed, the nature curists or vitalists sometimes disparagingly refer to the biomedically oriented naturopaths as "green allopaths." In turn, both members of both factions often refer to the graduates of the naturopathic correspondence program as UNDs (pronounced "un-dees") or "mail order people."

Efforts to Legitimize Naturopathy

Graduates of the JBCNM and NCNM as well as other naturopathic physicians formed the American Association of Naturopathic Physicians (AANP), which was incorporated in Oregon and held its first annual convention in Scottsdale, Arizona, in 1986. The AANP has 32 state associations and reportedly has about 1,800 members—a figure that includes retirees, supporting members, and students (Hough, Dower, and O'Neill 2001:12). It published the *Journal of Naturopathic Medicine* for several years and hopes to resume publication in the near future. The association recognizes the eclectic nature of naturopathic medicine in its delineation of several naturopathic treatment modalities: (1) clinical nutrition, (2) botanical medicine, (3) homeopathy, (4) hydrotherapy, (5) physical medicine, (6) behavioral medicine, and (7) Oriental medicine. The AANP, which is headquartered in Washington, D.C., is governed by a board and a House of Delegates that consists of representatives from the various state associations. Initially, it had been headquartered in Seattle but relocated to McLean, Virginia, and later to its present site for lobbying purposes. The AANP established the Council of Naturopathic Medical Education (CNME), which in turn granted accreditation to Bastyr University, NCNM, and SCNM and is in the process of evaluating possible accreditation of the College of Naturopathic Medicine at the University of Bridgeport. The CNME created the Naturopathic Physicians Licensing Examination (NPLEX) that is utilized by all licensing jurisdictions. The CNME lost is designation as an official federal accrediting body for a few years ago due to alleged noncompliance with federal guidelines but regained this designation on September 10, 2003, for a two-year period ("U.S. Department of Education," 2003).

Naturopathic licensing laws now exist in twelve states (Alaska, Arizona, California, Connecticut, Hawaii, Maine, Montana, New Hampshire, Oregon, Utah, Vermont, and Washington) as well as Puerto Rico. Naturopathic physicians are "registered" in Kansas and the District of Columbia. The AANP led the drive for licensure of naturopathic physicians in Montana (1991), New Hampshire (1995), Utah (1996), Maine (1996), and Vermont (1996). Licensing laws entitle practitioners to utilize "natural methods," "natural substances," and "natural therapeutics." The New Hampshire law defines naturopathic medicine as "a system of primary health practice by doctors of naturopathic medicine for the prevention, diagnosis, and treatment of human health conditions, injuries, and diseases that uses education, natural medicines and therapies to support and stimulate the individual's intrinsic self-healing processes" (quoted in Sale 1995:13). In the case of the District of Columbia, the naturopathic registration statute "authorizes the mayor to qualify for registration as a naturopath, and permits the mayor in doing so to adopt the standards of a national professional association of naturopaths" (Cohen 1998:37). Whereas the district has several practitioners who are graduates of the four-year naturopathic colleges, it also has registered other naturopaths who have acquired their N.D.'s from other institutions, including the Capital University of Integrative Medicine.

A few states permit naturopathic physicians to perform minor surgery and/or obstetrics. There are approximately 1,500 licensed naturopathic physicians in the United States but another several 100 or so graduates of the four-year naturopathic colleges practicing in unlicensed states. While naturopathic physicians were "sunsetted" in California in 1964, they often practiced under an acupuncture or a chiropractic license there. According to English-Lueck (1990:51), "[n]aturopathic medicine is widespread for a practice that does not officially exist in Paraiso [pseudonym]." Following a ten-year struggle, the California Association of Naturopathic Physicians, along with assistance from Bastyr University, successfully lobbied for licensure of the graduates of the four-year colleges. Just weeks before his recall in a special election, Democratic governor Gray Davis signed on September 22, 2003, Senate Bill 907, which would go into effect as the Naturopathic Doctors Act on January 1, 2004. It is expected that licenses for N.D.'s will be issued beginning in late fall 2004 ("Legislative Update," 2003). SB 907 does permit other alternative practitioners to refer to themselves as "naturopaths," "traditional naturopaths," or "naturopathic practitioners." Bastyr University plans to establish a branch campus in California.

Naturopathic physicians are presently licensed to prescribe drugs in Arizona, Oregon, Utah, Washington State, Vermont, New Hampshire, and Maine, but are restricted in what they may prescribe in the latter three (Hough, Dower, and O'Neil 2001:27). Senate Bill 907 will permit naturopathic physicians in California to prescribe drugs with the oversight of an M.D. or D.O., a scenario identical to that for nurse practitioners. Some naturopathic physicians, however, have reservations about the implications of the new legislation. Robert Broadwell, one of the icons of the naturopathic medical profession and a California practitioner, stated in an interview:

> A lot of the graduates in more recent years have been taught to depend a lot on the formularies and the prescription items. My personal opinion is that anytime we go and insist upon prescription rights, what we're in effect saying is that our methods don't work, therefore we have to use the prescription drugs. My personal opinion is that they have no place in naturopathy. (quoted in Chowka 2003a:3)

Naturopathic physicians are licensed to perform acupuncture in Arizona, Maine (without certification), New Hampshire (without certification), and Vermont (Hough, Dower, and O'Neil 2001:27). Utah became the first state to require a one-year residency for naturopathic licensures, but graduates of the four-year naturopathic colleges are pursuing residencies in other states (Pizzorno and Snider 2001:186).

Various hospitals and health care systems, including the Alternative and Complementary Medical Program at St. Elizabeth's Hospital (the teaching component of Tufts University Medical School), Centura Health (the largest health care system in Colorado), and the American Complementary Care Network, employ naturopathic physicians in both inpatient and outpatient settings. Ironically, some of these health care settings are situated in states where naturopathic physicians do not enjoy licensure.

U.S. naturopathic medicine has been gradually achieving legitimacy and recognition in the larger society. In 1994, the Office of Alternative Medicine of the prestigious National Institute of Health granted Bastyr University, now located in Bothell (a suburb of Seattle), a grant of over $900,000 to conduct research on alternative approaches to HIV and AIDS. The Natural Medical Clinic (founded in 1996) in Kent, Washington, is funded by the King County Department of Public Health, making it the first alternative medical clinic to be publicly funded. In 1999, NCNM became a partner in the Oregon Center for Complementary and Alternative Medicine. Other partners in the center include Kaiser Permanente's Center for Health Research, the Oregon College of Oriental Medicine, Oregon Health Science University's School of Dentistry, the Oregon School of Massage, and Western State Chiropractic College. The Washington State Board of Insurance ruled in favor of paying claims for naturopathic treatment. Indeed, some one hundred insurance companies, most of them situated in Washington State, Connecticut, and Alaska, cover naturopathic care (Stackel 1998:108). Seattle's American Wellness Life offers its subscribers a "wellness plan" that employs naturopathic physicians (Cassileth 1998:52).

Also in 1999, two naturopathic physicians were given seats on the eighteen-person Advisory Council for the National Center for Complementary and Alternative Medicine (formerly Office of Alternative Medicine). Presently, Konrad Kail, a Phoenix practitioner, is the sole naturopathic physician on the council. Growing biomedical interest in at least the sociopolitical status of naturopathy is indicated by a report titled "Profile of a Profession: Naturopathic Practice" published by the Center for Health Professions at the University of California, San Francisco (Hough, Dower, and O'Neil 2001). Harborview Hospital, a teaching hospital of the University of Washington Medical School, and the Seattle–King County Board of Health have naturopathic physicians on their boards (Weeks 2001:10).

Building on its stronghold in the Pacific Northwest, the naturopathic profession has been able to obtain licensing in various other western states as well as Alaska and Hawaii, outliers of a sort. A few states permit naturopathic physicians to perform minor surgery and/or obstetrics. Given that the naturopathic profession never lost its licensing law, which was drafted in the 1920s, in Connecticut, it has in the past decade been able to use its base there as a foothold for obtaining licensure in New Hampshire, Vermont, and Maine. Despite the fact that naturopathic associations now exist in thirty-two states as well as the District of Columbia and Puerto Rico, the profession has thus far been unable to obtain licensure per se in any state outside the West and New England. Naturopathic physicians practicing in these states, other than Kansas and the District of Columbia where they have "registration," in essence do so outside the pale of the law and have sometimes had to face prosecution and expensive legal battles for practicing medicine without a license.

The Alliance for Licensing of Naturopathic Physicians consists of unlicensed naturopathic physicians who in cooperation with the American Association of Naturopathic Physicians and the four-year naturopathic colleges seek strategies for obtaining licensure for the graduates of the four-year schools. The California Association of Naturopathic Physicians (n.d.: 3) successfully campaigned for licensure on the grounds that it assures patients that graduates of the four-year colleges have "met rigorous standards for education, training, and testing." The Colorado Association of Naturopathic Physicians (1998:5) in its campaign for licensure asserts that "[w]ithout licensing, anyone can hang out a shingle and claim to be a naturopath." The AANP and its allied organizations had for a while aimed to achieve licensure in all fifty states by 2008, a goal that at least some naturopathic physicians viewed as unrealistic. Nevertheless, the recent passage of naturopathic medical legislation in California holds out the promise that other states may grant the graduates of the four-year colleges the same privilege. According to Chowka (2003b:1), "the success of the effort to license naturopaths in the nation's largest state, with a population of 35 million, reflects the new power of the relatively small segment of the American naturopathic medical community that favors licensing and regulation of naturopaths (NDs)."

ORIENTAL MEDICINE AND ACUPUNCTURE: LEGITIMATION WITHIN AN UNCERTAIN CONTEXT

Some nineteenth-century European and U.S. M.D.'s were drawn to acupuncture (Whorton 2002:259). The revival of acupuncture and Oriental medicine in the United States in part was a byproduct of the hippie movement's interest in Eastern spiritual traditions. The reopening of diplomatic relations between the People's Republic of China and the United States with Nixon's visit to the former in 1971 served as a major impetus for a growing interest in acupuncture in this country. In July 1971, during his tour to the PRC, *New York Times* columnist James Reston received acupuncture treatment in conjunction with surgery for acute appendicitis. Later in the same year, four U.S. M.D.'s gave favorable reports on their observations of applications of acupuncture in the PRC (Whorton 2002:256). The first demonstration of acupuncture in San Francisco in May 1972 packed the meeting. A month later, "a symposium on acupuncture held at Stanford University drew 1,400 physicians, [so] many more registrants than expected that the meeting had to be moved to a larger hall" (Whorton 2002:266).

Despite a marked interest on the part of some biomedical physicians in acupuncture, the development of this therapy on the part of heterodox practitioners proved to be more slippery. The Acupuncture Center of New York opened its doors in summer 1972 and offered therapy for migraine, arthritis, hypertension, asthma, and other ailments, but it was closed by state department of education after a week (Whorton 2002:267–68). Despite this setback, as part of their endeavor to professionalize themselves, acupuncturists established schools around the United States. The first acupuncture schools opened in Boston and San Francisco in the mid-1970s (Whorton 2002:269). The Office of Alternative Medicine (1992:71) reported that many acupuncture schools transformed themselves into "colleges of Oriental medicine" by adding courses in massage, herbalism, and dietary therapy. There are more than fifty schools of acupuncture and Oriental medicine located in seventeen states. Fifteen of these are located in California alone ("Resources," 2001).

The San Francisco Bay Area has two well-known schools of traditional Chinese medicine (TCM) that offer an M.Sc. degree: the American College of Traditional Chinese Medicine in San Francisco and the Academy of Chinese Culture and Health Sciences in Oakland. Both of these institutions orient their graduates to pass the California licensing examination. According to Grossinger (1990:404), the former "has a tough medical-school level program in many holistic disciplines, integrating Oriental techniques with Western physiology, biochemistry and laboratory work." The Academy of Chinese Culture and Health Sciences (established in 1982) offers three programs of study: an M.Sc. in TCM, a one-year program leading to acupuncture certification, and a program for licensed acupuncturists. The curriculum includes a heavy emphasis on Western scientific courses. The Meiji College of Oriental Medicine in the Japantown section of San Francisco offers an M.Sc. in Oriental Medicine. It traces its origins to Kyoto, where the first Meiji college was established, and seeks to integrate Western and Eastern medicine.

The Council of Colleges of Acupuncture and Oriental Medicine (CCAOM; founded in 1982) is a voluntary membership association of acupuncture and Oriental medicine colleges (Mitchell 2002:378). It has forty-two member schools, develops academic and clinical guidelines and core curriculum requirements, and supports research and other academic endeavors in Oriental medicine ("What Is CCAOM?" 2001). The CCAOM in turn established the Accreditation Commission for Acupuncture and Oriental Medicine (ACAOM) as an accrediting body for acupuncture and Oriental medicine schools (Council of Colleges of Acupuncture and Oriental Medicine 2001). The ACAOM is recognized by the U.S. Department of Education as an official accrediting body, which permits students at its accredited schools to qualify for federally guaranteed loans. The ACAOM accredits two types of programs: a three-year master's level program in acupuncture and a four-year master's level program in Oriental medicine. It has developed standards for a doctorate in Oriental medicine. As of 1999, twenty-nine schools had achieved ACAOM accreditation and eleven candidacy status (Lyons 2000:428). Table 2.3 provides a partial listing of colleges offering a master's degree in acupuncture.

There are numerous other acupuncture and Oriental medicine organizations with varying missions. They include the National Accreditation Commission for Schools and Colleges of Acupuncture and Oriental Medicine (NACSCOM); the National Acupuncture and Oriental Medicine Alliance (NAOMA); the Acupuncture and Oriental Medicine Alliance; the American Association of Teachers of Oriental Medicine; the American Organization for

Table 2.3.   Selected Listing of Colleges Offering a Master's Degree in Acupuncture

College	Location
Acupuncture and Herbal Medicine College, Tai Hsuan	Honolulu, Hawaii
American College of Traditional Chinese Medicine	San Francisco, Calif.
Emperor's College of Traditional Chinese Medicine	Santa Monica, Calif.
International Institute of Chinese Medicine	Santa Fe, N.M.
Meiji College of Oriental Medicine	San Francisco, Calif.
Midwest Center for the Study of Oriental Medicine	Racine, Wisc.
New England School of Acupuncture	Watertown, Mass.
Phoenix Institute of Herbal Medicine and Acupuncture	Phoenix, Ariz.
Oregon College of Oriental Medicine	Portland, Ore.
Texas College of Traditional Chinese Medicine	Austin, Tex.
Traditional Acupuncture Institute	Columbia, Md.
Yo Sa University Traditional Chinese Medicine	Santa Monica, Calif.

the Bodywork Therapy of Asia; the International Veterinary Acupuncture Society; the North American Acupuncture and Oriental Medicine Council; the National Acupuncture Foundation; the National Sports Acupuncture Association; the Society for Acupuncture Research; the National Commission for the Certification of Acupuncturists (NCCA); and the National Academy of Acupuncture and Oriental Medicine (NAAOM) (Mitchell 2002:376). The National Acupuncture Detoxification Association provides thirty hours of classroom instruction and forty hours of work in detoxification.

Beginning in the early 1970s, acupuncturists, the majority of them Asian, began lobbying for licensure (Kao and McRae 1990). Organized biomedicine resisted this effort by initiating a twofold strategy that included (1) research designed to incorporate acupuncture into biomedicine and (2) promoting legislation and propaganda to wrest acupuncture from nonconventional physician acupuncturists (Wolpe 1985).

The Nevada legislature granted practice rights to acupuncturists in July 1973 and Oregon and Maryland passed similar laws shortly afterward. Two more western states followed suit in 1974 and another eight states had adopted acupuncture licensing laws by 1980. By 1978, California had five hundred nonconventional physician acupuncturists (Wolpe 1985:419); in 1979, they were declared primary health care practitioners who could be covered by Medi-Cal, California's Medicaid program. In 1984, Nevada became the first state to establish a Board of Oriental Medicine. Initially, most of the states along the Atlantic and Pacific coasts implemented acupuncture practice laws whereas most of the interior states did not (Baer and Good 1998:51). Thirty-eight states and the District of Columbia now have acupuncture and Oriental medicine practice acts that license, certify, or register acupuncturists. Whereas most of these states grant the designation "Licensed Acupuncturist," Arkansas grants the designation "Doctor of Oriental Medicine," Florida the designation "Acupuncture Physician," Rhode Island the designation "Doctor of Acupuncture," and several states simply the designation "Acupuncturist" (Mitchell 2002:382–83). Acupuncturists and Oriental medicine physicians are overwhelmingly concentrated in California. In 2001, there were 4,421 licensed acupuncturists in California alone. The next leading states in terms of numbers of licensed acupuncturists were Florida with 921, New York with 576, Maryland with 507, Massachusetts with 418, Colorado with 375, Texas with 372, New Mexico with 359, Oregon with 306, Pennsylvania with 301, Illinois with 266, Washington state with 260, and Arizona with 199 ("Resources," 2002). Many states that have not passed acupuncture licensing laws tolerate *sub rosa* practices.

Graduates of acupuncture and Oriental medicine schools are not the only practitioners who provide acupuncture treatment. Some states permit M.D.'s and D.O.'s to practice acupuncture without additional training. Other states require them to obtain some additional acupuncture training. New Mexico requires M.D.'s to obtain a separate license to practice acupuncture and to pass the same examination required of graduates of acupuncture and Oriental medicine schools (Morton and Morton 1996:172). An estimated three thousand conventional physicians have taken short courses in acupuncture (Milbank Memorial Fund 1998:9). Some states permit, at least with additional training, physicians' assistants, dentists, podiatrists, chiropractors, and naturopathic physicians to practice acupuncture. Despite a tendency by many alternative practitioners toward professionalization, others resist this process for a variety of reasons. Some acupuncturists ignore or circumvent licensing requirements. Practitioners of Chinese medicine often are located in Chinatowns and practice in back rooms of gift shops, where they treat low-income Chinese patients.

Whereas in its homeland, acupuncture and Chinese medicine is used to treat many ailments, in the United States, partly among non-Chinese patients, it tends be used primarily to relieve pain, stress, anxiety, and fatigue (Katz 2000:192). Acupuncture treatment has also become popular with HIV patients to alleviate some of the side effects, such as neuropathy, of antiretroviral medications

(Sanders 1989). Acupuncturists generally insert small needles at points along the meridians that are believed to be the conduits for *chi*, or energy essential for balanced health. Many practitioners use acupressure or shiatsu, moxibustion, cupping, and electromagnetic energy to stimulate the flow of *chi*. Chinese medicine relies heavily on the administration of herbs in treating diseases and generally entails blending several herbs into one mixture. Acupuncture has been increasingly used to treat drug addiction. Lincoln Hospital in New York City has been treating drug addicts with acupuncture for over twenty-five years ("The Fine Points of Acupuncture," 2003). The Lincoln model has been adopted in over four hundred detoxification centers in the United States and Europe. Oregon law requires that addicts can enter methadone treatment only after they have been unsuccessful in treatment with a combination of acupuncture and counseling treatment for a year.

Oriental medicine physicians often view their practices as holistic and comprehensive alternatives to biomedicine. Based on ethnographic observations in the Boston area, Barnes (1998) maintains that many non-Chinese practitioners of traditional Chinese medicine have incorporated psychotherapeutic concepts into their treatments of what they term "blocked emotions."

> For some practitioners, these associations lead to a more explicit redefinition of their own practice as overlapping with psychotherapy. . . . For other practitioners, acupuncture is a plausible alternative to psychotherapy. Indeed, they feel it is possible to perform interventions for psychological problems that would eliminate the need for psychotherapy altogether. Still other practitioners who distinguish between what one does as an acupuncturist and as a psychologist choose not to blend the two. (417)

Lee, Berde, and Kemper (1999) administered a questionnaire to 147 out of 227 licensed acupuncturists in the Boston area. They found that 70 percent of the practitioners were white, 29 percent Asian, and 1 percent African American, and 61 percent were female. Ninety-five percent of the patients who obtained services from these acupuncturists paid out of pocket with the remaining five percent covered by insurance plans, including Medicaid. Cassidy (1998) conducted the most comprehensive survey of Chinese medicine users thus far. Based on a sample of 575 patients drawn from six clinics in five states, she found that 411 (72.1 percent) were female, and 89.3 percent were white (as opposed to 2.1 percent who were black and 2.9 percent who were

Asian) (Cassidy 1998). Patients tended to be middle-aged, to be highly educated, and to have relatively high incomes.

Acupuncture and Oriental medicine have enjoyed a pattern of growth within the larger context of the holistic health movement. It offers a relatively safe and generally inexpensive form of health care that appears to provide relief from a wide variety of chronic ailments. As a professionalized heterodox medical system that defines itself as a form of primary care, acupuncture and Oriental medicine poses increasing competition for biomedicine as well as chiropractic and naturopathy. Robert Anderson (1991:466) asserts that acupuncturists and Oriental medicine physicians are "encroaching in part on chiropractic territory, in part on an area of competence claimed by a variety of mental health professionals, and in part on the domain of family practitioners." One key factor that naturopathic physicians cite for their profession's failure to obtain licensure in California, in contrast to most other Western states, is the strength of acupuncture and Oriental medicine in the former state. While licensing laws and other forms of state recognition have legitimated acupuncture and Oriental medicine, at least in part, these measures have forced its practitioners to accommodate their training programs and therapeutic procedures to the biomedical model.

HOMEOPATHY

Samuel Hahnemann (1755–1843), a German physician, became frustrated with the ineffectiveness of regular medicine. In the course of translating both classical and contemporary medical works into German, he began to consider how drugs affect the human body and developed the first principle of homeopathy, the "law of similars," which states that "like cures like." On the basis of his own experiments, Hahnemann concluded that an efficacious medicine is one that induces in a healthy person symptoms similar to those of the disease for which it is administered. In the course of applying this principle, he developed the second principle of homeopathy, the "law of infinitesimals," which asserts that the potency of a medicine increases the more that it is diluted. Homeopathic medicine can be derived from plants, poisonous substances, minerals, animals, reptiles, and insects. Homeopaths administer remedies for both preventive and curative purposes. Because homeopathic remedies are highly individualized, people with the same diagnosis may be treated with different substances.

In due course, homeopathy not only became fashionable among the aristocracy and higher social classes in Europe but also diffused to many other countries, including the United States, where it developed into the foremost competitor to regular medicine during the nineteenth century (Kaufman 1971). By 1898, homeopathic physicians had established nine national societies, thirty-three state societies, eighty-five local societies, thirty-nine other local organizations, sixty-six general hospitals, seventy-four specialty hospitals, and thirty-one journals in the United States (Rothstein 1972:236). Homeopaths operated twenty-two colleges in 1900, including ones affiliated with Boston University, the University of Michigan, and the University of Minnesota (Coulter 1973:450). With the evolution of regular medicine into biomedicine as the clearly dominant medical system in the United States during the early twentieth century, homeopathy underwent a rapid decline that included the closure of homeopathic schools or their conversion into biomedical schools. Hahnemann Medical College had transformed itself more or less into a biomedical school by making its sole remaining course on homeopathy an elective in 1947 and by dropping it in 1958 (Rogers 1998:196). Organized U.S. homeopathy, however, managed to linger on until the mid-twentieth century. The International Hahnemannian Association discontinued publishing its proceedings in 1947 and ceased operations in 1957 when its few remaining members joined the struggling American Foundation for Homeopathy (Coulter 1973:450). Although the foundation's postgraduate course was offered into the 1960s, it trained only small numbers of physicians in homeopathy. Fewer than one hundred U.S. M.D.'s were practicing homeopathy in the early 1970s (Whorton 2002:273).

In contrast to homeopathy during the nineteenth century and chiropractic and naturopathic medicine at the present time, present-day homeopathy functions to a large degree as an adjunct to biomedicine, osteopathic medicine, chiropractic, naturopathic medicine, dentistry, nursing, and clinical psychology. Some practitioners in these fields make homeopathy the focus of their practice. While apparently some laypersons also practice homeopathy, most of the homeopathic certification programs cater to health professionals. An estimated three thousand homeopaths are practicing in the United States, some five hundred of whom are M.D.'s or D.O.'s (Freeman 2001a:348). Most of the remainder are dentists, podiatrists, veterinarians, nurse practitioners, physician assistants, naturopathic physicians, chiropractors, acupuncturists, and even laypeople.

Despite its small size, homeopathy is represented by a multiplicity of or-ganizations. The American Institute of Homeopathy (founded in 1844) grants a diplomate to biomedical and osteopathic physicians and dentists who have passed a written and an oral examination. The American Board of Homeotherapeutics offers a "Diplomate in Homeopathy" to M.D.'s and D.O.'s (Lyons 2000:438). The North American Society of Homeopaths provides a written and practical competency examination for "nonphysician home-opaths" and has been urging the passage of state legislation so that they can receive health insurance reimbursement (Collinge 1987:163). The Council for Homeopathic Certification certifies individuals who have undergone five hundred hours of homeopathic training from either homeopathic schools or a combination of homeopathic schools and seminars (Lyons 2000:438). The North American Society of Homeopaths (established in 1990) also certifies health professionals as homeopaths, publishes a journal of classical homeop-athy, and makes a clear distinction between professional homeopaths and lay homeopaths (Lyons 2000:439). The National Center for Homeopathy in Alexandria, Virginia, offers training programs and seminars in homeopathy for both health practitioners and the public and publishes *Homeopathy Today,* a monthly magazine (Lyons 2000:452). Other homeopathic associations in-clude the National Center for Homeopathy, the Society for the Establishment of Research in Classical Homeopathy in Phoenix, the American Institute of Homeopathy, the Homeopathic Academy of Naturopathic Physicians, and the Chiropractic Academy of Homeopathy. The American Association of Homeo-pathic Pharmacists represents the majority of companies that produce home-opathic formulations. The Council on Homeopathic Education (founded in 1982) evaluates homeopathic training programs in the United States and Canada (Lyons 2000:230).

Table 2.4 provides a partial list of homeopathic training institutions in the United States. In addition to these, natural healing schools, such as the Amer-ican University of Complementary Medicine in California, and naturopathic colleges, such the Southwest College of Naturopathic Medicine, and the Na-tional College of Chiropractic offer courses in homeopathy.

In contrast to the popular orientation of the Pacific Academy in San Fran-cisco, the Hahnemann College of Homeopathy exemplifies the efforts of various homeopaths either to professionalize themselves or to further legitimize their endeavors, especially in instances where they already hold biomedical credentials

Table 2.4.   A Partial Listing of Homeopathic Training Institutions

School	Established	Location
Atlantic Academy of Classical Homeopathy	1989	New York, N.Y.
Colorado Institute for Classical Homeopathy	1991	Boulder, Colo.
Desert Institute School of Classical Homeopathy	1999	Phoenix, Ariz.
Hahnemann College of Homeopathy	1986	Richmond, Calif.
Institute of Classical Homeopathy	1992	St. Helena, Calif.
National Center for Homeopathy	1922	Alexandria, Va.
Northwestern School of Homeopathy	1994	Plymouth, Minn.
Pacific Academy of Homeopathic Medicine	1985	San Francisco, Calif.
School of Homeopathy	1998	New York, N.Y.
Teleosis School of Homeopathy	1997	New York, N.Y.

(Lyons 2000:87–80). It offers an 864-hour program in classical homeopathy to licensed health professionals, including chiropractors, naturopathic physicians, physician assistants, and acupuncturists, "in four-day sessions per year for four years," but does not admit clinical psychologists. The Desert Institute School of Classical Homeopathy offers a "Homeopathic Practitioner Certification Program" for M.D.'s, D.O.'s, naturopathic physicians, and nurse practitioners and a "Homeopathic Medical Assistant Certificate Program" for "nonmedically licensed practitioners" who "have either a bachelor's degree or an associate's degree with two years of experience in allied health" (Desert Institute School of Classical Homeopathy brochure). The school's core faculty consists of two M.D.'s, a licensed acupuncturist, and a chiropractor. Naturopathic colleges and the National College of Chiropractic also offer courses on homeopathy. The National Center for Homeopathy conducts a summer school where it provides classes designed for health care professionals as well as individuals interested in acquiring homeopathic knowledge for family or personal use ("About NCH," 2003). The center lists nineteen U.S. institutions that offer courses in homeopathy, although this figure probably does not include all such institutions (National Center for Homeopathy Education Directory, 2003).

Arizona, Connecticut, and Nevada have homeopathic licensing boards. Medical boards regulate homeopaths in Delaware and New Hampshire (Milbank Memorial Fund 1998:10). Nevada licenses Advanced Practitioners of Homeopathy who collaborate with M.D.'s or D.O.'s (Lyons 2000:14). Some states regulate homeopaths through "scope of practice" guidelines. Obviously, states vary greatly in their tolerance for homeopathy. In this regard, Borre and Wilson (1998) present a case study in which they compare and contrast the climate for homeopathy in Pennsylvania and North Carolina. In 1995, Penn-

sylvania, with a population of over twelve million, had twenty-two listed practicing homeopaths (thirteen licensed physicians, three veterinarians, one
nurse practitioner, two physician assistants, two naturopaths, and one chiropractor) and fourteen homeopathic study groups; North Carolina, with a
population of over seven million, had six listed homeopaths (two physicians,
a naturopathic physician/nurse, two veterinarians, and a chiropractor) and six
homeopathic study groups. Although the numbers of practicing homeopaths
in both states are quite small, Borre and Wilson (1998:79) explain the pro-
portionally greater number of practicing homeopaths in Pennsylvania in
terms of a stronger "history of tolerance of diverse beliefs and practices" than
exists in North Carolina. In contrast to the "social context in which complementary medicine can be successfully integrated into community life" that exists in Pennsylvania, North Carolina exhibits a social climate of "apathy and
rejection" toward heterodox practitioners in which "biomedical physicians
know little about homeopathy and do not teach alternative therapies in medical schools" (Borre and Wilson 1998:79–80). There actually may be more
laypeople and unlicensed providers practicing homeopathy than licensed
homeopaths. According to Baer and Good (1998:63), "[m]any lay homeopaths limit their practices to family and friends. Others practice without legal sanction, charging for services and building professional practices."

Licensed health professionals who practice homeopathy in the United
States are listed in a directory sold by Homeopathic Educational Services and
the National Center for Homeopathy based in Berkeley (Ullman 1991). Relatively little is known about the manner in which homeopathy is practiced and
who utilizes it in the United States. Jacobs, Chapman, and Crothers (1998)
conducted a study of twenty-seven conventional physicians (M.D.'s and
D.O.'s) who practice homeopathy and the social characteristics of their patients. They found that these physicians tend to spend more time with their
patients, order fewer tests, and prescribe fewer biomedical drugs than their
more conventional counterparts. The homeopathic patients tended to be
younger, more affluent, and more likely to present with long-term complaints
than patients seeking conventional treatment.

CONCLUSION

Of the four professionalized heterodox medical systems discussed in this
chapter, chiropractic constitutes the most accepted example of alternative

medicine in the United States today, despite the fact that its history has been marked by considerable factionalism. Moore (1993:138) contends that chiropractic "has moved into position as the orthodox, nontraditional approach to health—a type of orthodox unorthodoxy" that occupies a niche between biomedicine (and, I would add, osteopathic medicine) and the popular holistic health movement. In contrast, naturopathic medicine and Chinese medicine and acupuncture have not yet achieved licensing in all fifty states, whereas chiropractic has, and thus these can be termed secondary professionalized heterodox medical systems within the context of the U.S. dominative medical system.

Finally, in contrast to its distinguished status during the nineteenth century, the status of homeopathy as a professionalized heterodox medical system is quite ambiguous given that it is practiced, on the one hand, by some biomedical physicians as well as other biomedical health professionals and, on the other hand, by partially professionalized and lay practitioners of various sorts, including ones who term themselves "homeopaths."

Partially Professionalized Therapeutic Systems

The Struggle for Legitimacy

In addition to chiropractic, naturopathic medicine, acupuncture and Oriental medicine, and homeopathy, the holistic health movement encompasses a wide array of other heterodox healing systems, which I term "partially professionalized heterodox therapeutic systems," some of which are depicted in figure 3.1. These therapeutic systems generally entail training through apprenticeships, correspondence or distant learning courses, workshops, and/or relatively short intensive-training programs. Their practitioners also have created professional associations and conduct periodic conferences. Although massage therapists are licensed in most states, practitioners affiliated with virtually all the other partially professionalized and lay heterodox therapeutic systems either have created certification programs of their own or eschew professionalization per se (e.g., many herbalists and at least some midwives).

Space precludes a detailed discussion of most of the partially professionalized or lay therapeutic systems listed in figure 3.1. Virtually no social scientific or historical research has thus far been conducted on various partially professionalized heterodox therapeutic systems such as reflexology, Rolfing, Reiki, bioenergetics, and polarity. Fortunately, numerous resource guides on alternative medicine include discussions of these systems, although primarily in terms of their philosophies and treatment modalities (Rosenfeld 1996; Bratman 1997; Freeman and Lawlis 2001). The remainder of this chapter focuses on selected partially professionalized and lay heterodox healing systems: "traditional naturopathy," herbalism, massage therapy as an example of bodywork, Ayurveda and yoga as examples of mind–body medicine, and various forms of New Age healing. The glossary provides a brief description of various partially professionalized heterodox, religious, and folk medical or therapeutic systems.

Emerging heterodox therapeutic systems have repeatedly embarked on a process of professionalization in that they have sought to obtain legitimacy, generally in the form of legal recognition of some sort from the state or recognition from an accrediting body, even one internal to a specific therapeutic system. English-Lueck (1990:155–58) delineates four steps in the process by which heterodox practitioners in Paraiso (a pseudonym for a small southern California city) and elsewhere undergo professionalization: (1) full-time activity as a healer or therapist; (2) establishment of a school or accredited academy; (3) establishment of an association, such as the American Massage

---

"Traditional Naturopathy"

Herbalism
Bodywork
   Acupressure
   Alexander Technique
   Applied Kinesiology
   Feldenkrais Method
   Massage
   Reflexology
   Rolfing
   Shiatsu
Mind–Body Medicine
   Ayurveda
   Bioenergetics
   Biofeedback
   Guided Visualization
   Hypnotherapy
   Iridiology
   Meditation
   Polarity Therapy
   Reiki
   Therapeutic Touch
   Yoga
Lay Midwifery
New Age Healing
   Channeling
   Crystal Therapy
   Neoshamanism

FIGURE 3.1.
Selected Partially Professionalized and Lay Heterodox Therapeutic Systems

Therapy Association; and (4) establishment of an umbrella organization, such as the California Health Practitioners Association. Heterodox practitioners in the United States obtain legal recognition through licensing, certification, or registration (Milbank Memorial Fund 1998:14).

"TRADITIONAL NATUROPATHY"

Despite its organizational rejuvenation, the future of American naturopathic medicine as a more or less fully professionalized heterodox medical system remains tenuous for several reasons. These include the fact that it still has not achieved licensure in the vast majority of states, growing competition from other natural healers who often label themselves "traditional naturopaths," and the danger of co-option of its scope of practice by biomedicine—an issue that other alternative medical systems also face. Ironically, some of the very forces that allowed naturopathy to recover its footing—namely, a significant growth in popular interest in naturalistic approaches to health care—might well lead to a loss of organizational momentum.

Increasingly, the graduates of the four-year naturopathic colleges are encountering competition from partially professionalized or lay naturopaths. The partially professionalized or lay naturopaths often obtain training through apprenticeships and from various naturopathic or natural therapeutic schools that require a shorter program of study. Many of these schools, but not all, have also been established since the 1970s in response to the growing interest in the general public in natural healing strategies. This development, as an outgrowth of popular values that concretized during the late 1960s and early 1970s—values that are a product of the confluence of the ecology movement, the self-actualization movement, and healthy diet concerns—created a demand for alternative, naturalistic, and herbal healing approaches by the mid- to late 1970s. New rapid-education natural healing or naturopathic schools include (or have included, given that some of them have closed their doors) the Academy of Natural Therapies; the American Institute of Holistic Theology in Youngstown, Ohio; the California Naturopathic College in Del Mar; the First National University of Naturopathy; the Gateways College of Naturopathy in Shingle Springs, California; the Trinity School of Natural Health in Warsaw, Indiana; the University of Natural Medicine; Arizona College of Naturopathic Medicine; the American College of Naturopathic Medicine in Oregon; the Natural Therapeutics College in Mesa, Arizona; Dr. Jay

Sherer's Academy of Natural Healing in Santa Fe, New Mexico; the New Mexico School of Natural Therapeutics in Albuquerque; the North American College of Natural Sciences in Mill Valley, California; the International College of Naturopathy in Santa Barbara, California; the Clayton College of Natural Health in Birmingham, Alabama; the Hallmark Naturopathic College in Sulfur Springs, Oklahoma; the Natural Healing Institute in Encinitas, California; the University of Natural Medicine in Santa Fe; the Yamuni Institute of Healing Arts in Lafayette, Indiana; the Southern College of Naturopathy in Arkansas; and Westbrook University in Aztec, New Mexico (Hough et al. 2001:66–72).

Many of these institutions have created websites as a means of attracting students. The Clayton College of Natural Health, which was established by Lloyd Clayton (a naturopath) in 1980, describes itself as "the world's leading college of natural health" and claims that it has over fifteen thousand students and graduates ("Introduction to Clayton College of Natural Health," 2000). Its School of Natural Health offers a B.S. and M.S. in natural health, a doctor of naturopathy, a doctor of natural health, and a doctor of philosophy in natural health. Clayton also offers a naturopathic medical doctor (N.M.D.) for biomedical and osteopathic physicians and a doctor of naturopathy for chiropractors. The Hallmark Naturopath College offers correspondence courses in naturopathy, herbology, reflexology, aromatherapy, Native Medicine, and biologic ionization technology ("Welcome to Hallmark Naturopath College," 2000).

Westbrook University offers various degree programs, including ones in clinical nutrition, holistic nursing, integrative medicine, feng shui, and homeopathic medicine. Norbert E. Matts, the institution's chancellor, holds a doctorate in education, and Nita Resler, its president, holds a bachelor's degree in art education, a master's degree in ageless wisdom and spirituality from Westbrook, and a honorary Ph.D. from Faith Bible College and Seminary. Completion of its doctor of naturopathy program requires completion of a baccalaureate degree, "174 credit hours of personal studies and/or life/work experiential credits in fields of Natural Healing and Nutrition," "completion of 35 credit hours (525 actual) of independent research, observations and practicals in the field of natural health sciences," and "completion of 70 credit hours (1050 actual hours) in a clinical externship in the region where the student resides" ("Westbrook University—A World Leader," 1999). Furthermore,

Westbrook University offers a "special adaptation of our Naturopathic program to Allopathic, Chiropractic, Osteopathic and other professional practitioners who are seeking to expand their knowledge and expertise in the field of wholistic natural healing" ("Westbrook University," 1999). In 1999, the listed "maximum cost" for earning the doctor of naturopathy degree was $16,201.64. In addition to accreditation from the New Mexico Commission on Higher Education and various other bodies, Westbrook University has been accredited by the American Naturopathic Medical Association. Partially professionalized and lay naturopaths obtain much of their training in apprenticeships with practicing naturopaths, but little information is available on the nature of these apprenticeships. Hough, Dower, and O'Neil (2001) report the following:

> While many of the [naturopathic] programs provide residential and on-site coursework, a significant number of them offer distance learning opportunities via traditional correspondence or electronic means. Length of programs varies considerably. A few programs are 3–4 years long but the majority offer degrees for 2 years or less of education. (65)

The partially professionalized or lay naturopaths have come to refer to themselves as "traditional naturopaths" and disparagingly refer to the graduates of the four-year colleges as "allopathic naturopaths" or "medical naturopaths." Various groups consisting of partially professionalized and lay natural healers, but also holistic M.D.'s, osteopathic physicians, and chiropractors, oppose the efforts of the American Association of Naturopathic Physicians to obtain licensing for the graduates of the four-year schools. Organizations such as Citizens for Health, the Coalition of Natural Health, the American Naturopathic Medical Association, and the Naturopathic Association of America have played a role in recent years in blocking the passage of naturopathic licensing laws in California, Texas, Minnesota, Kentucky, Iowa, Massachusetts, Kansas, Minnesota, and Texas. In Texas, the reportedly eight-hundred-member Texas Naturopathy Association opposed licensure for the few graduates of four-year schools in that state.

The American Naturopathic Medical Association (ANMA), which is based in Las Vegas and holds annual conventions, appears to function as a loose consortium of representatives from the correspondence schools, partially professionalized and lay naturopaths, and some holistic M.D.'s, osteopathic physicians, and chiropractors who are practicing alternative therapies. It claims to have some two thousand members in the United States, Canada, and fourteen other countries and to constitute the "largest natural medical association in America today" (American Naturopathic Medical Association 1999b). In March 1998, ANMA formed an affiliate called the Texas State Naturopathy Medical Association that has opposed licensure for graduates of the four-year naturopathic colleges in Texas. ANMA favors certification of naturopaths rather than licensing per se and views the former as recognition of "expertise and proven ability without limiting entrance into or employment in the field" (American Naturopathic Medical Association 1999a). It also favors a national certification program rather than certification regulations in the various states. ANMA refers to the AANP as a "very small group of approximately 350 N.D.'s who share a misguided belief that they are 'primary care physicians'" (American Naturopathic Medical Association 1999c). George A. Freibott (1990), an ANMA member, accuses the graduates of the four-year naturopathic colleges of practicing "pseudomedicalism."

ANMA has created the American Naturopathic Medical Certification and Accreditation Board as an instrument to provide the partially professionalized and lay naturopaths with some semblance of legitimacy and "supports the current registration of Naturopaths in Washington, D.C., regulated by the Department of Regulatory Affairs/Corp. Div." (American Naturopathic Medical Association 1999c). The American Naturopathic Medical Certification and Accreditation Board charges $550 for certification as a naturopathic physician and only requires the applicant to provide information on education, internships/residencies, and other certifications and two letters of reference. ANMCAB certification is currently not recognized by any state. In 2001, it reported a total of 3,679 certified practitioners, including 660 in California, 330 in New York, and 462 in Texas (Hough, Dower, and O'Neil 2001:55). An unspecified number of "traditional naturopaths" apparently have not opted to obtain certification from the ANMCAB. At any rate, the number of "traditional naturopaths," a fair number of whom hold M.D.'s or D.O.'s, greatly outnumbers the number of graduates of the four-year naturopathic schools.

Wendall W. Whitman (1999) states in an editorial titled "Licensure Laws Seek to Restrict Freedoms for Naturopaths":

Licensure is a program which provides a monopoly for those it licenses. . . .
There is no need to restrict traditional naturopathy with licensure laws. Such
laws are not in the best interests of the public, but cater only to the selfish desires of a tiny minority of special interest lobby groups attempting to wag the
dog by the tail. (1)

A representative of ANMA maintains in a letter to *Prevention* magazine that
ANMA regards naturopathy as "a practice of noninvasive therapies and life
style counseling" that does not require licensing (American Naturopathic
Medical Association 1999c). The AANP opposes certification on the grounds
that it "does not carry with it the scrutiny of a licensing board nor regulation
of any sort, save that of the certifying organization itself" (American Association of Naturopathic Physicians n.d.:1).

The Coalition for Natural Health (CNH) also claims to represent the "traditional naturopaths." It has been involved in campaigns to deny the "allopathic
naturopaths" licensure in Minnesota, California, New Jersey, Texas, and Massachusetts and has opposed efforts on the part of the graduates of the four-year
schools to obtain payments from insurance companies. CNH claims to have
some six hundred members in Texas alone. In an article titled "Licensing Natural Health Is Bad Medicine" (Coalition for Natural Health 2000:1), it asserts
that whereas "naturopathic physicians and dieticians advocate diagnostic care,
. . . traditional naturopaths and holistic nutrition counselors emphasize healthy
lifestyle choices and wellness care." In other words, CNH claims that graduates
of the four-year colleges have adopted the biomedical emphasis on curing illness, while it claims for itself an emphasis on prevention and the maintenance
of good health. CNH laments the fact that "traditional naturopathy" is illegal
in eleven states and "holistic nutrition counseling" is illegal in nineteen states.
As this account indicates, the growing popular acceptance of the natural healing approach has helped to spawn an easy-access paraprofessional route to
naturopathic healing. This development flows naturally from the very anti–big
institution, antihierarchy values that led to expanded popular interest in alternative healing. Ironically, however, this development has become a threat to established naturopathic colleges and their full legitimation.

In reality, despite considerable rhetoric on the part of both the graduates of
the four-year naturopathic schools and the partially professionalized naturopaths, it is virtually impossible without considerable ethnographic research

to determine how their respective philosophies are implemented in their scopes of practice. Bradley (1999) summarizes the wide array of therapies practiced by the professionalized naturopaths or graduates of the four-year schools as follows:

> For example, there are still practitioners who adhere to the strict "nature cure" tradition and focus only on diet, "detoxification," lifestyle modification, and hydrotherapy. There are also those who specialize in homeopathy, acupuncture or natural childbirth. At the other end of the spectrum are found naturopathic physicians who extensively use natural medicinal substances to manipulate the body chemistry and physiology. Finally, there is the majority who practice an eclectic naturopathic practice that includes a little of everything. (41)

Although many graduates of four-year colleges speak disparagingly of the training and alleged incompetence of the graduates of the correspondence schools, one graduate of a four-year college who practices in Colorado told me that she respects the abilities of at least some of the latter whom she has encountered. Given that tuition at the four-year naturopathic schools is relatively high, it is very likely that individuals with fewer funds at their disposal and possibly of a lower socioeconomic status may opt to obtain their training from one of the correspondence schools. For example, tuition and fees came to $15,279 and books and supplies came to an estimated $1,445 for the 1999–2000 academic year at Bastyr University (Bastyr University 1999:16). In contrast, Westbrook University offers a program of study leading to the Doctor of Naturopathy (N.D.) for a maximum cost of $16,201.64 ("Westbrook University—Registration," 1999:2).

Some graduates of the four-year colleges have proposed the creation of a two-tiered regulatory system, similar to the one that exists in Puerto Rico, that would make a distinction between themselves as "naturopathic physicians" and "naturopaths" who must meet board-approved educational requirements of some sort. It seems unlikely, however, that many members of the general public will be able to make a distinction between a "naturopathic physician" and a "naturopath" any more than they are able to make a distinction between a "chiropractic physician" and a "chiropractor." As a result, a two-tiered regulatory system may not serve as an effective way by which the graduates of the four-year colleges could effectively counter growing competition from the graduates of the correspondence schools.

HERBALISM

Herbalism, or the utilization of plants for medicinal purposes, is one of the oldest healing practices and exists in virtually all sociocultural systems around the world. It is also referred to as *herbal medicine, herbology, phytomedicine*, and *botanical medicine*. In the nineteenth century, herbalism was an integral part of Thompsonian botanical medicine and later eclectic medicine. Herbalism contains subfields that draw on either biomedicine or energy medicine and is a prominent part of the holistic health movement and specific professionalized heterodox therapeutic systems, particularly naturopathy, homeopathy, Oriental medicine, Ayurveda, aromatherapy, and Bach Flower remedies. Herbalists, along with many other many alternative practitioners, view herbs as sacred and utilize them in the form of capsules, tinctures, extracts, or teas.

Hoffman (1992:1–24) maintains that "Medical Herbalism has the most to offer to holistic medicine when used within the context of a coherent philosophical system" and advocates a "model of Holistic Herbal Medicine." In addition to being part of various professionalized heterodox medical systems, herbalism is also an integral part of folk medical systems, such as southern Appalachian and Ozark folk medicine, African American medicine, *curanderismo* among Mexican Americans, *santería* among Cuban Americans, and Native American healing systems. Compared to European countries, such as Germany and Britain, Hoffman (1992) asserts:

> The United States of America is surprisingly backward when it comes to Medical Herbalism. Whilst much plant biochemistry is done, the practice of Herbalism as a branch of medicine is rare because of legal constraints. New schools are being established and an organization for professional herbalists has been formed; however, America is still in the herbal "dark ages"! (1)

Ethan Nebelkopf (1980), a family therapist who has used herbs in treating drug addicts, developed an alternative medical program at the White Bird Clinic in Eugene, Oregon, in the 1970s, and later worked as an herbalist at the Berkeley Holistic Health Center, however, views the arrival of a "new herbalism" as an integral component of the holistic health movement. He asserts that the "seeds plants planted by the New Herbalism today will produce fruit tomorrow for our children" (Nebelkopf 1985:155).

Herbalism is taught in numerous workshops, correspondence courses, and herbal academies as well as in natural healing, naturopathic, Oriental medicine, and Ayurveda schools and increasingly in biomedical colleges. Due to its widespread popularity among various types of practitioners and the general public, Cohen (2000:107) asserts that herbal medicine may constitute the fastest-growing form of alternative medicine. The *Alternative Medicine Herbology School Directory* (2003) lists sixty-three U.S. institutions that teach herbal medicine, two of which are located in Arizona, twelve in California, three in Colorado, one in Connecticut, one in Florida, two in Georgia, two in Hawaii, two in Illinois, one in Maine, one in Maryland, one in Massachusetts, three in Michigan, two in Montana, three in New Jersey, seven in New Mexico, nine in New York State, one in North Carolina, four in Oregon, one in Tennessee, one in Utah, two in Vermont, one in Virginia, and one in Washington State. Some of the institutions listed in the directory are schools of acupuncture and Oriental medicine, such as Tai Sophia Institute in Maryland, or natural healing schools, such as the American University of Complementary Medicine in California and the New Mexico College of Natural Healing in Silver City, but most of them are primarily schools of herbalism or botanical medicine. Thirty-four of the institutions listed are located in western states, a region of the country where alternative therapeutic systems are most popular and legitimized. Nonphysician herbalists are permitted to diagnose and prescribe on Native American reservations in the United States (Lyons 2000:12). In other contexts, herbalists may provide advice or teach about wildcrafting, growing, and preparing herbs.

One of the best known of the herbalism schools is the Southwest School of Botanical Medicine, established in 1985 in Bisbee, Arizona, and directed by Michael Moore, who has practiced herbalism since 1968 and has authored several books, including *Medicinal Plants of the Desert and Canyon West, Medicinal Plants of the Mountain West,* and *Medicinal Plants of the Pacific West* (Southwest School of Botanical Medicine 2002). This institution offers an annual five-hundred-hour, twenty-week training class in "Professional Herbology" and courses in botanical *materia medica,* physiology for the herbalist, herbal pharmacy, herbal therapeutics, herbal botany, constitutional medicine, and herbal formulating. The Southwest School also trains individuals "who wish to learn wildcrafting, herbal pharmacy and dispensing in order to supply practitioners and stores or to themselves retail herbs and allied products with a sound knowledge of herbs, the trade, and craft" (Southwest School of Botanical Medicine 2003). It distributes medicinal plant images, manuals, and distribution maps and reproduces classical botanical medicine texts. The school's website includes an article by Laurel Luddite (2002:2–3) titled "This Is Anarcho-Herbalism: Thoughts on Health and Healing for the Revolution," which critiques the manufacture of botanicals in capsule form and calls for a "green herbology" that relies on plants found in "vacant lots and neglected gardens."

The North American College of Botanical Medicine (established in 1996) in Albuquerque offers a three-year bachelor of science degree in botanical medicine and a nine-month certificate program in botanical medicine (North American College of Botanical Medicine 2003). Its students obtain clinical training at the New Mexico Herb Center. The East West School of Herbology in Ben Lomond, California, offers distance learning courses that integrate Western, Ayurvedic, and Chinese herbology ("Natural Healers," 2003). Other herbalism schools include the Australasian College of Herbal Studies with a U.S. office in Oswego, New York; the Pacific School of Herbal Medicine in Oakland; the Herbalist Certification School in Scottsdale, Arizona; the California School of Traditional Hispanic Herbalism; the Institute of Chinese Herbology in Oakland; the American Herbal Institute in Salem, Oregon; and the Rocky Mountain Herbal Institute in Mission Range, Montana.

Herbalists and other alternative practitioners interested in herbalism obtain additional training at a variety of conferences and workshops, such as the American Herbalists Guild Symposium, Medicines from the Earth Annual Symposium, the Pacific Northwest Herbal Symposium, and the Southwest Conference on Botanical Medicine sponsored by the Southwest College of Naturopathic Medicine in Tempe, Arizona. The Voyage Botanica Herbal Intensive was held on October 10–12, 2003, at Indian Hot Springs near Safford, Arizona (Plant Planet 2003). Featured speakers included author Michael Moore; Jonathon Sparrow Miller Weisberger, an ethnobotanist reared in Ecuador who worked among five indigenous communities in the Upper Amazon area; Pablo Cesar Amaringo Shuna, a "visionary painter" and "spiritual master" from the Peruvian Amazon; Michael Cottingham, the founder of Bear Creek Herbs in Silver City, New Mexico, and cofounder of the Herbal Medicine Program at the New Mexico College of Natural Healing; Ryan Eggleston, a clinical herbalist and co-owner of Tucson Herbs; and Sarah Roots, an herbalist and specialist in primate communication.

Herbalists have also formed several professional associations. The American Herb Association functions as an educational and research organization

(Lyons 2000:450). The Herb Research Foundation (established in 1983) bills itself as the "world's most comprehensive source of accurate scientific information on medicinal plants" (Herb Research Foundation 2001:1) and fosters research on them. The American Botanical Council (founded in 1988) seeks to inform the public about the value of medicinal plants and herbal preparations and publishes a quarterly publication, *HerbalGram* (American Botanical Council, 2003). The American Herbalists Guild (established in 1989) headquartered in Canton, Georgia, certifies trained herbalists and promotes research on herbalism (American Herbalist Guild 2003). The Herb Growing and Marketing Network (founded in 1990) is the largest herbal trade association in the United States (Lyons 2000:451).

Unfortunately, relatively little ethnographic research has been conducted on the culture of herbalists in the United States, but some preliminary studies suggest a countercultural strain among at least some, if not many, of its practitioners. While at least some herbalists refer to themselves as "clinical herbalists," it appears that they generally do not operate on a fee-for-service basis in clinical settings per se. Instead, most herbalists appear to operate more through herb shops and consultations with customers. Conversely, at least some herbalists treat clients in their homes. Neil McGoldrick (1994), an undergraduate student who conducted a miniethnography on herbalists for a course on "Medical Pluralism in Europe and North America" that I taught in spring 1994, interviewed Sharon (pseudonym), an herbalist of Hungarian Jewish and Native American ancestry who practiced without a license in her East Bay home. She studied herbalism for eight years, first at the New York School of Botanical Medicine and later at the California School of Herbal Studies. Sharon avoided prosecution by referring to herbs as "nutritional supplements" and disclaiming that she is a "diagnostician."

Janneli Miller (1990) describes the Winter Sun Trading Company in Flagstaff, Arizona, as an enterprise that consists of two rooms—one of which displays Native American art objects and Native American tapes and the other of which contains over three hundred bulk herbs stored in gallon jars, over two hundred tinctures or fluid extracts, herbal teas, various body products (such as massage oils and facial rinses), and copies of books on herbalism by Michael Moore and other authors. Phyllis and Denise Hogan, a mother/daughter team, owned the store and define themselves as "clinical herbalists." In 1995, Dee Ann Tracy, Phyllis's younger daughter, took over co-ownership of the store from Denise.

Phyllis "began her study of herbs in 1973, after having her interest in ethno-botany piqued by an anthropology class text, Alfred Whiting's *Ethnobotany of the Hopi*" (Miller 1990:18). She established the Winter Sun Trading Company in Coolidge, Arizona, and moved it to Flagstaff in 1978. Phyllis also serves as the director of the Arizona Ethnobotanical Research Association, an organiza-tion that disseminates knowledge about medicinal plants. She often presents public lectures and classes on herbalism. The association also operates an herbarium, which contains over one thousand pressed plant specimens, and publishes a journal that appears periodically. Miller (1990) provides the fol-lowing social profile of the Winter Sun clientele:

> All sorts of people walked in the door, the age range being babes in arms to old folks hobbling in with a cane or on the arm of a relative. . . . It was apparent that wealthier customers came in as often as those who did not appear to be well off. Again, it could not be said that the customers shared a lifestyle, as "yuppies," "hip-pies," "businessmen," "Indians" or "students" were all equally liable to walk in. (41)

Based on the client's description of his or her specific ailment, Phyllis or Denise would recommend a specific tea or make up a tincture from various herbs or provide a premixed product. Phyllis and Denise also provided advice over the phone and mailed herbal products to their clients. Denise Hogan now owns the Super Salve Company near Mogollon, New Mexico, and is no longer affiliated with Winter Sun but is still involved with it.

While I was a visiting professor in the Medical Anthropology Program at Arizona State University in 1997–1998, J. D. Baker (1998), one of my students, conducted observations in a small herb shop in the Phoenix area owned by Sarah (pseudonym), a middle-aged woman who had worked as a medical technician. She had received training in herbalism from Brenda (pseudonym), the shop's previous owner. Jennifer, Sarah's daughter, had learned herbalism from her mother and grandmother, took a basic certified course in herbalism, and works in the shop. Baker (1998) provides the following social profile of the shop's customers:

> The clientele I observed consisted almost entirely of white Euroamericans who appeared to be middle class or higher. Most of the customers were women be-tween the ages of 30 and 50, although a small number of customers were stu-dents around 20 years old. Many of the older women were accompanied by their

children, and were often buying herbal remedies for other sick family members. The customers could fairly easily be differentiated into two main groups.... The first group consists of customers who have a large knowledge of herbal remedies acquired through personal research and years of experience. The other group consisted of people with little experience with or knowledge of herbal remedies. Overall, it appears that the latter group makes up the larger part of the clientele at this herb shop. (8–9)

Both Sarah and Jennifer refer to their clientele as "customers" rather than "patients," avoid making therapeutic claims about herbal products, and avoid words like *prescription, treatment,* and *cure.*

While on another visiting position at Arizona State University in fall 2002, I had the privilege of accompanying Janneli Miller to the Fifth Annual Meeting of the Arizona Ethnobotanical Research Association (established in 1983) on September 21, 2002, in Flagstaff. The association publishes a newsletter, *The Plant Ambassador,* as well as a periodic journal. Phyllis Hogan moderated the meeting, which had "Medicinal Plants of the Mountain West" as its theme and was attended by ninety people who were either herbalists or interested in herbal medicine. She paid a tribute to the "wisdom keepers," a reference to some members who had "passed over into the spirit world." Hogan referred to Michael Moore, the director of the Southwest School of Botanical Medicine, who was present in the audience, as the "Jerry Garcia of the plant herb world." She noted, "We are applied ethnobotanists and work with indigenous people" and referred to the San Francisco Peaks to the immediate east of the meeting site as the "sacred mountains of the West." Alluding to the Navajo and Hopi goddesses of the area, Hogan stated, "We come here as outsiders. We have to give back to the land. We have been in a really big drought. There are over 3,500 flowering plants in Arizona. Medicines of all types grow here." She went on to tell the audience that the meeting was a "hands-on symposium"—"taste things, smell things."

Hogan presided over a panel in which various herbalists who had studied under Moore described the qualities of specific medicinal plants. In 2003, she received a lifetime achievement award for botanical research at the annual meeting of the American Herbalists Guild in Albuquerque (personal communication with Phyllis Hogan and Janneli Miller).

Donna Chesner, Moore's wife, noted that she met Moore in 1990 and has been working as an administrator at the Southwest School of Botanical Medicine for the past ten years, and explained that her father, who had been a hunter, fisherman, and carpenter, had connected her with nature. Donna went on to describe Western sweet root that does not grow in Arizona, noting that it is a "feminine plant—it gets big and round." She passed a tincture of sweet root around the audience and said that it is used as a bitter tonic that settles stomach problems. Donna also noted that sweet root can be used as an enema or female douche. She said, "It is warmy. It is used by some tribes as love medicine."

Pamela Nakai, the next speaker, stated that her interest in the plant world began in 1975 when she moved to the Navajo reservation. She met Moore in Santa Fe, studied with him in 1988, and went on to open the Sonoran Herbal Institute in Tucson. Pamela noted that she had discovered valerian in Hyde Park and described it as being "good for the adrenaline-stressed person" in that it has a calming quality and acts as a "smooth muscle relaxant." Dee Ann Tracy, the owner of Peak Scents Aromatherapy Company in Flagstaff, spoke about arnica, and Dee Ann Tracy spoke about red root.

In the afternoon, Michael Moore—a rotund man with long, graying, balding hair and a long beard—told stories about his experiences with medicinal plants to the audience. He noted that he was sixty-one years old and had grown up around the music industry, which included playing in a symphony orchestra, in Los Angeles. Moore said that he discovered in his late twenties or early thirties that he wanted to get away from people and "got hooked" on medicinal plants after reading some "serious plant books." He began to concoct "herbal smoking mixtures" for hippies and came to realize that he might lose his love for music if he had to do it for a living. Moore said that he opened an herb store in 1970, noting that "it may have been the first herb store in the western United States." He referred to himself as a "white guy from L.A. who has no rituals." Moore continued by describing herb shops that he established in Santa Fe and then Albuquerque. He disseminates his research findings through several books that he has authored and by speaking at many herbal workshops and conferences.

MASSAGE AS THE PREEMINENT FORM OF BODYWORK

In contrast to chiropractic, naturopathy, acupuncture and Oriental medicine, and certain other heterodox healing systems that have been the focus of at least some social scientific and historical research, bodywork in its various guises has received very little such attention. An exception to this paucity in the literature is an unpublished paper on massage therapy and other body-work modalities by Lisa Mertz (1996), an anthropologist, and a forthcoming essay on massage therapy by Susan Walkley (2004), a massage therapist and anthropologist. Although massage, entailing manipulation of soft tissues to alleviate muscular tension, is an ancient therapeutic technique found in many societies throughout the eons, two New York physicians who had obtained training in massage in Sweden introduced it in the United States during the mid–nineteenth century (Milbank Memorial Fund 1998:11). In the 1870s, Swedish physicians established massage clinics in New York City. Baron Nils Posse operated the Posse Institute in Boston, and Harwig Nissen operated the Swedish Health Institute in Washington, D.C. (Greene 2000:338). Between 1880 and 1910, a fair number of M.D.'s employed massage in their practices. Undoubtedly due to its labor-intensive nature, they eventually delegated massage to nurses and physical therapists. Although conventional physicians often refer patients to massage therapists in much the same way as they refer patients to physical and occupational therapists, the growing interest in alternative therapies that began in the early 1970s appears to have revitalized massage therapy. Reference sources on holistic health or complementary and alternative medicine routinely include chapters or sections on massage therapy.

The American Massage Therapy Association (established in 1943) is the oldest and largest massage organization in the United States and claims over thirty-seven thousand members (Lyons 2000:430). It has a commission that accredits massage schools and specifies a minimum of five hundred hours of coursework. The Commission on Massage Therapy Accreditation recognizes seventy massage schools. In reality, there are fewer than one hundred massage schools (*Global Directory of MT Schools, US* 2003) or natural healing schools, such as the Southwest Institute of the Healing Arts in Tempe (Arizona) and the Natural Academy of Natural Therapy in Colorado, that teach massage therapy.

One of the best-known massage schools is Dr. Jay Scherer's Massage Academy. Scherer syncretized massage therapy, naturopathy, I Am mysticism, and anthroposophy and established the Niagra Health Center in Santa Fe in 1953, where he treated many Hispanics. According to Fox (1997:150–51), "Scherer, who died in 1991, estimated his graduates at fifteen hundred, some of whom have founded four other therapeutic academies in Santa Fe and Albuquerque."

The National Certification Board for Therapeutic Massage and Bodywork established a national certification program in 1992. Most states that license massage therapists employ its examination (Greene 2000:346). Massage therapy is licensed in twenty-nine states, the District of Columbia, and various localities (Greene 2000:346). In Maryland, the chiropractic board oversees licensing of massage therapists, whereas in Texas massage therapists are required to be registered. There reportedly are more 120,000 massage therapists and other bodyworkers in the United States (Weeks 2001:5).

Although massage therapists have associations, schools, certification programs, and licenses of their own, chiropractors, naturopathic physicians, physiatrists, physical therapists, and occupational therapists may employ massage in their respective practices. Even among massage therapists, as Walkley (2004) notes here, one finds wide variation in practice:

> Massage practitioners can take a wide range of continuing education classes and be inspired by body theorists like Alexander, Rolf, Feldenkrais, Pilates, Travell, Chaitow, and Trager. Individual therapists inevitably develop eclectic and unique hybrids of styles and movements that make it very difficult to generalize what a massage *is* in the United States. Using myself as an example, my own massage work combines elements of massage school training that included Western and Eastern techniques, selective elements of continuing education classes, the overarching body philosophies of Alexander and Rolf, and my experiences as a receiver of massage. (57–58)

In addition to Sweden massage and other Western massage techniques, acupressure constitutes a Chinese form of massage in which finger or thumb pressure is applied to specific points along the meridians in order to facilitate the flow of *chi*. Shiatsu is a Japanese variant of acupressure. The American Oriental Bodywork Therapy Association represents acupressure and shiatsu practitioners. In her ethnography of the holistic health/New Age movement, English-Lueck (1990:55) notes the "gamut of bodywork therapies is practiced in Paraiso," including Esalen and Swedish massage, shiatsu, zone therapy/reflex massage, Rolfing, and polarity-tomasic. Bodyworkers in Paraiso treat primarily pain, chronic pain or tension, and postural abnormalities.

Over the past decade or so, massage and other forms of bodywork have attained some legitimacy as a result of research that Tiffany Field and her collaborators are conducting at the Touch Research Institute (established in

1992) at the University of Miami School of Medicine. She has been involved in ongoing research on massage therapy (Freeman 2001b:380–83).

AYURVEDA AND YOGA AS IMPORTED FORMS
OF MIND–BODY OR ENERGY MEDICINE

Ayurveda is a South Asian medical system based on ancient Vedic texts. The word *ayurveda* means the knowledge (*veda*) of life (*ayu*). According to tradition, the *rishis* (enlightened sages) held a convocation in which they sought to discover the mysteries of human physiology and health in order to prevent or alleviate suffering. Bharadwaja, one of the *rishis*, came up with the essence of Ayurveda during the course of a convocational meditation. Ayurveda posits that the human body consists of five elements—space, air, fire, water, and earth. Combinations of these elements result in three humors or *doshas*: *vata* (consisting of air and space), *pitta* (consisting of fire and water), and *kapha* (consisting of earth and water), which in turn result in ten different body types. The combination of these *doshas* in each person determines his or her body type and temperament. *Vata* is found in people who are active and changeable; *pitta* in people who are assertive, explosive, and efficient; and *kapha* in people who tend to be sluggish, conservative, stable, and sometimes overweight. Health results from a balance in each person of these three *doshas*, which can be increased or decreased through eating, sleep, lifestyle, and other physical and mental endeavors. Conversely, an imbalance in the levels of the *doshas* results in illness or disease. An excess of *dosha* in its original site affects the entire body, creating lesions in the tissues and interfering with metabolism.

Ayurveda focuses on restoring bodily balance rather than illness per se. As Alter (1999:S43) observes, Ayurvedic medicine is "proactive and concerned with overall fitness rather than reactive and primarily concerned with either disease or illness." Ayurvedic physicians attempt to determine the patient's constitution and to rebalance his or her *doshas* through careful observation and questioning. They seek a detailed history of the patient's health, emotional state, diet, and social environment.

Sita Reddy (2002) appears to be the only social scientist thus far to have conducted an extensive study of Ayurveda in the United States. She maintains that Ayurveda exemplifies "broad changes in definitions of health and illness—such as holistic phenomenology, humanistic mode of practice, and increasingly client-centered health markets" (Reddy 2002:99). In contrast to other Asian medical transplants, such as Chinese medicine, *kanpo* among Japanese Americans, and Hmong folk medicine, that initially appeared in ethnic enclaves, Ayurveda as a medical transplant found its initial appeal among non–South Asians and has become merged with New Ageism. Reddy (2002:100–1) asserts that transplanted Ayurveda has come to encompass a "wide-ranging plurality of subtraditions in practice, each of which reflects articulations with the New Age."

Ayurveda made its debut in the United States in the mid-1980s under the sponsorship of the Maharishi Ayur-Veda Association of America, an arm of Maharishi Transcendental Meditation. Shortly afterward, in 1986, Vinod Seth established the Ayurvedic Center and Ted Warren established the National Center for Ayurvedic Medicine.

Until recently, Ayurvedic practitioners did not seek to professionalize themselves by pursuing licensure (Reddy 2002:102). At least six Ayurvedic training programs have been established. Ayurveda practitioners have tended to establish its practices in "spa-like therapeutic centers" and add non-Ayurvedic techniques, such as meditation and yoga (Reddy 2002:103). Like other alternative therapeutic systems, Ayurvedic practitioners have adopted New Age aspects, including concepts such as *vibrations* and *energy* and an emphasis on individual responsibility and self-mastery. In their efforts to gain legitimacy, Ayurvedic practitioners have tended to follow one of two routes: (1) "using their status as biomedical physicians to obtain insurance coverage and gain scientific legitimacy of their state and as New Age shamans or religious healers and herbalists to escape medical regulation altogether" (Reddy 2002:106–7). As I demonstrate in chapter 5, the neo-Ayurvedic guru Deepak Chopra has at various times incorporated both strategies in his career trajectory that led him to become the most renowned and apparently financially successful holistic/New Age figure in the United States and probably in the world. Indeed, in her ethnography of holistic health/New Age practices in Paraiso, English-Lueck (1990:42) reports that in that community, Ayurveda tends to assume an eclectic cast. For example, a Ayurvedic/Unani therapist has incorporated aspects of homeopathy into his practice.

Reddy (2002) cites four examples of U.S. Ayurvedic subtraditions: (1) the Maharishi Ayurveda Association, (2) the Southwestern Ayurvedic school founded by Vinod Seth, (3) the Ayurvedic Center established by Swami Krishnandanda, and (4) the National Center for Ayurvedic Medicine operated by Ted Warren. Maharishi Ayurveda evolved into the focal point around which the other variant of transplanted Ayurveda came to define themselves. In the early 1980s, the Maharishi Mahesh Yoga, the founder of Transcendental Meditation, asked several prominent Ayurvedic physicians to assist him in rejuvenating Ayurveda (Sharma and Clark 1998:2). Maharishi Ayurveda synthesizes traditional Ayurveda and Transcendental Meditation and regards "unfolding consciousness as the single most important strategy of both prevention and cure" (Sharma 1996:247). It developed into an international phenomenon practiced in India, Europe, Japan, Africa, Russia, Australia, and South and North America. The Transcendental Meditation organization started the College of Maharishi Ayur-Ved as a degree- and non-degree-granting operation in 1993 as a part of Maharishi International University in Fairfield, Iowa (Collinge 1996:68).

Maharishi Ayurveda became embroiled two fraud cases, one in 1992 as the plaintiff and the other in 1995 as the defendant, against the *Journal of the American Medical Association* (*JAMA*).

> In [the 1995 case], despite the best efforts of the plaintiff's lawyers to frame Ayurveda as a fraudulent medical system, what consistently emerges is how Ayurveda escapes these definitions as a cultural commodity, as an Indian import with an ambiguous status as an alternative medical system. Similarly, in [the 1992 case], the Ayurvedic plaintiffs, despite being medical physicians, relied on their Indian background to excuse ignorance of scientific journal ethics including financial disclosure and conflicts of interest with manufacturers of the Ayurvedic articles promoted in their article. (Reddy 2002:110)

These two cases shaped to what extent the various Ayurvedic subtraditions aligned themselves with or distanced themselves from Maharishi Ayurveda. Reddy (2002:111–12) maintains that the Ayurveda have pursued several promotional strategies, "including scientific credibility, prosperity consciousness, and the appeal of powerful rejuvenating tonics." In each case, however, transplanted Ayurveda has undergone a shift from an esoteric South Asian medical system to a New Age healing system. Like the larger New Age movement, New Age Ayurveda has preferred to situate itself in seminars, spas, and retreats rather than clinical settings and has positioned itself between "medicine and metaphysics" (Reddy 2002:115). As a result, some Ayurvedic practitioners present themselves as scholars of a classical South Asian medical tradition, others as holistic scientists, and still others as spiritual teachers.

Other Ayurvedic training institutions include the Ayurvedic Institute, established by Vesant Lad in Santa Fe in 1984 and relocated to Albuquerque in 1986; the American Institute of Ayurvedic Studies in Bellevue, Washington; the California College of Ayurveda in Grass Valley; the New England Institute of Ayurveda in Cambridge, Massachusetts; the National Institute of Ayurvedic Medicine in Brewster, New York; and the Florida Vedic College (Trivieri and the American Holistic Medical Association 2001:328–29). Homeopathic training programs vary from one to two years of study and often entail part-time classroom instruction and independent study (Halpern 2000:254). The American Institute of Vedic Studies offers home-study programs in Ayurveda. Graduates of the California College of Ayurveda obtain certification as a "clinical Ayurvedic specialist." Various biomedical physicians, nurses, acupuncturists, Chinese medicine physicians, naturopathic physicians, and chiropractors have also incorporated aspects of Ayurveda into their practices.

Yoga (meaning "union") constitutes another transplanted South Asian therapeutic system and seeks to integrate body, mind, and spirit in order to enhance health and wellness through the uses of *asanas*, or postures, diet and nutrition, meditation, regulated breathing, and relaxation. While there are many forms of yoga, *hatha yoga* (meaning "force") is the most common one and the one that is most closely related to Ayurveda (Pelletier 2000:245). An estimated three to five million Americans practice some form of yoga (Lyons 2000:28).

Lyons (2000:48) lists twenty-two schools for training yoga instructors, but this by no means encompasses all such institutions. Training to become a yoga teacher may last as little as a few weeks or as long as three years. Yoga instructors are represented by the California Yoga Teachers Association, the 3HO International Kundalini Yoga Teachers Association (headquartered in Espanola, New Mexico), and the Himalayan Institute Teachers Association (headquartered in Honesdale, Pennsylvania). The America Yoga Association (established in 1968) is headquartered in Sarasota, Florida.

In addition to thousands of yoga studios around the country, yoga is practiced at various yoga retreat centers which "transfer the everyday social space of the yoga studio to one of two generalized sites—either serene, wooded forest or lush, tropical islands" (Lau 2000:117). Yoga is also conducted in many hospitals and centers of CAM or integrative medicine. Yoga has increasingly entered into the mainstream as a commodity that often has been stripped of its hippie and New Age connections. As Lau (2000) observes:

> [Y]oga studios and health clubs offering yoga classes are careful to find instructors who will play up yoga's physical benefits while downplaying the more philosophical, mystical aspects. . . . In many cases, innovative yoga instructors go further in making yoga familiar by setting it to music, making it intensely aerobic, combining yoga positions with dance moves, and creating classes which bring yoga together with more conventional strength training and stretching. (124–25)

LAY OR "DIRECT ENTRY" MIDWIFERY

Lay midwifery is an ancient practice found in all sociocultural systems. It entails prenatal care, birthing, and postpartum care and in reality does not constitute a medical or healing system per se since birth is a natural process rather than a medical one. Historically, biomedical dominance has forced lay midwifery to function politically, legally, and economically in much the same way as other alternative medical or health care systems. In reality, as DeVries (1996:16) observes, "[a]lthough midwives are now seen as adjunct to physicians, historically midwifery was an autonomous profession" or, perhaps more properly speaking, endeavor. Cobb (1981:77) delineates four types of birth attendants in the United States: (1) obstetricians; (2) nurse-midwives; (3) lay "granny" midwives, who historically were particularly predominant among African Americans in the South; (4) and "modern lay midwives," who emerged out of the feminist and natural birthing movements of the late 1960s. Robbins (1976:76) distinguishes between traditional or "direct-entry" midwives who obtain their skills through apprenticeship and nurse-midwives who are licensed in all fifty states.

Modern lay midwives became increasingly popular in California in the late 1960s and early 1970s, and elsewhere shortly afterward (Robbins 1996:67). The Birth Center of Santa Cruz (est. 1971) functioned for five years as a collective of lay midwives who provided prenatal care at the center and delivered babies in mothers' homes (Rooks 1997:62). The Fremont Women's Clinic (established in 1971) in Seattle developed a birth collective in 1975 when two family physicians offered to train five women to become midwives. "The first seven months of their training included weekly classes and use of a classic midwifery textbook and books and journals from the University of Washington Health Science Library. A midwife with extensive home birth experience joined the collective and was the primary teacher in the 'home' aspects of childbirth" (Rooks 1997:62).

The Farm, a hippie commune started by Steve Gaskin and his followers in middle Tennessee in the early 1970s, established a well-publicized lay midwifery program (Traugot 1998:46). Ida May Gaskin, Stephen's wife, assumed the task of becoming community midwife and obtained advice from a local physician. The Farm published *Spiritual Midwifery*, a book that became very popular in lay midwifery circles and reportedly sold over 450,000 copies worldwide (Daviss 2001:78). Lay midwifery appealed to others besides hippies or countercultural people. As Cobb (1981:82) observes, "at precisely the time when members of low income and rural populations have been persuaded to give up home births, certain segments of the white American middle-class are seeking birth at home, and it is the home birth couples themselves and modern lay midwives as well as selected physicians and nurse-midwives demand." In her study of forty-nine lay midwives in a West Coast community, Reid (1989:224) reports that the majority of them had at least started a college education and that all of them, except two, were white. Midwives in this network had incorporated much of the birthing ideology of Steve Gaskin's Farm.

Many lay midwives have obtained training through a combination of apprenticeship and self-education. Conversely, a growing number of lay midwives are undergoing formal training in university or direct-entry programs, distance learning, and private midwifery schools (Davis-Floyd 1998a). By the late 1970s, at least ten direct-entry midwifery-training programs existed in the United States (Rooks 1997:76). These included the Arizona School of Midwifery, which operated between 1977 and 1981 in Tucson, and the Seattle Midwifery School (established in 1978), affiliated with the Fremont Birth Collective. Apprentice Academics, started by Texas midwives but now based in Oklahoma, offers a correspondence course intended to complement apprenticeship training in midwifery. Informed Home Birth, a Colorado-based enterprise, conducts workshops on childbirth to birth attendants, prospective parents, and childbirth educators at various sites around the United States. Eight U.S. midwifery schools are accredited by the Midwifery Education Accreditation Agency that follows principles and competencies established by the Midwifery Alliance of North America (MANA) (Lyons 2000:22).

MANA was formed in 1982 and played a significant role in creating the North American Registry of Midwives (NARM) in 1991 as a measure to facilitate licensure for direct-entry midwives (Davis-Floyd 1998a:78–79). According to Davis-Floyd (1998b:79), "[o]nce it existed, the NARM written exam was quickly picked up by midwifery associations and state agencies which had been needing such an exam but did not wish to develop it themselves." MANA advocates the notion of "pure apprenticeship," which is defined as a "long-term (usually three-year) learning process involving one teacher and one student with a focus on out-of-hospital birth" (Benoit et al. 2001:144).

Arizona passed the first law regulating lay midwifery in 1957 when some one hundred midwives were serving Hispanics or Mormons (DeVries 1996:55). Pennsylvania and Oregon have been two states that provided a supportive legal environment for lay midwives (Robbins 1996:81). As has been the case for other heterodox medical systems, licensure for lay midwives has proven to be a mixed bag in that it, on the one hand, has provided them with a certain legitimacy and legal protection, and, on the other hand, placed certain restrictions on them. Not surprisingly, midwifery licensure has been dominated by organized biomedicine and has required midwives to abandon certain traditional practices and adopt some modern procedures. DeVries (1996:83) describes laws regulating lay midwifery as examples of "hostile licensure" in that they require midwives to obtain approval from biomedicine in order to practice.

> The Texas and Arizona laws place authority over midwives in a committee or agency comprised of a majority of nonmidwives. In California, the proposed Midwifery Examining Committee was dominated by midwives, but that Committee was under the jurisdiction of the Board of Registered Nursing. . . . S.B. 670 in California stated: "All applicants for certification shall be required to submit [with their] application for licensure a written plan describing a mechanism for providing to clients continuity of care. The plan shall include a working agreement with current training and practice in obstetrics." Other laws create a dependence on physicians for such things as education or certification of physical and mental health. (DeVries 1996:83–84)

Rooks (1997:251) provides a summary of state laws regulating direct-entry midwives up to the mid-1990s. Seventeen jurisdictions—Alabama, Delaware, the District of Columbia, Georgia, Hawaii, Illinois, Indiana, Iowa, Kentucky,

Maryland, Missouri, New Jersey, North Carolina, Ohio, Rhode Island, Virginia, and West Virginia—limited midwifery to nurse-midwives and regarded "all other midwifery practice to be illegal, or require a license or permit that is no longer available." Eight states—Idaho, Kansas, Nebraska, Nevada, North Dakota, Oklahoma, South Dakota, and Wisconsin—either did not explicitly outlaw direct-entry midwifery or had laws that were "silent, vague, or internally inconsistent" (Rooks 1997:232). Direct-entry midwifery was legal but unregulated in nine states: Connecticut, Maine, Massachusetts, Michigan, Mississippi, Pennsylvania, Tennessee, Utah, and Vermont. Thirteen states licensed direct-entry midwives but did not require extensive formal training. Twelve states—Alaska, Arkansas, Colorado, Louisiana, Minnesota, Montana, New Hampshire, New Mexico, Oregon, South Carolina, Texas, and Wyoming—had "regulatory boards, which usually include physicians and CNMs [certified nurse midwives], as well as licensed midwives, and require[d] applicants to pass a state-administered examination" (Rooks 1997:232). Washington State, New York, and California required direct-entry midwives to have undergone three years of formal education. Lay midwives in certain areas lacking licensing laws practice illegally but in many cases have adopted self-regulation (DeVries 1996:152). As of August 2003, the Midwives Alliance of North America (2003) reports that twenty-one states are licensed, certified, or registered. Lay (2000:4) estimates some two thousand to three thousand direct-entry practicing midwives in the United States.

Some bodies, such as the National Association of Parents and Professionals for Safe Alternatives in Childbirth (NAPSC), are cognizant of the pitfalls associated with licensure (DeVries 1996:144). Based on her research on direct-entry midwives in Minnesota, Lay (2000:108–9) found that many of them expressed concern that professionalization would erode their autonomy through normalization of birthing procedures and contribute to further divisions within their ranks. Reid (1989:257) maintains that licensure tends to erode the intimacy of informal midwifery circles. At any rate, as DeVries (1996:150) observes, "[t]he supporters of midwifery and home birth, aware of the hegemony of medicine, have begun to employ the criteria of scientific medicine in defense of their cause."

Based on in-depth interviews with twenty-six direct-entry, licensed, and certified nurse-midwives in Florida, Foley and Faircloth (2003) argue that the biomedical model is a resource that their subjects used to validate their endeavors.

Because licensing inevitably entails some degree of biomedical supervision, lay midwifery faces the danger of being co-opted by biomedicine, despite the fact that in large part it emerged as a counter-hegemonic response to it. Conversely, as a result of increasing numbers of malpractice suits and the cost of malpractice insurance premiums, conventional physicians are increasingly opting out of practicing obstetrics. Nurse midwives, but also lay midwives, have been filling a niche that many obstetricians have vacated.

NEW AGE ENERGY HEALERS, CHANNELS, AND NEOSHAMANS
New Age healing incorporates many therapeutic techniques and practices, including centering, channeling, astral projection, chromotherapy, rebirthing, and healing with the power of pyramids and crystals. It often incorporates techniques from earlier therapeutic systems, such as Ayurveda, yoga, shiatsu, reflexology, polarity therapy, iridology, shamanism, and other indigenous healing systems. Fuller (2003:115) asserts that the New Age movement exhibits three dimensions that have implications for health and healing: "(1) avid interest in Eastern philosophy and meditation practices, (2) continuing belief in the existence of subtle energies that connect the human body with higher cosmic planes, and (3) faith in the power of the mind or thought to influence external reality." New Age healing draws on earlier healing practices, including mesmerism, which sought to facilitate the flow of energy into patients; Spiritualism, which attempted (and still attempts) to connect with spirits who can diagnose illness and prescribe remedies; theosophy; New Thought; and the work of the psychic Edgar Cayce.

New Age energy healers draw on the South Asian notion of *chakra*, which was first popularized in the West by Charles W. Ledbetter, a leading British theosophist who wrote a book titled *The Chakras* in 1927. He referred to the *chakras* (Sanskrit for "wheels") as "points of connection at which energy flows from one vehicle or body of a man to another" (quoted in Albanese 1999b:314). Barbara Ann Brennan, a physicist who worked from the National Aeronautics and Space Administration at the Goddard Space Flight Center from 1965 to 1971, makes use of chakra movement in her bioenergetic counseling (Albanese 2000:31–36). She wrote two best-sellers titled *Hands of Light* (1987) and *Light Emerging* (1993). Brennan asserts that most diseases originate in disrupted energy fields. She maintains that chakras or energy vortices are opened during therapy, which entail an alteration of the patient's consciousness or belief system. Valerie Hunt, a retired UCLA physiology professor and the author of *Infinite Mind: Science of the Human Vibrations of Consciousness* (1996), is another advocate of New Age energy healing who refers to the importance of chakras in her work.

Some New Age energy healers also draw inspiration from the work of the Institute of Noetic Sciences, a nonprofit organization established by Edgar D. Mitchell, a retired naval officer, in 1973. The Institute "conducts and sponsors research into the potentials and powers of consciousness—including perceptions, beliefs, attention, and intuition" (Institute of Noetic Sciences 2003). The Religious Movements Homepage (2004) at the University of Virginia states the following about similarities between the Institute and New Ageism:

> The interest of the IONS in alternative practices of health makes it easily identifiable with New Age. . . . Like many New Age groups IONS gives great consideration to parapsychology, consciousness, communication with the dead, and seems to expect, if not a new age, some kind of change in the near future. Edgar Mitchell put it as an "evolutionary crossroads."

New Agers may have derived crystal therapy from Native Americans and other indigenous peoples. Many New Age energy healers believe that crystals are excellent receptors that can channel divine white light from the etheric or spiritual plane into the patient's body (Fuller 2002:116–17). Others maintain that crystals "amplify personal energies or harness extrapersonal energies" (Fuller 2002:117). Crystal healing entails various procedures, such as placing crystals around one's dwelling, wearing them around the neck as ornaments, or touching them (Cassileth 1998:295). Crystal healers or facilitators take care in choosing particular crystals that they believe will enhance their own personal vibrations and generally undergo a process of purification by eradicating carnal desires and negative emotions and centering themselves through breathing exercises, relaxation exercises, meditation, visualizations, and affirmations. Nauman (2002:771) claims that "[c]rystal therapy is as varied as the training of the crystal facilitator." Crystal healers generally use six-sided crystals but prefer four-sided crystals. Many crystal healers and users maintain that the color of the crystal is of significance in healing. For example, "[r]ed-orange agate . . . is thought to energize, amethyst is said to calm the conscious and unconscious mind . . . , and blood-stone (or heliotrope) is believed to purify the blood" (Cassileth 1998:295). New Age energy healers attempt to alter broken and disfigured auras in their clients and use crystals to treat physical, mental, emotional, and spiritual problems. Crystal healers generally claim that crystals alter thoughts and emotions underlying illness rather than curing specific illnesses.

While there are no crystal healing schools as such in the United States, crystal healing is taught in workshops and seminars or self-taught from books. The Crystal Awareness Institute is based in Kingwood, Texas, and there is an International Association of Crystal Therapists based in Manchester, England (Nauman 2002:773).

While New Ageism is often associated with numerous places on both the West Coast and East Coast or in interior cities, such as Santa Fe, Sedona, Boulder, and Asheville, the New Age movement has even found its way to rather conservative places such as the state of Arkansas. The Quachita Mountains, probably due to their extensive natural deposits of quartz crystals, and Eureka Springs in the Ozarks have evolved into minor New Age centers. Hot Springs is the site of the Golden Leaves Book Store, which in addition to selling New Age books and articles offers classes in astrology and on dreams, angels, and relationships. It also offers lectures by traveling New Age speakers, including spiritual messengers from exotic places. Dr. Bernadine R. Stockwell, an eclectic spiritual healer and teacher based in Mount Ida, does counseling, rebirthing, hypnotherapy, inner child and regression therapy, Reiki, and craniosacral therapy (brochure). Pyramid Village in Mena is operated by Reiki master Michael McCormack and "consists of seven small pyramids and one 5,400 square feet, four story pyramid, on twenty acres of cleared land, surrounded by the Quachita National Forest" (brochure). In addition to Reiki, Pyramid Village staff employ astrology, hypnotherapy, and past life energy. The Village conducts three-day retreats that include a "fireside meditation at the medicine lodge teepee" (brochure).

Channeling has become part and parcel of the New Age movement and in many ways is a late incarnation of American spiritualism, a movement that was particularly strong during the mid–nineteenth century. Edgar Cayce (1877–1945), known as the "sleeping prophet" who delivered information on health and metaphysics in the form of individual readings, was also a progenitor of New Age channeling. Although he considered himself a devout Christian and delivered "Christ-centered" readings, Cayce also believed in reincarnation (York 1995:61). The A.R.E. [Association for Research and Enlightenment] Clinic, Inc., in Phoenix conducts research on Cayce's readings and seeks to incorporate them into health care.

Channels assert that they can establish contact with spiritual guides from earlier eras and mythological sites. J. Z. Knight, a renowned channel, believes that her body serves as a conduit for Ramtha, the Enlightened One, an Atlantean warrior and deity. Ramtha claims that earthquakes, volcanic eruptions, floods, and climatic shifts will propel humanity into a New Age. Channels conduct workshops throughout the country where they teach their clients how to contact spiritual guides and guardian angels. Trance channels claim to undergo a complete separation from their bodies and become possessed by spiritual beings who transmit therapeutic messages for clients. Conscious channels have powerful intuitive abilities and remain aware of their surroundings while channeling.

Anthropologist Michael F. Brown (1997) conducted an ethnographic study of channeling in Santa Fe and western New England. He also visited channeling sites in Arizona, California, Florida, New York, and Virginia. Brown presents the following social profiles of channels and their clients:

> People involved specifically in channeling fit the general profile of Boomers who find their way into other NRMs [new religious movements]. There is, however, a significant demographic split between the producers and consumers of channeled information. The consumers—those who attend channeling workshops or seek individual counseling—are well educated and often affluent. Channels—the producers in this exchange—have educational backgrounds similar to their clients, but their economic situation is often precarious because of their unusual career. Some channels use channeling as their primary means of income. Others have ordinary jobs and try to fit channeling activities into their free time. The professional channels who enjoy the most stable incomes are those who manage to integrate channeling into a conventional occupation, often as psychotherapists or motivated trainers. (7–8)

Women tend to be more involved in channeling, both as channels and as clients, than men, sometimes by a ratio of 3:1 or greater (Brown 1997:95). Fellowship tends to occur within the context of informal self-help groups and counseling sessions or workshops. Few channeling congregations have been created. The Temple of Ascendant Light, one of the two channeling congregations that Brown visited, is led by a charismatic female channel but also has other channels who deliver messages during Sunday services (Brown 1997:135). The Festival is a channeling fellowship in New Mexico that conducts weekly meetings in a rented auditorium. Services incorporate singing, readings, a healing meditation, an inspirational message, a candle-lighting ceremony, and affirmations (Brown 1997:136–37). In that a fair number of members are therapists, bodyworkers, and counselors, "the time for 'personal sharing' in the weekly service is a tempting platform for members who wish to advertise their services" (Brown 1997:138). Indeed, channels during the mid-1990s reportedly charged anywhere between $25 and $1,500 for a session (Kyle 1995:179).

Many New Agers are enthusiasts of neoshamanism. Anthropologist Michael Harner, a former professor at the New School for Social Research, has become a New Age guru as a result of his book *The Way of the Shaman* (1990) and his creation of the Foundation for Shamanic Studies. He became knowledgeable about shamanism among the Jivaro and Conibo Indians of South America and has developed a synthesis of universal shamanic practices, called "core shamanism," which he teaches in workshops around the globe. Unlike shamans in indigenous societies, neoshamans are generally urbanites and not incorporated into a tight-knit community per se, although they belong to a drumming group. According to Jakobsen (1999):

> Through the courses and reading *The Way of the Shaman*, it is possible to become an apprentice. There is no prior demand such as special birth, inheritance of supernatural skills, special behavior verging on insanity, illness, near death experience or any other spiritual insight, although it is likely that the people commencing a course of shamanism have had just that and do not know how to relate to such experiences, to their "normal" role in society as teachers, architects, nurses, psychotherapists, and so on. (163)

Neoshamanic organizations include the Dance of the Deer Foundation, located in Soquel, California, in the Santa Cruz Mountains, which promotes the shamanic tradition of the Huichol Indians of northern Mexico; the Foundation for Shamanic Studies in Mill Valley, California (Cassileth 1998:317); and the Shamanic Healing Institute based in Maryland and established by Paul M. Sivert, who claims to have been initiated into the healing traditions of the Q'ero of Peru (Shamanic Healing Institute 2003).

In early 1994, the National Congress of American Indians declared war on "non-Indian 'wannabes,' hucksters, cultists, commercial profiteers and self-styled New Age shamans" (quoted in Glass-Coffin 1994:A48) for exploiting Native American religious traditions. The American Indian Movement (AIM) has also condemned neoshamanism. Conversely, some young, college-educated Native Americans refer to themselves as the "New Native Shamans" and have joined forces with New Agers interested in indigenous healing rituals. Leslie Gray, a faculty member in both the Department of Native American Studies at Berkeley and the California Institute of Integral Studies in San Francisco, teaches "self-help shamanism" to her clients so they can learn how to enter altered states of consciousness and to gain health and personal empowerment (Geertz 1997:544). Various Native American figures such as Sunbear (or Vincent LaDuke), Ed McGass, Jamie Sams, and Wallace Black Elk have acted as guides for New Agers who have incorporated the Native American sweat lodge into their ceremonial repertoire (Clements 2001:148).

4

The Emergence of Complementary and Alternative Medicine and Integrative Medicine

Historically, what constituted regular or allopathic medicine in the nineteenth century and what evolved into biomedicine in the twentieth century adopted a policy of staunch and often vigorous opposition to a wide variety of alternative or heterodox medical systems. Ironically, as Wolpe (1999) so eloquently states:

> Over the last thirty years, as alternative medicine has increased its profile, many of the very therapies that were being continuously ridiculed by orthodox opponents have been finding their way into the orthodox regimen. The importance of nutrition, low-fat diets, and vitamin supplements; the concept of stress as a pathogen; techniques like meditation, yoga, massage, and biofeedback; the use of magnets to cure pain, acupuncture, and a host of pharmaceuticals drawn from traditional medicines—all were once marginalized ideas that were considered by many as quackery. (229)

Although the great majority of biomedical physicians maintained either an indifferent or hostile attitude toward the holistic health movement, certain biomedical scientists in various countries, including Britain, France, and Germany, as early as the beginning of the twentieth century subscribed to the concept of holism well before the emergence of the holistic health movement per se (Lawrence and Weisz 1998).

THE BEGINNINGS OF AN INTEREST BY CONVENTIONAL PHYSICIANS AND NURSES IN THE HOLISTIC HEALTH MOVEMENT

Some biomedical and osteopathic physicians began to exhibit an interest in the holistic health movement relatively shortly after its emergence. Osteopathic physicians have long claimed that they treat the person rather than the disease, in part as a strategy to justify their distinctiveness from biomedical physicians (Bezilla 1997). Indeed, in a random national survey of D.O.'s that produced 955 usable questionnaires, 40.9 percent of the 707 respondents who cited philosophical differences that distinguish them from M.D.'s referred to their "holistic approach" (Johnson and Kurtz 2002:2143). It should be noted, however, that making this assertion and carrying it out are quite different matters and would require more empirical research to assess. In reality, at least in the U.S. context, osteopathic medicine has by and large evolved into a parallel medical system to biomedicine, with an emphasis on family medicine and in which manipulative therapy tends to function as an adjunct modality (Baer 2001:50–56). In contrast, osteopathy in various Anglophone countries, particularly Britain, Australia, and New Zealand, continues to function as a professionalized heterodox medical system that emphasizes manipulative therapy (Baer 1984).

Despite an interest in the concept of holism on the part of biomedical physicians and scientists in various countries prior to the advent of the holistic health movement per se, various biomedical practitioners have functioned as pioneers in introducing holistic health or alternative approaches into biomedicine. Although a growing number of biomedical practitioners have come to express an interest in holistic or alternative medicine, patients and other health professionals, both heterodox and biomedical practitioners, contributed to the climate that sparked the holistic health movement. According to Porter (1999:65), "Orthodox medicine [or biomedicine] has often assimilated a fringe practice rather than lose patients en masse to marginal medicine. This usually happens through an astute filtering process: the metaphysical claims of the fringe practice are abandoned, while its practical techniques are absorbed." In the case of late-twentieth-century U.S. society, nurses and allied health professionals constituted the vanguard among biomedical practitioners in terms of an interest in holistic health—a development that has received relatively little attention (Kuhn 1999; Dossey, Keegan, and Guzzetta 2000; Fontaine 2000). Furthermore, as Alster (1989:161) observes, "It is important to recall that physicians were latecomers, arriving to find other groups well established and claiming to offer different and even superior services than those available from physicians or physician-controlled agencies." Within the corridors of biomedicine itself, nurses, occupational therapists, and physical therapists expressed an interest in holistic health before M.D.'s did. These practitioners have asserted for some time that holism is a part and parcel of their approach to health care. Barbara Blattner, for example, incorporated holistic principles in her conceptual model of nursing education and practice that was discussed in her book *Holistic Nursing* (1981). Effie Poy Yew Chow (1984) is another prominent nurse who has been part of the holistic health movement, largely in her role as the president of the East West Academy of Healing Arts in San Francisco.

KEY HOLISTIC BIOMEDICAL PHYSICIANS

A precursor of the interest of biomedicine in the holistic health movement was Flanders Dunbar, a psychiatrist at Columbia-Presbyterian Medical Center, who did pioneering work in psychosomatic medicine and authored *Psychosomatic Diagnosis* (1945). Another precursor was Halpert Dunn, who has been credited as the founder of the "wellness movement" and authored *High Level Wellness* (1961). Evarts Loomis reportedly had a dream in which the phrase "treat the whole person" appeared while on assignment in Newfoundland in 1940 and went on to establish Meadowlark in 1958, which Morton and Morton (1996:158) refer to as the "first holistic medical retreat center" in the United States.

Herbert Benson, a cardiologist and professor at Harvard Medical School, achieved fame in the 1970s following the publication of *The Relaxation Response* (1975). He maintained that the "relaxation response" has been likened to a secular version of transcendental meditation and can be induced by repetition of a word, phrase, sound, or prayer and by the passive return to these when intrusive thoughts reoccur. Benson asserted that the relaxation response could be useful in the treatment of chronic pain, insomnia, anxiety, hypertension, depression, and the side effects of various cancer and AIDS therapies. He was one of the first U.S. biomedical physicians to enter the People's Republic of China after diplomatic relations were restored there during the Nixon administration. When Benson obtained a large grant to study the mind–body connection, Harvard Medical School colleagues debated as to whether he should be permitted to accept it. He threatened to resign and went on eventually in 1988 to establish the Mind/Body Institute affiliated with both Harvard and the Beth Israel Deaconess Medical Center in Boston.

David Eisenberg accompanied Benson on his trip and went on to become one of the first of a new generation of U.S. biomedical students to master Chinese and to attend the Beijing College of Traditional Chinese Medicine. He wrote *Encounters with Qi*, in which he discusses the Chinese concept of *chi* or energy and Chinese healing methods (Eisenberg 1995). After completing his M.D. degree and specializing in internal medicine, Eisenberg established himself at Harvard as a staunch proponent of alternative medicine, and he directs the Division of Research and Education in Complementary and Integrative Therapies—an endeavor in mind–body medicine that interfaces with "such disciplines as social medicine, medical anthropology, and comparative religions" (Taylor 2000:34). He directed two national surveys on the utilization of "unconventional medicine" (Eisenberg et al. 1993, 1998). Eisenberg also served as the principal consultant on the PBS series *Healing and the Mind with Bill Moyers*.

Bernard Siegel, a surgeon, had his cancer patients read books on meditation and psychic phenomena in order to tap into their higher healing energies. He authored *Love, Medicine and Miracles* (1986) and *Peace, Love, and Healing* (1989) and served for several years as the president of the American Holistic Medical Association.

Norman Shealy established the Shealy Wellness Center, the first pain and stress management clinic, in the United States in 1971. He was the founding president of the American Holistic Medical Association (Morton and Morton 1996:170). Shealy directs the Pain and Health Rehabilitation Center in Springfield, Missouri, which integrates relaxation therapies, fitness training, dietary changes, hypnosis, biofeedback, and psychotherapy with biomedical therapies in the treatment of chronic diseases (Gordon 1988:92). He presents seminars and workshops around the globe.

James Gordon (1996:30), a graduate of Harvard Medical School and a clinical professor in the departments of psychiatry and family medicine at Georgetown University, became disenchanted with the limitations of the biomedical model in his practice. He eventually became the director of the Center for Mind–Body Medicine in Washington, D.C., and served for a while as the chairperson of the NIH's Office of Alternative Medicine. The Center for

Mind–Body Medicine has developed a "comprehensive program of self-awareness, movement, meditation, massage, yoga, dietary education, and breathing exercises" in biomedical schools in Washington, D.C. (Gordon 1996:256). He has authored *Holistic Medicine* (1988) and *Manifesto for a New Medicine: Your Guide to Healing Partnerships and the Wise Use of Alternative Medicines* (1996).

Marc Micozzi is the executive director of the College of Physicians of Philadelphia and the former director of the National Museum of Health and Medicine. He also served as a senior investigator at the National Cancer Institute. In addition to training as a biomedical physician, Micozzi has a Ph.D. in anthropology. He was the founding editor of the *Journal of Alternative and Complementary Medicine* and edited *Fundamentals of Complementary and Alternative Medicine*, which first appeared in 1996 and appeared in a second edition in 2001. He advocates "tolerance and medical pluralism" in health care and egalitarianism in the physician–patient relationship (Redwood 1995a:1).

Larry Dossey was an internist at the Dallas Diagnostic Center and the former chief of staff of Medical City Dallas Hospital ("Larry Dossey, M.D.," 2003). He is the past president of the Isthmus Institute in Dallas, an organization dedicated to synthesizing science and religion, and is the former cochair of the NIH Office of Alternative Medicine's panel on Mind/Body Interventions. He has written several books on the power of prayer, including *Healing Words: The Power of Prayer and the Practice of Medicine* (1993), *Prayer Is Good Medicine* (1996), and *Reinventing Medicine: Beyond Mind, Body to a New Era of Medicine* (1999). Dossey has dismissed the need for randomized control trials or double-blind studies of prayer. He serves as the executive director of the journal *Alternative Therapies in Health and Medicine*.

Andrew Weil, a Harvard-trained family physician at the University of Arizona medical center, and Deepak Chopra, an Indian-trained biomedical physician, have emerged as the two foremost holistic M.D.'s not only in the United States but around the world. Because of their prominence, the following chapter is devoted to biographical sketches of these two figures as well as their respective views on health, illness, and health care.

Lewis Mehl-Madrona, a family physician–psychiatrist–clinical psychologist who is one-quarter Cherokee, has gained both prestige and notoriety as a result of his decision to integrate biomedicine, Native American healing rituals, and other alternative therapies. He has served as a director of alternative medical clinics at various institutions, including the University of Hawaii School of Medicine, the University of Pittsburgh, and Beth Israel in New York City. Presently Mehl-Madrona is the coordinator of Integrative Psychiatry and Systems Medicine for the University of Arizona's Program in Integrative Medicine. He is the author of *Coyote Medicine* (1996), a chronicle about his journey to "shaman-hood," and most recently *Coyote Healing* (2003), a compilation of "healing miracles" that he personally witnessed.

HOLISTIC MEDICAL AND NURSING ASSOCIATIONS AND SOCIAL PROFILES OF HOLISTIC M.D.'S AND D.O.'S

Holistic biomedical physicians have also formed various organizations. One of the earliest is the American College for Advancement in Medicine based in Laguna Hills, California. Its website states that it is "dedicated to educating physicians on the latest findings and emerging procedures in complementary/ alternative medicine, with special emphasis on preventive/nutritional medicine" (Federal Trade Commission 2003).

Norman Shealy, Gladys Taylor McGarey, Bill McGarevy, and Gerald Looney laid the groundwork for creation of the American Holistic Medical Association (AHMA) in 1977 at Meadowlark, Evart Loomis's holistic health center ("In Honor of Holistic Medicine Pioneer," 2004). The organization held its first meeting in Denver the following year. AHMA adopted a list of "Principles of Holistic Medical Practices" in 1993 (Davis-Floyd and St. John 1998:209). Individuals who are state licensed, certified, or registered health practitioners or social workers can become associate AHMA members but do not have the right to vote. The headquarters of AHMA initially was located in Seattle but now is located in McLean, Virginia, close to the nation's capital. Caplan and Gesler (1998:224) report that "[u]sing U.S. census regions, the highest proportion of physicians who were members of the AHMA was found in the West." Robert S. Ivker, D.O. (2004:1), maintains that holistic medicine is "based on the integration of allopathic (MD), osteopathic (DO), naturopathic (ND), energy, and ethno-medicine" and lists "love applied to body, mind, and spirit with: diet, exercise, environmental measures, attitudinal and behavioral modifications, relationship and spiritual counseling, bioenergy enhancement" as its "primary care treatment options" and "botanical (herbal) medicine, homeopathy, acupuncture, manual therapies, physical therapy, drugs, and surgery" as its "secondary treatment options." The AHMA created the American Board of Holistic Medicine in 1996, which in turned established board certification for M.D.'s and D.O.'s in holistic medicine (Trivieri and the American Holistic Medical Association 2001:402).

Charlotte McGuire, a Texas nurse, founded the American Holistic Nurses Association (AHNA) as a result of her disillusionment with biomedicine, including its emphasis on profit making. In 1994, the association adopted the following description of holistic nursing:

> Holistic nursing embraces all nursing practice that has healing the whole person as its goal. Holistic nursing recognizes that there are two views regarding holism: Holism involves studying and understanding the interrelationships of the bio-psycho-social-spiritual dimensions of the person, recognizing that the whole is greater than the sum of its parts, and holism involves understanding the individual as an integrated whole interacting with and being acted upon by internal and external environments. Holistic nursing accepts both views, believing that the goals of nursing can be achieved within either framework. (quoted in Kowalak 2003:69)

The AHNA created the American Holistic Nurses Certification Corporation in 1995 in order to offer programs in aromatherapy, therapeutic touch, Amma therapy, and imagery (American Holistic Nurses Association 2004). The association also publishes the *Journal of Holistic Nursing*. Several other nursing journals, such as *Alternative Health Practitioner* and *Holistic Nursing Practice*, also focus on alternative therapies. While an interest in holistic health or alternative medicine has clearly made inroads into nursing, it is difficult to determine how extensive this impact has been. Barnum (1998:183) reports that "[t]he National League for Nursing does not differentiate approved schools according to whether or not their curricula are holistic."

While specific biomedical physicians and nurses and biomedical and nursing schools have taken the lead in introducing alternative therapies, the rather conservative American Medical Association has shifted its stance from staunch antipathy to cautious openness toward it (Patel 1998:66). In December 1995, the Resident Physician Section of the AMA passed a resolution that encourages its members to support the scientific evaluation of alternative therapies. The *Journal of the American Medical Association* devoted its November 11, 1998, issue to "Alternative Medicine."

Several studies have provided social profiles of holistic conventional physicians (M.D.'s and D.O.'s). Goldstein et al. (1985) interviewed thirty members of Physicians in Transition, a support group for holistic physicians that was established at the Center for Healing Arts in Los Angeles in 1975. All of the physicians in the study expressed dissatisfaction with biomedicine on matters such as limitations in the treatment of chronic diseases, iatrogenesis, and barriers in physician–patient interaction. Seven PIT members became predisposed to holistic medicine as a result of psychotherapy, encounter groups, or other personal growth situations (Goldstein et al. 1985:329). Fourteen subjects reported that personal rather than professional experience with illness had contributed to their interest in holistic medicine.

In a later study, Goldstein et al. (1987, 1988) compared 340 members of the American Holistic Medical Association with 142 family practice physicians (FPs) in California. Although both groups were matched in terms of age, gender, and social class, there were significant differences between them.

> AHMAs are significantly less likely than FPs to have been raised in metropolitan environments and to have attended an American medical school; roughly equal proportions graduated from foreign medical schools (9.9% versus 5.1% of the FPs) and from American osteopathic medical schools (10.2% versus 2.2% of FPs). Thus foreign medical graduates, who constitute about one-fifth of all physicians in the United States, are underrepresented among both groups, while osteopaths, who make up 3.9% of all U.S. physicians, are underrepresented among the FPs and overrepresented among AHMAs. (Goldstein et al. 1987:107)

These findings indicate that D.O.'s may overall exhibit a greater predilection for holistic medicine than M.D.'s do, thus bearing out in part the osteopathic profession's contention that D.O.'s "treat the person rather than the disease." More empirical research needs to be conducted to further investigate this assertion. At any rate, whereas 59.8 percent of the AHMA members regarded religion and/or spirituality as a "very important" dimension in their lives, only 17.6 percent of the FPs did so (Goldstein et al. 1987:110). Two-fifths (40.5 percent) of the AHMA members described their practices as "holistic," in contrast to 3.6 percent of the FPs (Goldstein et al. 1988:856).

Davis-Floyd and St. John (1998:208) conducted intensive interviews with thirty-four holistic physicians. None of their subjects were AMA members, and most did not belong to state, county, or local medical societies. Davis-Floyd and St. John (1998:150–69) identify the following factors that prompted their subjects to shift from "technocratic medicine" to "humanistic medicine" or "holistic medicine": (1) experiences with the limitations of biomedicine; (2) encounters with patients who informed them about the merits of holistic medicine; (3) personal illnesses that biomedicine failed to adequately address; and (4) social and spiritual experiences that altered their relationships with friends, family, and society.

Caplan and Gesler (1998) attempted to survey the entire 1988 membership list of the AHMA, which numbered some two hundred U.S. M.D.'s and D.O.'s at the time. Eighty-nine members returned questionnaires. In terms of geographic distribution, "[t]he West clearly had substantially more members than expected. The Northeast was somewhat underrepresented, the North Central region achieved near parity, and the South was the most underrepresented" (Caplan and Gesler 1998:194). In terms of gender, the sample of holistic practitioners resembled the general population of biomedical physicians. Ironically, as we saw earlier, the vast majority of prominent holistic physician spokespersons are males—a phenomenon that also needs further investigation. Caplan and Gesler (1998:195) report that "holistic MDs earn approximately the same income as their nonholistic counterparts when medical specialties are taken into account."

Diehl et al. (1997) compared a sample of 312 U.S. conventional physicians who practice acupuncture, namely members of the American Academy of Medical Acupuncture (AAMA), with national data on conventional physicians. Compared with national data, the AAMA physicians were more likely to be generalists, in private practice, and ages thirty-five to fifty-four. Males and females were more or less equally represented among AAMA members, yet another manifestation of the greater predilection of females for alternative medicine both among health practitioners and patients. Jacobs, Chapman, and Crothers (1998) conducted a study that compared twenty-seven conventional physicians (M.D.'s and D.O.'s) using homeopathy in 1992 with physicians included in the National Ambulatory study of 1990.

Of the 27 participating AIH [American Institute of Homeopathy] physicians, 22 (81.5%) were men; the average of the entire group was 46 years. United States geographical distribution was as follows: 7 (26%), northeast; 2 (7.4%),

South; 3 (11.1%), Midwest; and 15 (55.5%), west. This compares with 76 (72.6%) men; 38 (37.4%), northeast; 12 (11.7%), south; 18 (17.5%), Midwest; and 34 (33.5%), west of the total AIH membership of 102 physicians in 1992. (537)

Whereas female biomedical physicians, proportionately speaking, have a greater predilection for holistic medicine in general, this does not seem to be the case for homeopathy, perhaps in large part because historically homeopathic medicine, like biomedicine, had been a male-dominated preserve.

INCORPORATION OF CAM INTO THE CURRICULA OF BIOMEDICAL AND NURSING SCHOOLS AND CONTINUING EDUCATION PROGRAMS

A growing number of biomedical and nursing students have come to express interest in holistic health, CAM, or integrative medicine (Kreitzer et al. 2002). In 2002, at least 81 out of 125 biomedical schools offer instruction in CAM, either in required courses or as electives or both ("Courses on Complementary Medicine," 2002). Since 1997, the Special Interest Group on Complementary and Alternative Medicine of the Association of American Medical Colleges has discussed the importance of incorporating CAM into biomedical colleges (Wetzel et al. 2003:191). The Consortium of Academic Health Centers has been seeking to introduce programs of integrative medicine in U.S. biomedical schools (Rees 2001).

The first teaching program in alternative medicine at a U.S. biomedical institution was established in the 1970s at Montefiore Medical Center in Bronx (Abrams 1994:99). Andrew Weil directs the Program in Integrative Medicine at the University of Arizona, which provides continuing medical education (including quarterly miniconferences) and a two-year fellowship for M.D.'s and D.O.'s who have completed residencies in primary care specialties (Goldstein 1999:120). C. Everett Koop, a former surgeon general, is developing a center at Dartmouth that combines biomedicine and CAM. While many schools offer courses on alternative medicine as electives, many other schools, including Harvard, Cornell, and Columbia, incorporate lectures on alternative medicine into required courses. Conversely, Wallace Sampson, a retired oncologist, teaches a course at Stanford University designed to discredit alternative medicine. The Department of Family Medicine at the University of Colorado School of Medicine in Denver is planning to establish a holistic track within a four-year family medicine residency officially planned to begin in June 2004. The track will include modules in physical and environmental health, emotional and mental health, and spiritual and social medicine.

A growing number of biomedical schools and university hospitals have created centers of integrative or complementary and alternative medicine where they treat patients. The Stress Reduction Center at the University of Massachusetts–Worcester Medical School teaches Buddhist meditation and yoga to its patients. The Rosenthal Center for Complementary/Alternative Medicine at Columbia University provides physicians and patients with information on CAM therapies. The UCLA Center for East–West Medicine was created in 1993 to merge principles of Chinese medicine and biomedicine (Hui et al. 2002). Thomas Jefferson University Hospital in Philadelphia operates a Center for Integrative Medicine. The University of Texas Anderson Center offers "complementary/integrative medicine" to its patients (flyer).

In March 2003, I had the opportunity to visit the Center for Integrative Medicine at George Washington University Medical Center while teaching a course on "Comparative Health Systems" in the anthropology department at that university and to speak with the center's founder and director, John C. Pan, M.D. Pan is an obstetrician/gynecologist who established the center in 1998 to "fulfill his mission of promoting optimal health and preventing disease" (professional profile flyer). In 1995, "he embarked upon a multi-dimensional journey of self-education in the healing arts to understand how to heal the whole patient rather than just treat a disease" (professional profile flyer). The staff at the center includes an M.D. with a specialty in mind–body medicine, a nurse practitioner, a licensed acupuncturist who also works with Western herbs, a doctor of Oriental medicine, a chiropractor, a Reiki practitioner, a massage therapist, a hypnotherapist, a nutritional counselor, and an Alexander technique/yoga practitioner. Most of the health staff work at the center on a part-time basis and maintain other practices. The center offers seminars in "PreConception," "Healthy Aging for Women," "Pain Management," and "Healthy Weight for You"; classes in tai chi, meditation, and hypnosis; continuing medical education lectures; and lectures for the general public. Although the center is seeking arrangements whereby its services would be covered by health insurance and managed health care plans, most of its patients and clients pay out of pocket. Wolpe (2002:169) states: "The conventionalization of CAM into the academic medical center is part of a long history of medicine gaining control over modalities by co-opting them." In the process, he maintains that the CAM that conventional physicians adopt strips it of the "very ritual and therapeutic philosophy that made it attractive to many patients in the first place" (Wolpe 2002:171).

Many nursing schools have established programs in "holistic nursing." The New York University Advanced Practice Holistic Nursing Graduate Program (established in 1998) offers a master's degree as holistic nurse practitioner and teaches meditation, therapeutic touch, and homeopathy (Dean 2001). The University of Minnesota School of Nursing has incorporated CAM into its curriculum and offers instruction in storytelling, journaling, aromatherapy, energy healing, herbal therapies, imagery, acupuncture, traditional Chinese medicine, tai chi, yoga, massage, and prayer (Halcon et al. 2001). Other holistic nursing programs include the Beth-El College (Colorado Springs) Master's Program in Holistic Nursing and the College of New Rochelle (New York) Master's Program in Holistic Nursing. The University of Washington School of Nursing offers instruction in CAM with input from Bastyr University (Sierpina 2003).

Many nursing schools have incorporated therapeutic touch, a healing technique developed by Dolores Krieger, a now-retired nursing instructor at New York University. She has a background in theosophy and devised hands-on techniques for nurses to direct *prana*, a Hindu term referring to a cosmic energy, into patients. She claims that "during the healing process both patient and healer experience tingling sensations, pulsation of energy, and a radiation of heat—all tangible evidence of the activation of *prana*" (Fuller 2001:112). Despite Krieger's metaphysical interests, the "power of therapeutic touch, however, is derived not from a religious concept of God's presence, but rather from the idea of energy fields within and surrounding the body" (Cassilith 1998:318). Therapeutic touch practitioners assert that this technique induces relaxation, reduces anxiety, and stimulates the patient's self-healing capacities.

A growing number of biomedical and nursing schools have adopted research on CAM or integrative medicine. Harvard Medical School operates the Division for Research and Education in Complementary and Integrative Therapies that is directed by David M. Eisenberg (Harvard Medical School 2003). In addition to education and clinical services in CAM, the Hennepin County Medical Center, one of the teaching hospitals of the University of Minnesota Medical School, conducts research on CAM approaches in treatment of substance abuse (Canfield and Faass 2001:124). The University of

Virginia College of Nursing (2003) has a Center for the Study of Complementary and Alternative Therapies that is funded by the NIH. Out of sixteen research sites funded by the NIH's National Center for Complementary and Alternative Medicine, nine of them are situated in biomedical colleges.

In addition to CAM training at biomedical and nursing schools, many M.D.'s, nurses, and other health professionals are receiving training in CAM at a wide assortment of conferences and workshops. Acupuncture in particular has captured relatively wide appeal among U.S. conventional physicians (Kotarba 1975; McQueen 1985). UCLA enrolls some five hundred to six hundred M.D.'s a year in a three-hundred-hour acupuncture training program (Brunk 2000). The American Academy of Medical Acupuncture was established by a group of biomedical physicians who had graduated from the "Medical Acupuncture for Physicians" training programs sponsored by the UCLA School of Medicine. Out of the estimated ten thousand licensed or certified acupuncturists in the United States in 1995, about one-third reportedly were M.D.'s (Pearl and Schillinger 1999:180). Wolpe (1985:421) maintains that nurses have been more open to acupuncture than have conventional physicians.

The American College for Advancement in Medicine (established in 1973), which is committed to informing conventional physicians about CAM, conducts annual conferences on "New Advances in Complementary Medicine." While most of the speakers at the 2002 conference in Phoenix were M.D.'s, Konrad Kail, a naturopathic physician and a member of NCCAM's Advisory Council, spoke about "Toxification and Cancer." Marc Micozzi offers a conference called "World Med" and James Gordon offers a conference on "Comprehensive Cancer Care" for M.D.'s and other health professionals (Haynes 1999:134). In May 2003, the Columbia University College of Physicians and Surgeons offered a two-day course titled "Integrative Pain Medicine" (flyer). The course included a discussion of current pain pharmacology; psychological evaluation of pain; mind–body medicine for pain; acupuncture and Chinese medicine for pain; nutritional, manual physical, and bioenergetic therapies for pain; and yoga for pain. The Institute for Health and Healing sponsored by consortium of hospitals, health services, and the University of California–San Francisco has been sponsoring for several years an "Integrative Medicine Mini Medical School" that combines the "best of conventional and holistic medicine." The series ran from April 11 to June 6 in 2002 and featured lectures by various M.D.'s, nurses, alternative practitioners, and a nurse-anthropologist (Meg Jordan, who has done ethnographic research on "healing circles") (flyer).

I attended portions of the Fifth Cancer Conference sponsored by the Center for Mind–Body Medicine for an assemblage of a few hundred health professionals and other interested parties at the Washington Hilton in April 2003. James Gordon, the center's director, started out the opening session with a moment of silence to "see what can we do to bring peace and healing to the people of Iraq, the U.S., and Great Britain." Gordon told the audience that the center stresses mind–body approaches, spirituality, exercise, and nutrition and has been working on healing the effects of war and terrorism, such as stress and trauma in war zones, particularly in Kosovo. He added that the center is interested in creating a model of "comprehensive, integrative cancer care." Gordon then introduced Senator Tom Harkin (Democrat–Iowa) as the "initiator of the Office of Alternative Medicine [now National Center for Complementary and Alternative Medicine]." Harkin told the audience that "Americans want medicines that are holistic" and referred to biomedicine as "traditional medicine." He noted that "we need to figure out what really works instead of debating what is conventional or alternative" and called for putting CAM therapies through peer-reviewed tests. Harkin stated that there is a critical need to teach conventional physicians and nurses about the use of CAM and that "there is a lot out there on CAM information and that it is difficult to figure out what works and what is a fad." He said that this was the case with the acupuncture treatment that his brother had received for cancer.

Steve Bonner, another speaker in the opening session and the CEO of the Cancer Treatment Center of America, told the audience that his organization offers both "traditional" and CAM therapies or an integrative approach to cancer treatment and has published *Fighting Cancer: Mind, Body, and Spirit.* Michele Kahn, a British biomedical physician and complementary therapies adviser, stated that she works with Prince Charles in promoting complementary therapies and has worked with HIV patients who utilize alternative therapies. She read a message from Prince Charles and referred to the Prince of Wales Center for Integrative Medicine. Jeffrey White, a medical oncologist at the National Cancer Institute, noted that his organization is involved in CAM research. Stephen Straus, M.D., the director of the NIH's National Center for Complementary and Alternative Medicine, told the audience that this conference was the third Center for Mind–Body Medicine event that he had attended and noted that NCCAM funding for cancer research had increased tenfold between 1999 and 2002.

The following day, I attended a session in which Caroline Peterson from the Thomas Jefferson University for Integrative Medicine spoke about "Mindfulness-based Art Therapy for Cancer Patients" and Lewis Mehl-Madrona spoke about forty-three patients who had experienced miraculous cures with Native American healers.

David Hess (2003), a renowned medical anthropologist who has done extensive research on CAM cancer therapies, makes the following observations about the annual cancer conference sponsored by the Center for Mind–Body Medicine:

> The registration fee structure, availability of continuing education credits, and generally high scientific quality of the research reflect the orientation toward the health care professions, in contrast with the populist, patient-to-patient advocacy orientation of the Cancer Control Society's annual meeting. The Washington, D.C.–based conference also has a higher participation from federal research agencies (including the armed forces, NCI [National Cancer Institute], and NCCAM) . . . from nutritional and mind–body protocols to their practices, and from cancer hospitals that were adding off-site CAM facilities. (242)

Conventional physicians and other health professionals, both biomedical and heterodox, may acquaint themselves with CAM or integrative medicine by consulting a growing number of research journals, such as *Alternative Medicine,* the *Journal of Alternative and Complementary Medicine, Advances in Mind–Body Medicine, Alternative & Complementary Therapies, Alternative Therapies,* and *Alternative Healthcare Management,* and *Focus on Alternative and Complementary Therapies: An Evidence-Based Approach.*

THE INCORPORATION OF PRAYER AND SPIRITUALITY INTO CONVENTIONAL MEDICINE AND NURSING

Although holistic health proponents and New Agers have often viewed healing and spirituality as intricately intertwined, an increasing number of conventional physicians and nurses have come to express an interest in the role of Christian prayer or other forms of spirituality in the healing process. A growing number of biomedical researchers and psychologists are conducting research on the impact of religious commitment on health (Chamberlain and

Hall 2000). Herbert Benson and Jared Klass have been conducting research on the impact of prayer on health at the Mind/Body Medical Institute at New England Deaconess Hospital since 1988 (Trivieri and the American Holistic Medical Association 2001:117). The National Institute for Healthcare Research (established in 1991) reviews the biomedical research on impact of religious commitment on health and has been introducing spirituality into the curriculum of U.S. biomedical schools (Pelletier 2000:253). Harold Koenig (1999) directs the Program on Religion, Aging, and Health at Duke University Medical Center and is a major proponent of the claim that religiosity fosters both physical and mental health and wellness.

As noted earlier, Larry Dossey has been the foremost biomedical proponent of the significance of prayer, including at-a-distance prayer, and spirituality in general in the promotion of health and addressing disease. According to Dossey, the number of biomedical schools teaching courses that explore the role of religious devotion and prayer increased from three to fifty in a matter of four years (interviewed in Lawlis 2001:490). There is now a substantial body of research literature on the role of prayer, religiosity, or spirituality in coping with specific diseases (e.g., leukemia, cancer, arthritis), recovering from illness, preventive health, wellness, longevity enhancement, and the prevention of specific diseases or health-related problems (e.g., heart disease, hypertension, substance abuse, suicide) (Lawlis 2001).

Cohen (2003:9) refers to various therapeutic modalities such as Reiki, therapeutic touch, polarity therapy, shiatsu, and kinesiology as genres of *energy medicine* or *energy healing*—a category that he defines as "that subset of therapies within the spectrum of complementary and alternative therapies that primarily are based on the projection of information, consciousness, and/or intentionality to patients." He observes that energy medicine constitutes a bridge between medicine and religion in that it postulates the presence of a human energy field or aura surrounding the body and "containing information, in the form of consciousness, relevant to disease and healing" (Cohen 2003:17). Indeed, Cohen draws parallels between developments of psychology and medicine. Whereas psychology has evolved from Freudian theory to behaviorism to humanistic psychology to transpersonal psychology, medicine has evolved from biomedicine to complementary to alternative medicine to integrative medicine to energy medicine, which he describes as "future medicine" (Cohen 2003:95). Indeed, NCCAM classifies energy therapies as forms of "frontier medicine." As Cohen (2003:206–7) observes, energy healing may defy standard double-blind, controlled scientific experimentation given that energy healers often claim to work with spirit guides and angels, see deceased relatives around patients, and heal "past life" traumas. In his effort to project future developments in health care, he asserts that "[f]uture medicine will mean that health care provides and governments internationally collaborate to synthesize technological medicine with different healing systems and traditions from across the globe and to more deeply incorporate spirituality across a range of traditions in the care for human health."

While some biomedical physicians and nurses have become staunch, at times even uncritical, advocates of the impact of prayer and other religious or spiritual practices on health, Cassileth states that literature reviews of research in this area indicate mixed results. According to Cassileth (1998:312), "In an analysis of 115 studies, thirty-seven studies found that religious belief seemed to have a positive effect on health, forty-seven studies produced a negative effect, and thirty-one found no effect."

> As for the health benefits of religious belief, there are some studies that appear to indicate that religious belief does correlate with better health. However, it is important to note that correlation is not the same as causation: other factors, such as social support, may explain the better health of those with religious belief. The evidence is not yet clear that religious faith causes better health. (Cassileth 1998:313)

Aside from these points, it is important to note that the vast majority of studies arguing that prayer and other forms of religiosity or spirituality on health, at least in modern societies, has been conducted in the United States and may reflect the fact that this country has the highest level of belief in a God, a Higher Power, or a Supreme Being than any other advanced capitalist society in the world. Ironically, most of these studies fail to note that overall health statistics—for example, infant mortality and life expectancy—lag behind those of highly secularized societies, such as the Scandinavian countries and other Western European countries, where the percentages of "nonbelievers" (atheists or agnostics) are far higher than in the United States and where the vast majority of people rarely or never attend religious services, even if they hold a belief in God or an afterlife. Whereas about 95 percent of Americans believe in God, 45 percent of Swedes, 65 percent of Norwegians, 63 percent of West Germans, 57 percent of French, 61 percent of Dutch, and 71 percent of Britons reportedly do (Ashford and Timms 1992:40). In contrast to predominantly Protestant countries, belief in God tends to be higher in the predominantly Catholic countries. Whereas approximately 40 percent of Americans claim to attend church on a regular weekly basis (Hadaway, Marler, and Chaves 1993:741), Ashford and Timms (1992:46) report that 13 percent of Britons, 19 percent of West Germans, and 21 percent of Dutch claim to attend church on a weekly basis. Elsewhere, Inglehart, Basanez, and Moreno (1998) report that 10 percent of Swedes, 13 percent of Norwegians, 17 percent of French, 24 percent of Britons, 34 percent of West Germans, 44 percent of Austrians, 51 percent of Italians, and 88 percent of Irish claim to attend church "at least monthly."

Due to a number of factors, such as geographic mobility, relatively weak family and community ties, and suburbanization, many Americans often find themselves socially isolated and often discover a sense of social connectedness within the context of a religious congregation. In contrast, Lambert (1996) reports that whereas 19 percent of West Europeans rate religion "very important" in their lives, 81 percent rate family, 53 percent rate work, 43 percent rate friends and acquaintances, and 38 percent rate leisure with this designation. Much more than in many European countries, particularly northern ones, churches appear to provide countless numbers of Americans with quasi-communities or lifestyle enclaves.

In a society characterized by social isolation and geographic mobility, religious groups, including ones that incorporate healing rituals, often provide members with social support and a sense of well-being. In contrast to many Americans, Western Europeans are more inclined to retain strong family and community ties and find social contacts in the public life or street life or even political parties and labor unions. The literature on the impact of prayer and religiosity/spirituality on health or wellness needs to take on a more multidisciplinary and cross-cultural research orientation than it has at the present time (Levin 1994; Becker 2001). While I do not wish to dismiss the corpus of literature that suggests that prayer and religiosity or spirituality contribute to health, I strongly suspect that much of this research has a culture-specific or ethnocentric bias.

SURVEYS OF PATIENT UTILIZATION OF COMPLEMENTARY AND ALTERNATIVE MEDICINE

Numerous studies examining patient utilization of CAM have been published over the past fifteen years or so. David Eisenberg and his colleagues have been involved in a couple of renowned and frequently cited national surveys of patient utilization of CAM therapies (Eisenberg et al. 1993, 1998). The first study, which entailed a 1990 telephone survey of 1,539 English-speaking adults, estimated that one-third of the U.S. population used some type of CAM therapy. Respondents most often noted the use of exercise and prayer, but approximately one-third said that they had used at least one CAM therapy during the past year, such as relaxation techniques, self-help groups, biofeedback, hypnosis, chiropractic, massage, imagery, spiritual healing, lifestyle diets, herbal medicine, energy healing, homeopathy, acupuncture, and folk remedies. Almost two-thirds of CAM users did not consult a provider but treated themselves. The remainder consulted a provider, making an average of nineteen visits each over the twelve-month period. Forty-four percent of CAM users had attended college, 39 percent were middle-class adults with incomes exceeding $35,000, and 44 percent resided in western states. Virtually all respondents (96 percent) utilizing CAM consulted a conventional physician (M.D. or D.O.). None of the respondents saw a CAM practitioner for treatment of serious medical complications, such as cancer, diabetes, lung ailments, hypertension, urinary tract problems, and dental problems. Based on their findings, Eisenberg et al. projected that sixty-one million Americans used at least one of sixteen CAM therapies and that twenty-two million Americans consulted a CAM practitioner in 1990.

The follow-up study conducted in 1997 found that the use of CAM had increased to 42.1 percent. Eisenberg and his colleagues report that in 1997:

> Use was more common among women (48.9%) than men (37.8%) ($P = .001$) and less common among African Americans (33.1%) than members of other racial groups (44.5%) ($P = .004$). People aged 35 to 49 years reported higher rates of use (50.6%) than people either older (39.1%) ($P = .001$) or younger ($P = .003$). Use was higher among those who had some college education (50.6%) than those with no college education (36.4%) ($P = .001$) and more common

among people with annual incomes above $50,000 (48.1%) than with lower in-
comes (42.6%) ($P = .03$). Use was more common in the West (50.1%) than elsewhere in the United States (42.1%) ($P = .004$). (Eisenberg et al. 1998:1571)

The percentage of users paying out of pocket for CAM services had decreased
somewhat from 64.0 percent in 1990 to 58.3 percent in 1997. Total expendi-
tures for CAM therapies came to an estimated $27.0 billion, $12.2 billion of
which was paid out of pocket.

Paul Ray (1996), a sociologist, conducted a systematic study of CAM utilization in the United States as part of his Integral Cultural Survey. Based on
1,036 usable questionnaires obtained from a random sample of some 1,500
respondents who are part of a panel of 350,000 persons associated with the
National Family Opinion, Inc., Ray divided the U.S. populace into three primary subcultures: (1) the Heartlanders (29 percent, fifty-six million); (2) the
Moderns (47 percent, eighty-eight million); and (3) the Cultural Creatives (24
percent, forty-four million). The Heartlanders exhibited a predisposition toward "Traditionalism" entailing nostalgic images of the past; the Moderns
subscribed to "Modernism" or conventional day-to-day materialistic concerns
of the larger culture; and the Cultural Creatives value "Trans-Modernism" and
utopian images of a better world. Whereas 34.1 percent of the Heartlanders
and 32.0 percent of Moderns used "unconventional medicine" in 1994, 52.2
percent of Cultural Creatives used it. Ray notes (1996:41), however, "it must
immediately be said that since Cultural Creatives are only 23.6% of the population, they still cannot be a dominant part of the total population who use
alternative health care: They are 33% of all users." He makes an interesting distinction that sheds further light on the type of people more likely to use CAM
therapies—namely, one between Green Cultural Creatives and Core Cultural
Creatives. The Core Cultural Creatives (10.6 percent, twenty million) tended
to express a greater interest in "psychology, spiritual life, self-actualization,
[and] self-expression"—themes consonant with New Ageism—than do Green
Cultural Creatives (13 percent, twenty-four million) who tend to exhibit more
"values centered on the environment and social concerns from a secular view"
(Ray 1996:23).

Various other parties have conducted national surveys of CAM utilization.
Landmark Healthcare, Incorporated (1998), commissioned Interactive Solutions to interview a national random sample of 1,500 subjects in November

1997. The study found that 42 percent of the interviewees had utilized some type of CAM therapy in the past year. Some 17 percent of the interviewees had used herbal therapy, 16 percent chiropractic, 14 percent massage therapy, 13 percent vitamin therapy, 5 percent homeopathy, 5 percent yoga, 5 percent acupressure, 2 percent acupuncture, 2 percent biofeedback, 1 percent hypnotherapy, and 1 percent naturopathy.

Based on a survey involving forty-six thousand of its readers, *Consumer Reports* (2000) found that more than sixteen thousand, or almost 35 percent, were CAM users. Using data derived from the 1999 National Health Interview Survey, Ni, Simile, and Hardy (2002) estimate that 28.9 percent of U.S. "noninstitutionalized civilian adults" in the United States utilized at least one CAM therapy in the past year. Spiritual healing or prayer (13.7 percent), herbal medicine (9.6 percent), and chiropractic (7.6 percent) constituted the most prevalent CAM therapies. Furthermore, "The use of CAM was most prevalent among women, persons aged 35 to 54 years, and persons with an educational attainment of >= 16 years. The overall CAM use was higher for white non-Hispanic persons (30.8%) than for Hispanic (19.9%) and black non-Hispanic persons (24.1%)" (Ni, Simile, and Hardy 2002:354).

Sociologist Melinda Goldner (1999) conducted a small survey of "alternative practitioners and clients" in the San Francisco Bay area, primarily in Marin County. She compiled a list of alternative clinics in the area and called the clinics seeking volunteers. Out of Goldner's forty respondents, thirty were alternative practitioners and ten were clients, two of whom were studying to become alternative practitioners. "[R]espondents were overwhelmingly female (73%) and Caucasian (97%), and ranged in age from 35 to 63 (mean age = 47)" (Goldner 1999:59).

In another local survey that involved 113 family practice patients in the Portland, Oregon, area, 57 (50 percent) reported that they used some form of CAM, but only 30 had told their family practitioner (Elder, Gillcrist, and Minz 1997). The researchers note that there may be a greater predilection for CAM use in Portland than in many other U.S. cities because of the presence of a chiropractic college and a naturopathic college in the area.

Various studies have focused on CAM utilization among specific populations. Whitlock (2001) and his team surveyed HMO members affiliated with Kaiser Permanente about their use of CAM outside the HMO. Out of a random sample of members, 15 percent ($n = 380$) had used CAM providers such as chiropractors, naturopaths, and acupuncturists during the previous twelve months, and 35 percent had used CAM providers at some time in the past. CAM users were more likely to be females, more educated, and more dissatisfied with the HMO.

A survey based on 508 military veterans in the U.S. Southwest found that 252 (49.6 percent) reported CAM use. Much in keeping with other studies, the military veteran CAM users tended to be non-Hispanic whites, earn more than $50,000 a year, and have more than twelve years of education.

Arcury et al. (2002) conducted research on CAM use among rural older adults in North Carolina. They found that 11 percent of their respondents used chiropractic. Whereas "[s]ignificantly more Native American and African American than European respondents used home and folk remedies," "[s]ignificantly more Native American and European than African American respondents used vitamin and mineral supplements" (Arcury et al. 2002:177).

Lundy et al. (2001) conducted a survey of the utilization patterns of alternative therapies on the part of 516 low-income Hispanic and Anglo patients at eight community-based family practice clinics in the Phoenix area. Forty-one percent of the respondents indicated that they had visited an alternative practitioner, and 58 percent had used an alternative therapy within the previous two years. Whereas 45 percent of the Hispanic respondents and 31 percent of the Anglo respondents had visited an alternative practitioner, 65 percent of the Anglos used an alternative therapy as opposed to 55 percent of Hispanics (Lundy et al. 2001:208). Whereas Anglos were more likely to rely on chiropractic care, prayer, relaxation, meditation, acupressure, special diets, massage, hypnosis, and acupuncture, Hispanics were more likely to turn to naturopaths, *curanderas/curanderos* and other folk healers, herbalists, homeopaths, and various folk remedies.

Whereas most CAM utilization studies focus on the social characteristics of patients who actually seek out CAM therapies, Jain and Astin (2001) conducted a survey in which they focused on barriers to CAM utilization among respondents derived from a randomly selected sample of 1,680 Stanford University alumni. They found that those less inclined to use CAM are men; people in good health; and those who believe that CAM is generally ineffective or inferior to conventional medicine, that biomedical doctors are not supportive, and that they do not know enough about alternative therapies.

While most studies examining patient utilization of CAM therapies tend to focus on those provided by professionalized and partially professionalized heterodox practitioners, such as chiropractors, acupuncturists, and massage therapists, some studies have examined the utilization of various folk medical systems in the United States, particularly among ethnic minorities. Bailey (1991) found that among a sample of African Americans in Detroit that 24 percent of the women and 10 percent of the men reported using folk or "personal" care treatments for hypertension. Rivera (1988) reported, 32 percent of Mexican Americans in urban barrios in Colorado sought treatment from *curanderas* or *curanderos*. In a survey of 2,103 people born in Mexico but residing or working in San Diego, Chavez (1984:34) found that only 27 (1.3 percent) reported that they had actually used a *curandera* or *curandero*, but 429 (23.3 percent) were willing to do so.

THE GROWING POPULARITY OF CENTERS OF INTEGRATIVE MEDICINE

What were once termed *holistic health centers* are being replaced more and more by *centers of integrative medicine,* which tend to be directed by one or more conventional physicians (M.D.'s or D.O.'s) and staffed by an array of heterodox practitioners.

Sociologist June S. Lowenberg (1989) conducted an in-depth ethnography of the Mar Vista Clinic (pseudonym) in a major California city. Although its practitioners identified with the holistic health movement, they did not refer to the clinic as "holistic" or use the term because of negative connotations associated with it in the minds of some people. The clinic's director, a man with a family practice specialty and a master's degree in acupuncture, was a founding member of both the American Holistic Medical Association and the Association of Holistic Medicine. Mar Vista Clinic had two male family physicians, two female registered nurses, two clinical psychologists (one male and the other female), two bodyworkers (one female and the other male), an office manager, and a receptionist.

Patients at the clinic ranged from those who embraced holistic health as a lifestyle to those who were referred. The vast majority of its patients were middle- to upper-middle-class, and 60 percent were female. "Most clients had fairly high educational levels, and were extremely sophisticated consumers in medical matters" (Lowenberg 1989:183). The clinic's brochure stated that it provided family practice, preventive medicine, acupuncture, and psychological services (Lowenberg 1989:96). The vast majority of patients came to the clinic for a specific problem and because they were dissatisfied with biomedicine. Lowenberg (1989:102) notes that "[s]ome patients appeared to be on a moral crusade, and attempted to convert me to all the advantages of a more holistic approach."

While the clinic's physicians used conventional laboratory tests in diagnosing illnesses, they sought to minimize use of X rays and drugs and also to use alternative procedures, such as hair analysis and an extensive dietary intake history (Lowenberg 1989:106). Interactions among staff and between staff and patients tended to be more egalitarian and warmer than they tended to be in conventional medical clinics. Staff were on a first-name basis among themselves and with patients. Nevertheless, "there are still the markings of bureaucratic efficiency in the office" that are demanded of any medical practice, conventional or alternative, in U.S. society (Lowenberg 1989:111).

Another example of a center of integrative medicine is the Health Medicine Institute (HMI) located in Walnut Creek, California. It is directed by Len Saputo, an internist, and has a health team that includes a somatics educator, a licensed acupuncturist, and various practitioners with training in therapies such as bodywork, Reiki, and Native American and indigenous healing rituals. HMI periodically conducts Health Medicine Forums in part as a venue for recruiting new patients. I attended a forum on "Healing Pain Naturally" in Oakland on March 26, 2002. The audience consisted of about eighty people, most of whom were European Americans but a few of whom were Asians or Asian Americans and four of whom were African American women. Saputo told the audience that he became a convert to integrative medicine as a result of a severe illness that his wife had experienced. Various HMI practitioners spoke about their therapeutic specialties. A female acupuncturist and Chinese medicine practitioner noted that she had been a chronic pain sufferer herself and noted that emotions can block the flow of *chi*. A female naturopath said that various alternative therapies had helped her overcome back injuries that had made it difficult for her to sit and stand. Saputo spoke glowingly of the photon stimulator developed by a man in the audience in order to alleviate pain. The forum allowed various members of the audience to discuss their health problems, and HMI practitioners suggested some possible treatments. Saputo closed the forum by noting that the next one on April 23, 2002, would focus on nutrition and cuisine.

National Integrated Health Associates and the Center for Holistic Medicine situated in northwest Washington, D.C., is another example of a private center of integrative medicine (brochure). The health staff of this complex includes the M.D.-founder of the center, three other M.D.'s, three dentists, four doctors of naturopathy (N.D.'s), two "registered naturopaths," a "medical intuitive," a licensed acupuncturist, and several other health practitioners. The complex offers holistic dentistry; naturopathic and psychoemotional therapies; osteopathic, environmental, and primary care medicine; chronic pain modalities; and detoxifying and regeneration modalities. This "multispecialty health center" functions as an affiliate office of Capital University of Integrative Medicine (established in 1995). The latter offers a Doctor of Integrative Medicine Program, a Master of Integrative Health Science Program, and Doctor of Philosophy Programs (Capital University of Integrative Medicine, 2003). Since Capital University does not have its own campus, it conducts its classes at the Georgetown University Conference Center.

The Canyon Ranch Health Resort in Tucson constitutes an example of the luxury integrative health care center. It has a health and fitness assessment center, six gyms, a yoga and meditation dome, massage treatments, a beauty salon, an aquatic center, and other facilities (Canyon Ranch, 2003). Health specialists working at Canyon Ranch include M.D.'s, nurses, nutritionists, behavioral therapists, movement and aquatic therapists, acupuncturists, physical therapists, chiropractors, and podiatrists. The ranch offers four-night and seven-night "healthy vacations" that include health services, spa and sports services, fitness classes, hikes and excursions, and gourmet meals.

Established in 1989, the American Holistic Health Association (2003) serves as a resource center that seeks to educate the public about "holistic principles." It commissioned William Collinge to write *The American Holistic Health Association Complete Guide to Alternative Medicine* (1996). Although most of the members of the AHHA board are laypeople, James Gordon, M.D., serves on the board. The association lists several "healing centers" on its website, ranging from small clinics to hospitals.

IS BIOMEDICINE CO-OPTING ALTERNATIVE MEDICINE?

Various medical social scientists have warned that holistic health or alternative medicine faces the danger of being co-opted by biomedicine (Alster 1989:163; Lowenberg 1989:225; Montgomery 1993; Wolpe 1999:235). Wolpe

(1994:1144) asserts that "orthodoxies can force conformity through co-optation, isolation, subjugation, absorption, and suppression." Indeed, as we have seen, the terms *holistic health, holistic medicine,* or simply *alternative medicine* appear to have become increasingly displaced by the terms *complementary and alternative medicine* or *integrative medicine.* It should be noted, however, that nurses have tended to retain the notion of *holism* much more than biomedical physicians. Montgomery (1993:87) asserts that "holism will continue to exist along the margins of biomedicine and will slowly, selectively be absorbed into it."

While some holistic M.D.'s and D.O.'s subscribe to the philosophical underpinnings of various CAM therapies, others adopt their techniques without wholeheartedly subscribing to the ideology of the holistic health movement. As Morton and Morton (1996:151) observe, "the broad scope of practice granted to an M.D. by their license allows them to take short, consolidated courses on complex systems of alternative medicine and then immediately offer them to the public." Whereas some non-M.D. acupuncturists study their primary treatment modality for four years at institutions such as the American College of Traditional Chinese Medicine in San Francisco or the Academy of Chinese Culture and Health in Oakland, most have learned their specialty in much more abbreviated programs of study. Indeed Butch Levy, an M.D. acupuncturist in Lakewood, Colorado, argues:

> No one, not even an M.D., can just take a weekend course in acupuncture and really call him- or herself a competent acupuncturist. I think this practice of M.D.s taking quick classes and then practicing alternative techniques without responsible training is an important issue for both the public and the state licensing agencies to look at. (quoted in Morton and Morton 1996:151)

Biomedicine historically has often incorporated alternative therapies rather than losing patients en masse to heterodox practitioners. Alster (1989:163) maintains that biomedical calls for complementary and alternative therapies or integrative medicine may in reality "serve the purpose of preserving the hegemony of medicine by co-opting the most attractive components of holism." In a similar vein, Budd and Sharma (1994:4) assert that "[o]fficial medicine tends to colonize 'fringe' areas of medicine once they are popular and successful." At any rate, cross-cultural research has repeatedly indicated that the integration of biomedical and alternative medical systems tends to preserve rather than eradicate biomedical hegemony (Cant and Sharma 1999:183; Yoshida 2002). Indeed, David Rakel and Andrew Weil, both biomedical physicians and staunch proponents of integrative medicine, observe that biomedicine often views CAM as "tools that are simply added to the current model, one that attempts to understand healing by studying the tools in the tool box" (Rakel and Weil 2003:7).

The dominance of biomedicine often becomes apparent in CAM or integrative medicine centers. Goldner (2000) found this to be the case in her ethnographic observations in an integrative clinic in the San Francisco Bay area:

> At the integrative clinic, one practitioner mentioned that the "physician here likes to be the physician and wave her title. So I have to be respectful, but not necessarily back down." . . . On several occasions, members thanked physicians for attending workshops, especially since they were "putting themselves out there" when "they don't have to [do this]." The alternative practitioners seemed so appreciative that physicians were giving them any level of credibility, that they did not seem to mind differences in power. (228)

Despite the claim on the part of holistic health or CAM proponents that they wish to contribute to a process of demedicalization by shifting responsibility from the physician to the patient, the growing emphasis on holism or integrative health within biomedicine may actually be contributing to further medicalization of U.S. society. The holistic health or CAM/integrative medicine movement runs the risk of becoming a subtle crusade that equates specific lifestyles with moral failures and in essence depoliticizes the social origins of disease (Lowenberg 1989). As Lowenberg and Davis (1994:592) observe, "holistic health practices ultimately extend the control of medical definitions and even gatekeeping to incorporate far wider arenas of lifestyle, spirituality, work, and family."

Alternative practitioners vary in their stance toward biomedicine. Some are willing to collaborate with biomedicine and may even see incorporation into biomedicine as a desirable thing (Goldstein 1999:220). Tori Hudson (2001), a professor of gynecology at the National College of Naturopathic Medicine and the creator of an integrative medicine residency, states:

> As a naturopathic physician, it has always been important to me to work with physicians in mainstream medicine and to learn from them. While I was still in

medical school studying naturopathic medicine, I sought opportunities early in my education to preceptor with medical doctors. At that time, I chose two placements with family practice physicians because, as a student, I knew that the foundations I most needed were in basic science and diagnosis. (262–63)

Conversely, many alternative practitioners have strong feelings about the potential "medicalization" of their expertise (Davis-Floyd and St. John 1998:248). Saks (2000:235) argues that the professionalization of CAM "may draw therapists involved into undesirable roles in surveillance and control through state sponsorship."

At least some health practitioners and laypeople are resisting the biomedical co-optation of alternative medicine. As noted in chapter 3, the herbalists associated with various herbalism schools, such as the Southwest School of Botanical Medicine, constitute the strongest resisters to the culture of professionalism. Based on my observations at several naturopathic conventions and three of the four U.S. naturopathic colleges, the same could be said of at least some naturopathic physicians and students. Most naturopathic physicians, however, appear to accept collaboration with holistic conventional physicians, and a growing number of new naturopathic college graduates are accepting positions in centers of integrative medicine. Peter Chowka, who worked for a time as a consultant on media and public affairs for the American Association of Naturopathic Physicians, noted in an interview with anthropologist David J. Hess that "[while] I see naturopathic medicine as very promising, . . . the [biomedical and cancer] establishment is now increasingly interested in it and, from what I can see, in co-opting it" (quoted in Hess 1999:174).

Other parties resisting biomedical hegemony and supporting the rights of a patient to choose his or her health practitioner or therapeutic modalities include organizations such as the American Association for Health Freedom, the National Health Federation, the Betah Foundation, the Cancer Control Society, the Committee for Freedom of Choice in Medicine, and Citizens for Health (Goldstein 1999:146–48). The American Association for Health Freedom (2004:1), based in Great Falls, Virginia, and established in 1992, describes itself as the "political voice for health care practitioners who use nutritional and other complementary therapies in patient care." Murray R. Susser, M.D., serves as its president, and its board includes eight other biomedical physicians, a naturopathic physician (Thomas Kruzel, the former director of the

Southwest College of Naturopathic Medicine Medical Center in Scottsdale, Arizona), and several laypeople. Patch Adams and Bernie Siegel are members of the association's advisory board.

The Committee for Freedom of Choice (founded in 1972) is headquartered in Chula Vista, California; advocates "freedom of choice in medicine, with informed consent, for physician and patient"; and publishes a quarterly magazine called *The Choice* (2003). Robert Bradford, the founder of the committee, also established several other organizations, including the Robert Bradford Research Institute; the American Biologics–Mexico (a hospital in Tijuana); American Biologics (a pharmaceutical company); and the Capital University of Integrative Medicine in Washington, D.C. Stephen Barrett (2003:1), a psychiatrist and leading opponent of alternative therapies, maintains that the committee constitutes the "political arm of several interlocking corporations promoting and/or marketing questionable remedies for cancer and other serious diseases." The committee is part of the California-based laetrile movement, which has a reputation of being right-wing. Michael Culbert, a journalist who became involved in the alternative cancer therapy movement during the prosecution of John Richardson (a prolaetrile physician) and who had served as the chair of the committee, made the following observations:

> Of the people who headed up the original Committee for Freedom of Choice in Cancer Therapy, . . . half were indeed members of the John Birch Society, primarily because . . . Richardson, M.D., was himself a Birch Society member. But when we got into this fascinating area, freedom of choice, it cut through everything—left, right, and center. (quoted in Hess 1999:103)

While covering Richardson's trial in the early 1970s at the Berkeley municipal court, Culbert observed "McGovern-for-president left-hippies" who supported Richardson (quoted in Hess 1999:103). Indeed, alternative medicine has tended to be politically "highly plastic" in that it has curried favor among both, on the one hand, conservatives and moderates and, on the other hand, liberals and leftists or progressives (Goldstein 1999:113).

5

Deconstructing Andrew Weil and Deepak Chopra

While some holistic biomedical physicians, such as James Gordon, the director of the Center for Mind–Body Medicine in Washington, D.C., have captured some public attention, Andrew Weil and Deepak Chopra have emerged over the past two decades as the most visible spokespersons of the holistic health movement. They have been propelled into fame as holistic biomedical physicians as a result of their success at manipulating the organs of mass communication—books, audiotapes, videotapes, and appearances on television. Weil has published eight books, some of which have been best-sellers. Chopra has authored some twenty-five books and produced more than one hundred audio, video, and CD-ROM titles. In a special issue published on June 14, 1999, *Time* designated both Weil and Chopra as among the "Top 100 Icons and Heroes of the 20th Century" and referred to Chopra as the "poet-prophet of alternative medicine."

In this chapter, I provide brief biographical sketches of Weil and Chopra and compare and contrast their respective views on health, illness, healing, and health care. I also discuss the response of various biomedical parties to these two holistic gurus who have attempted to integrate biomedicine and various alternative healing systems. Finally, I argue that Weil and Chopra both represent the limitations of the holistic health/New Age movement, such as its tendency to downplay the role of social structural factors in the etiology of disease, particularly as it is manifested in the United States.

BIOGRAPHICAL SKETCHES OF TWO HOLISTIC/NEW AGE GURUS

Andrew Weil was born in Philadelphia in 1942. He earned a bachelor of arts degree in biology, with an emphasis on botany, from Harvard University in 1964, and a medical doctor degree from Harvard Medical School in 1968. Upon completion of an internship at Mount Zion Hospital in San Francisco, he worked for a year at the National Institute of Mental Health. After experiencing opposition to his research on marijuana and other drugs at NIMH, Weil retreated to his house in rural northern Virginia, where between 1971 and 1972 he began to practice yoga, vegetarianism, and meditation and composed *The Natural Mind* (1986; originally published in 1972). His disillusionment with biomedicine prompted him to investigate indigenous healing systems around the world. As a fellow of the Institute of Current Affairs from 1971 to 1975, he collected information about medicinal plants and healing in numerous countries around the world. From 1971 to 1984, Weil worked as a research associate at the Harvard Botanical Museum and investigated the properties of medicinal and psychoactive plants. Weil has written a respectable number of articles on ethnomycology, ethnobotany, and ethnopharmacology in journals such as *The Harvard Review* and the *Journal of Psychedelic Drugs* (now the *Journal of Psychoactive Drugs*).

Weil serves as the director of the Center for Integrative Medicine at the University of Arizona Medical Center and as the editor of *Integrative Medicine*. He established the Program in Integrative Medicine at the University of Arizona in 1994, which offered one-year fellowships to family practitioners and internists in order to teach them "how to combine the best ideas and practices of conventional and alternative medicine, with a strong emphasis on healing, natural healing, mind-body interactions, etc." (quoted in Redwood 1995b:2). Due to financial difficulties, the program was assumed under the fund-raising umbrella of the University of Arizona Foundation (MacClain 2000).

Weil settled in Arizona quite fortuitously, while awaiting the repair of his car when traveling through the state. As he observes in the following quote:

> I always had a vision of Arizona being very politically conservative . . . although Tucson is a liberal pole of it. But the regulatory laws in Arizona, including the medical licensing laws, have a kind of Wild West *laissez faire* flavor which is unique, except for Nevada. Nevada and Arizona are the only two states that have

a Homeopathic Board of Medical Examiners under which people doing unusual practices can get licensure that rivals the regular Board of Medical Examiners. So Arizona has been a haven for people producing alternative medicine. (quoted in Redwood 1995b:3)

Weil's first three books represent the "early Weil" in that they focus on his research on the role of drugs in raising human consciousness around the world as well as the dangers associated with the misuse of drugs (Weil 1986 [1972], 1980; Weil and Rosen 1983). Conversely, the publication of *Health and Healing* (1995a; originally published in 1983) marks the beginning of the "late Weil"—namely, the "good hippie doc" and a prominent holistic health guru. In addition to having written several books that elaborate and expand on points made in *Health and Healing*, Weil has evolved into a virtual one-man industry that includes a website (www.drweil.com) and "Andrew Weil's Self Healing" electronic newsletter, which reportedly has some 450,000 subscribers (Lemley 1999:2). Weil presents an image of a jovial, aging hippie doctor with his bald dome and full white beard. He generally wears casual clothes in portraits that appear on his books and websites.

Deepak Chopra was born in 1947 as the son of a New Delhi cardiologist and graduated as a biomedically trained physician from the All India Institute of Medical Sciences in 1968 (Chopra 1988). After completing an internship at a New Jersey hospital, he did a residency at the Lahey Clinic and the University of Virginia Hospital and obtained board certification in internal medicine and endocrinology. Chopra established a successful private practice and served as chief of staff at New England Memorial Hospital. His disenchantment with biomedicine prompted him to turn to Ayurvedic medicine in the wake of his conversion to transcendental meditation (Chopra 1988). After reading a book on TM, Chopra (1987:193) attended an introductory lecture on TM in Cambridge, Massachusetts. Like Weil, Chopra underwent a transformation in his lifestyle. He observes:

[M]y days were blurring into nights. I was drinking black coffee by the hour and smoking at least a pack of cigarettes a day. I had acquired a taste for whisky in the evening. My schedule kept my stomach upset all the time. . . . The idea of stress management was in the air. TM had abundant research to prove it relieved stress. (Chopra 1988:125)

Chopra maintains that TM helped him to stop drinking within a week and smoking within two weeks. Shortly after meeting Maharishi Mahesh Yogi in 1985, he followed his guru's instructions to establish the Maharishi Ayurveda Health Center for Stress Management in Lancaster, Massachusetts, and has dedicated his earliest books to the maharishi. Chopra also established and became the president of American Association for Ayurvedic Medicine and Maharishi Ayur-Veda Products International.

In 1993, Chopra abandoned his Massachusetts connections and apparently his connections with the TM movement. He moved to San Diego, where he became the executive director for the Sharp Institute for Human Potential and Mind/Body Medicine and the chief consultant to the Center for Mind/Body Medicine, a health care facility for stress management and behavioral medicine. The latter reportedly charges $1,125 to $3,200 for its week-long "purification" program (Barrett 2002:4). He left Sharp in 1996 and became the educational director of the Chopra Center for Well Being in La Jolla, a suburb of San Diego and one of the most affluent communities in the United States. He states on the center's website, "I am dedicated to sharing laughter, joy, abundance, and freedom that comes from access to the infinite ocean of energy and creativity that we carry within" (Chopra Center, 2002). The center advertises that it is "dedicated to a holistic view of life that sees human beings as networks of energy and information, integrating body, mind and spirit" and that it has four hundred instructors who offer courses and workshops to hospitals, corporations, and educational institutions. It offers five-day programs on topics such as the "Creating Health Program," "The Return to Wholeness Program" (for cancer patients), the "Emotional Wholeness Program," the "Creating Health Purification Program," and the "Vital Energy Program." The center also conducts courses, workshops, and seminars on topics such as the "Path of Inner Peace," "Ayurvedic Cooking and Nutrition," "Primordial Sound Meditation," "Knowing God," and "SyncroDestiny" (or "Spontaneous fulfillment of desire"). It also offers massage therapy, facials, meditation, and corporate stress management courses on a daily or weekly basis and operates the Quantum Shop Café and Infinite Possibilities Gift and Bookstore.

Chopra regularly presents lectures around the globe. His speaking schedule for the fall of 2000 included lectures in Rio de Janeiro, São Paulo, Curitiba (Brazil), Buenos Aires, Lima, Asunción (Paraguay), San José (Costa Rica), the University of Phoenix, Atlanta, three cities in India, the Hague, Tel Aviv, San

Francisco, and New York ("Calendar," 2002). He reportedly has spoken at the United Nations, the World Health Organization in Geneva, the Soviet Academy of Sciences in Moscow, the Royal College of Physicians and Surgeons in Australia, and the National Institutes of Health, and at biomedical schools around the globe (Redwood and Chopra 2001). In contrast to Weil's more casual presentation of himself, Chopra, with his ruggedly handsome appearance and full head of black hair, generally is shown wearing a conservative, but fashionable, business suit that exudes success and material prosperity.

In contrast to Weil, Chopra has been involved in several litigations relating to both his work and personal life. In 1995, Jonie Flint filed suit against Chopra, Brihaspati Dev Triguna, the Sharp Institute, and various other individuals for malpractice in treatment of her husband, who was suffering from leukemia and died four months after Triguna allegedly stated that his leukemia had been cured (Barrett 2000). Flint dropped her suit due to a lack of financial resources. Chopra sued Joyce Weaver, who had worked with Chopra at the Sharp Center for Mind/Body Medicine, for allegedly trying to blackmail him for $50,000 not to reveal a prostitute's assertions that she had engaged in sex with him (Krueger 2000). After the jury ruled in favor of Weaver, she sued him for alleged sexual harassment, a charge of which a jury cleared him (Dottinga 2000). Chopra sued the *Journal of the American Medical Association* over an article by Andrew Skolnick (1991) that is referred to later in this essay. On its website, Shameless Mind (2004) asserts that "[a]lthough the case was dismissed, sources inside *JAMA* suggest Chopra demanded silence to drop a prolonged and expensive appeal process: The article was not to be reprinted and the editorial staff were to avoid writings about Chopra in the future."

In yet another litigation, Chopra settled a plagiarism suit by Stanford University biologist Robert Sapolsky, who charged that the former in *Ageless Body, Timeless Mind*, along with Random House and several book retailers, had infringed his copyright in *Behavioral Endocrinology* (Shameless Mind 2004).

CONCEPTS OF HEALTH, DISEASE, HEALING, AND HEALTH CARE

Health and Disease

Weil (1997a:13) asserts that health is "wholeness and balance, an inner resilience that allows you to meet the demands of living without being overwhelmed" and that "optimum health" entails a sense of strength and exuberance.

He delineates "ten principles of health and illness": (1) "Perfect health is not attainable"; (2) "It is alright to be sick"; (3) "The body has innate healing abilities"; (4) "Agents of disease are not causes of disease"; (5) "All illness is psychosomatic"; (6) "Subtle manifestations of illness precede gross ones"; (7) "Every body is different"; (8) "Every body has a weak point"; (9) "Blood is a principal carrier of healing energy"; and (10) "Proper breathing is a key to good health" (Weil 1995a; originally published in 1983).

Like many other biomedical physicians, Weil incorporates the machine analogy into his concept of health: "Health represents efficient operation of all of [the body's] systems. A useful analogy is the engine of a car. When all components are doing what they should be doing in just the right way, efficiency is maximal, and operation is quiet, producing a 'contented' purr that you rarely notice" (Weil 1995b:129).

Weil (1997a:15) focuses on the "diseases of lifestyle" that, he argues, result from failure to eat and exercise properly and maintain one's body and mind. Again in keeping with his machine analogy, he asserts that "most bodies come with warranties for eighty years of productive, relatively trouble-free service, if basic requirements for preventive maintenance are followed" (Weil 1997a:19). While Weil tends to focus on lifestyle as the root cause of disease, here and there he does acknowledge the role in disease of environmental "toxins," such as air pollution, contaminated water, toxins in food, drugs and cosmetics, nuclear radiation, and X rays.

In contrast to Weil, who views health as a relative matter, Chopra (1991:3) asserts in *Perfect Health* that "perfect health" is a state found in every person "that is free from disease, that never feels pain, that cannot age or die" and is an entity that every person must choose for himself or herself. He maintains that the physical body functions as the portal to the "quantum mechanical body" that exists at a subatomic level where matter and energy are interchangeable. According to Chopra:

> The quantum mechanical body is the underlying basis for everything we are: thoughts, emotions, proteins, cells, organs. . . . At the quantum level, your body is sending out all kinds of invisible signals, waiting for you to pick them up. You have a quantum pulse underlying your physical one, and a quantum heart beating it out. In fact, Maharishi Ayurveda holds that all the organs and processes in your body have a quantum equivalent. (Chopra 1991:7)

In *Ageless Body, Timeless Mind* (1993), Chopra adopts an even more meta-physical view about the mind–body connection by stating that the human body consists of energy and information rather than solid matter. He asserts that "human aging is fluid and changeable; it can speed up, slow down, stop for a time, and even reverse itself," depending on one's mental framework (Chopra 1993a:5). At a more mundane level, Chopra believes that bodily toxins adversely promote biological aging.

Healing and Health Care

Weil views healing as a "spontaneous" process in that it is an "inherent capacity of life" existing within DNA (1995b:75) and comes from within a person. He asserts that "good doctoring requires all the wisdom of religion, all the techniques of magic, and all the knowledge of small-*m* medicine to be most effective" (Weil 1996:2). He asserts that most regular physicians focus on physical bodies while ignoring their patients' mental and spiritual states (Weil 1995a:83). He also criticizes biomedicine for performing an excessive number of surgeries and overdrugging its patients, adding that many prescription drugs are "worthless" (Weil 1995a:107).

Weil maintains that alternative medical systems offer worthwhile techniques, such as the spinal manipulation performed by chiropractors and some osteopathic physicians. Conversely, he correctly observes that "chiropractors often expose patients to frequent, large doses of X-rays, in order to monitor the changes in the shape of the spine as treatment progresses" and that many "chiropractors are quite successful in making patients dependent on them" (Weil 1995a:132). While Weil (1995a:139) feels that naturopathy tends to be somewhat disorganized in terms of philosophical premises and treatment modalities, he states that it "can offer a refreshing balance to the aggressive, invasive, and unnatural practices of modern allopathy." He particularly singles out Chinese medicine as an "elegant" complement to biomedicine that has "much to teach allopaths and scientists" (Weil 1995a:151). In contrast to biomedicine, which focuses on the structural systems of the body, he asserts that Chinese medicine focuses on bodily functions, especially those by which the body defends itself against external threats to its equilibrium (Weil 1997a:13–14).

Although Weil is often viewed as a major figure within the holistic health movement, he regards the term *holistic* as "a stilted, synthetic word, a cumbersome way of saying 'whole,' especially obnoxious in the phrase *holistic health*" (Weil 1995a:181). He also argues that, "like naturopathy, the movement has no theoretical unity or coherence besides [a] very general philosophy" (Weil 1995a:182). Like many other holistic M.D.'s, Weil prefers to refer to his approach to healing as "integrative medicine" in that it blends components of biomedicine and alternative medical systems of different sorts. He makes the following assertions about the nature of medical systems in general: (1) "No system of treatment has a monopoly on cures," (2) "No system of treatment has a monopoly on failures," (3) "There is a great inconsistency among existing systems of treatment," (4) "New systems of treatment work best when they first appear," and (5) "Belief alone can elicit cures" (Weil 1995a:191–95). He also maintains that practitioners of all medical systems need to focus more on preventive than curative approaches (Weil 1995a:272). He argues that biomedicine needs to reclaim its ancient roots in magic and religion (Weil and Toms 1997:31).

Since publication of *Health and Healing* in 1983, most of Weil's writings focus on preventive health measures such as nutritious eating, breathing, exercise, relaxation, rest, and sleep. In *Eight Weeks to Optimum Health*, he provides his readers with an eight-week program that will assist them in building the foundation of a healthy lifestyle (Weil 1997a). In his most recent book, titled *Eating Well for Optimum Health*, Weil (2000) provides his readers with the basic facts of human nutrition, information about weight reduction programs and diet aids, and menu plans for healthy eating. In keeping with his long interest in medicinal plants and work as a consultant to various organizations that promote herbal medicine, he recommends the use of various herbal remedies, such as ginseng, as well as vitamins and supplements. Weil asserts, however, that manufacturers of herbal products frequently make "unsubstantiated claims" about them (Weil 1995b:51). His *Your Top Health Concerns* (Weil 1997b) consists of answers to selected questions on health care advice posed to his website entitled "Ask Dr. Weil." This short book includes a discussion of the ways to treat chronic fatigue syndrome, the common cold, and migraines, and the advisability of consuming various products such as aspartame and decaffeinated coffee and soda products. It also gives advice on how to treat depression without the use of drugs.

In *Spontaneous Healing* (1995b), Weil calls for the creation of a new type of health care institution—one that would resemble a spa rather than a hospital and would integrate biomedicine and alternative medical systems. In this regard, he appears to be drawing on the Central European tradition of spas or *Kurorte* that diffused in the form of hydropathy to the United States in the nineteenth century (Legan 1987) and continues to thrive in Europe (Maretzki 1987; Rees 1988). Weil also favors a "radical reform of medical education" that would incorporate instruction of a philosophy of science based on quantum physics; a history of medicine that takes into account alternative systems; an emphasis on the "healing power of nature and the body's healing system" and mind–body interactions; and instruction in psychology, spirituality, nutrition, exercise, relaxation, meditation, visualization, and the "art of communication" (Weil 1995b:279–80). However, he admits being cynical about the possibility of incorporating such reforms into the biomedical curriculum. Weil asserts that physicians need to function as exemplars of healthy living. He argues that "the process of medical education now, in a way, encourages very unhealthy lifestyles and habits. I mean, how can a medical student possibly take time to meditate, for example, or even, let alone, to have good exercise habits or good nutrition habits?" (quoted in Weil and Toms 1997:8).

Weil (1995b:280–81) also suggests creating a National Institute of Health and Healing under the auspices of the National Institutes of Health and incorporating the Office of Alternative Medicine (now the National Center for Complementary and Alternative Medicine) within such an institute. He favors universal health care of some sort but has not been specific on the form that it should assume (Redwood 1995b:3).

In contrast to Weil, who attempts to synthesize biomedicine and an array of alternative medical systems in the healing process, Chopra initially privileged Maharishi Ayurveda and later came to promote his own brand of positive thinking as the primary vehicle for improving health and overcoming disease. In his autobiography, Chopra (1988:vii) asserts that "Ayurveda contains the spiritual element that Western scientific medicine jettisoned three hundred years ago." He particularly singles out Maharishi Ayurveda as offering to revolutionize health care around the globe:

> Transcendental Meditation and Ayurvedic medicine can become the core of health care anywhere and are affordable even in the poorest countries. As Maharishi presents it, Ayurveda complements the existing traditional medicine in every locale around the world. It can re-enliven these traditions, which are nearly

extinct in all but a few societies, by restoring the techniques and preparations that have been lost, making each system whole once more. (Chopra 1988:197)

Chopra is a staunch proponent of what he terms "quantum healing"—a method that entails a "shift in the fields of energy information, so as to bring about a correction in an idea that has gone wrong. So quantum healing involves healing one mode of consciousness, mind, to bring about changes in another mode of consciousness, body" (Bunk 1999:2).

In *Quantum Healing*, Chopra maintains that individuals need to identity their body type before commencing upon an effort to improve their health. According to Ayurveda, the human body consists of five elements: space, air, fire, water, and earth. Combinations of these elements result in three *doshas*: *vata* (consisting of air and space), *pitta* (consisting of fire and water), and *kapha* (consisting of earth and water), which in turn result in ten different body types. Some individuals are single-*dosha* types (*vata, pitta, kapha*), most are two-*dosha* types (*vata-pitta* or *pitta-vata, pitta-kapha* or *kapha-pitta*, and *kapha-vata* or *vata-kapha*), and some are triple-*dosha* types (*vata-pitta-kapha*) (Chopra 1991:32–45). Disease or illness results from an imbalance of one or more of the *doshas*. Balancing the *doshas* entails following certain dietary proscriptions, exercising, and engaging in certain daily or seasonal routines.

In recent years, Chopra has come to place increasingly less emphasis on Ayurveda in his publications, although his center does continue to rely on Ayurvedic techniques. According to Goldstein (1999:112), whereas Chopra makes sixteen page references to Ayurveda in *Quantum Healing* (1989), he makes only one page reference to it in *Ageless Body, Timeless Mind* (1993). As opposed to the first work, which is dedicated to the Guru Maharishi and asserts that Ayurveda constitutes the best alternative medical system, the second work places considerably less emphasis on Ayurveda and "is grounded in references to Western mind–body medicine, psychoneuroimmunology, and physics" (Goldstein 1999:112). Conversely, in *Boundless Energy* (1995), Chopra does recommend various Ayurvedic dietary procedures, exercises, breathing methods, sleeping patterns, and other techniques for overcoming chronic fatigue. His break with Maharishi Ayurveda per se is strongly suggested by his failure to make a single reference to this branch of Ayurveda. In keeping with Ayurveda, both the Maharishi and non-Maharishi genres, and

New Age healing approaches, Chopra continues to recommend meditation as a very significant technique of quantum healing and an important means for lowering one's biological age. He also views herbs, in contrast to drugs, as functioning as gentle agents for facilitating healing.

Although Chopra continues to promote Ayurvedic healing techniques at his center in La Jolla, he does not make reference to Maharishi Ayurveda per se in that context. Conversely, Hari Sharma (1996) makes no references to Chopra in his overview of Maharishi Ayurveda, nor does the College of Maharishi Vedic Medicine of the Maharishi University of Management in Fairfield, Iowa, refer to Deepak Chopra as a practitioner of Maharishi Ayurveda on its website (Maharishi Vedic Medicine 2000). It appears that Chopra may have cut his ties with the transcendental meditation movement and the maharishi after relocating his operations to California and following sharp criticisms of an article on Maharishi Ayurveda that he and two colleagues published in the *Journal of the American Medical Association* (Sharma, Triguna, and Chopra 1991; Skolnick 1991).

In contrast to Weil, Chopra has become the preeminent figure in a long tradition of positive thinkers in American society over the course of the past decade or so (Meyer 1965). In *Creating Affluence: Wealth Consciousness in the Field of All Possibilities* (1993), he delineates the steps that individuals can take in their efforts to attain material prosperity and success in various pursuits. In *The Seven Spiritual Laws of Success*, Chopra (1993b:2–3) asserts that the laws of "pure potentiality," "giving," "karma" or cause and effect, "least effort," "intention and desire," "detachment," and *dharma* or "purpose in life" will provide individuals with the ability to create "unlimited wealth with effortless ease, and to experience success in every endeavor." In *Unconditional Life: Discovering the Power to Fulfill Your Dreams* (1992), he presents case studies that purportedly demonstrate that "the outside world—even so-called 'material reality'—can be altered radically by changing the world within." In his audiotape *Journey in the Boundless*, Chopra (1999c) provides a set of techniques by which individuals can achieve their "full potential."

For Chopra, the path to a healthy and fulfilling life is integrally intertwined with prayer and the broader quest for spirituality. In *How to Know God: The Soul's Journey into the Mystery of Mysteries* (2000), he explores the significance of prayer and spirituality in achieving good health and happiness. Chopra asserts that "God is another name for infinite intelligence. To achieve anything in life, a piece of this intelligence must be contacted and used" (Chopra 2000:16). Other books in this genre include *Everyday Immortality: A Concise Course in Spiritual Transformation* (1999a) and *On the Shores of Eternity* (1999b), a collection of Tagore poetry edited by Chopra. In *The Path to Love* (1997), Chopra discusses romantic love and the human need for passion and ecstasy.

A CRITICAL PERSPECTIVE OF WEIL AND CHOPRA IN THE CONTEXT OF THE LARGER HOLISTIC HEALTH MOVEMENT

Like others in the larger holistic health movement, both Weil and Chopra engage in a rather limited holism in that they both focus largely on the individual rather than society and its institutions. Rather than encouraging people to become part of social movements that attempt to either reform or revolutionize society, they take the larger society as a given to which one must adjust. Indeed, Weil (1995b:103) asserts that healing of chronic illness may require a "total acceptance of the circumstances of one's life, including illness." He notes that most people eschew an "accepting mode" and adopt a "state of perpetual confrontation" with their illnesses (Weil 1995b:103). Both Weil and Chopra provide an alternative form of medical hegemony by reinforcing individualizing patterns in U.S. society. Like the discourse of many other holistic health practitioners, their discourse does not take into consideration issues of class, race, ethnicity, and gender and capitalism per se.

Like most holistic health practitioners, Weil and Chopra tend either to downplay or to ignore occupational and environmental factors such as air and water pollution and toxic waste. Although Weil acknowledges that environmental pollutants may play a role in producing disease, he does not encourage his readers to become involved in the environmental movement. Instead, he appears to resign himself to the status quo by noting, "Toxins, both chemical and energetic, are more and more a fact of life in our industrial world. . . . My suggestions for self-defense are reasonable and practical [such as the utilization of tonics]; even if you implement only some of them, you will be protecting your healing system from harm" (Weil 1995b:170). Weil's advice corresponds to Kopelman's (1981:215) observation that "[a]lthough holism gives providers the responsibility to teach individuals and society about these hazards, providers are not solely responsible for bringing about social and environmental change." As part of his eight-week program of optimal healing power, he advises his readers to gradually diminish their habit of listening or watching the news, apparently in order to avoid negative thoughts.

Weil and Chopra exemplify par excellence the increasing entrepreneurial-ization of the holistic health movement. Chopra's enterprises reportedly bring in about $15 million a year (Power 1997:55). Robert Todd Carroll (2003), on his *Skeptics Dictionary* website, observes the following about Chopra's finan-cial situation:

> Chopra spends much of his time writing and lecturing from his base in Cali-fornia where he is not licensed to practice medicine. He charges $25,000 per lec-ture performance, where he spouts a few platitudes and give[s] spiritual advice while warning against the ill effects of materialism. His audiences are apparently not troubled by his living in a $2.5 million house in La Jolla, California, where he parks his green Jaguar. (4)

Sociologist Michael Goldstein (1999) makes the following astute observa-tions about Chopra's rise to success:

> With their economic muscle, Chopra's books receive massive publicity and he receives best placement at the corporate owned bookstores like Borders and Barnes and Noble. The popularity of Chopra's work led to his appearance on the covers of both *Newsweek* and *Time*. . . . The precise impact of this success on Chopra's work is difficult to assess. But his reduced emphasis on Indian religion and increasing reliance on Western religious sources make his work more mar-ketable to a mass American audience. (192)

Practitioners such as Weil and Chopra indicate that the holistic health move-ment has evolved into a "marketed social movement" (Goldstein 1992:151). In a similar vein, Melton (1988:51) observes that the New Age movement "has wel-comed a large number of entrepreneurs—alternative health practitioners (from chiropractors to masseurs), publishers, organizers of retreat centers, indepen-dent writers and teachers, health-food store owners, etc." Gordon (1984:246), an enthusiast of holistic health centers, warns that there is a danger that they "will continue to be primarily a luxury for the wealthy, that their doctrine of self-help and individual responsibility will be perverted to public neglect." In that holis-tic health services are generally not covered by insurance policies, Medicare, and Medicaid, they tend to cater primarily to white, upper- and upper-middle-class people and to members of the counterculture who have chosen to funnel their often limited financial resources into alternative medicine. Surely, very few working-class people have the financial resources to visit Chopra's healing center in La Jolla. Indeed, he shocked the press during a visit to Italy in 1997 when he asserted that poor people are "obsessed by money much more than the rich" and thus incapable of genuine spiritual growth (quoted in Introvigne 2001:64).

In keeping with the general orientation of the holistic health/New Age movement, both Weil and Chopra either ignore or downplay community service, social reform, and other collective goals. Danforth (1989:260) asserts that the New Age movement legitimizes "utilitarian individualism" and a "materialist concern for upward social mobility" in contrast to the countercultural ideology that many of its adherents learned during the late 1960s. He asserts that despite their purported concern with social problems such as racism, poverty, and environmental degradation, New Agers generally

> fail to realize that it requires more than personal growth and self-transformation to change long-standing public policies and powerful social institutions, nor do they realize that their idealistic and utopian visions for social change are doomed because they fail to take into account the oppressive aspects of the social, political, and economic order that are ultimately responsible for the problems of so many people. (Danforth 1989:284–85)

The prominence of Weil and Chopra, both trained biomedical physicians, as the leading holistic health/New Age gurus constitute another indication that the holistic health movement as a grassroots phenomenon is being co-opted by biomedicine.

Within biomedical and scientific circles, both Weil and Chopra have their fans and detractors. The Center for Integrative Medicine at Thomas Jefferson University Hospital in Philadelphia asked Weil to present a lecture at a gala celebration in his honor as both a proponent of integrative medicine and a native of Philadelphia. Conversely, Arnold Relman, the editor emeritus of the prestigious *New England Journal of Medicine*, has been Weil's most virulent opponent. He pays his nemesis a back-handed compliment by noting:

> If Deepak Chopra is the mystical poet-laureate of the [holistic health] movement, then Weil is its heavy-duty theoretician and apologist. He directs a large

and astonishingly successful medical marketing enterprise that might be called Weil, Inc. No longer the angry young rebel, he has become the urbane and supremely self-assured CEO of alternative medicine, who is seeking to reshape the medical establishment that he once scorned. (Relman 1996:28)

While granting that Weil makes some valid points about the limitations of biomedicine, Relman criticizes him for his allegedly spurious castigation of the heavy use of drugs on the part of biomedical physicians and characterizes much of the advice that he dispenses in his various books, audiotapes, videotapes, newsletter, and website as anecdotal and scientifically suspect. He characterized Weil as "devious" and a "manipulator" in his remarks at a Science Meets Alternative Medicine conference in Philadelphia (Lemley 1999:1).

Indeed, in early 1999, Relman and Weil debated at the University of Arizona College of Medicine. Relman argued that efforts to integrate biomedicine and alternative medicine constitute a retrograde measure because "most alternative systems of treatment are based on irrational or fanciful thinking, and false or unproven claims" (quoted in Bunk 1999:1). In response to his assertion that "alternative methods have not been adequately tested," Weil countered that

> I don't agree at all there is no data to support this. There is a great deal of data scattered in far-flung places. . . . We [in the program of integrative medicine] are trying to go through this and sort it all out, and separate what is nonsensical and what is possibly harmful from what is potentially useful, and to teach both doctors and patients to do that. (quoted in Bunk 1999:2)

Biomedicine and mainstream science also have expressed mixed reactions to Chopra, but generally more negative ones than to Weil. The American College of Preventive Medicine accredited Maharishi Ayurveda courses for continuing education (Wheeler 1997:8). Chopra achieved some semblance of recognition when he, along with two colleagues, published an article touting Maharishi Ayurveda in the *Journal of the American Medical Association* (Sharma, Triguna, and Chopra 1991). Chopra came into contact with Triguna, a prominent member of the All India Ayurveda Congress, in 1981 and states that "Trigunaji's great specialty was to gain a full diagnosis of his patients simply by feeling their pulse" (Chopra 1988:105). Letters to the editor

(1991) of *JAMA* in response to this article ranged from enthusiastic support to those that asserted that Maharishi Ayurveda and transcendental meditation are mystical systems lacking scientific support.

Andrew Skolnick (1991:1741) published a scathing article in the same journal that portrays Maharishi Ayurveda as a "marketing scheme" and asserts that Chopra and his collaborators "are involved in organizations that promote and sell the products and services about which they wrote." Stephen Barrett, M.D., the principal spokesperson of the National Council against Fraud, accuses Chopra of engaging in "Ayurvedic mumbo jumbo" (Barrett 2002). Butler (1992:116) argues that Chopra has been the "ideal propagandist for Ayurveda because, as a medical doctor, he can give it a respectable scientific aura." Victor Strenger accuses Chopra and other "quantum mystics," such as Fritjof Capra in *The Tao of Physics*, of inappropriately applying quantum mechanics in their alleged assertion that the "physical universe is the product of a cosmic mind to which the human mind is linked throughout space and time." In his assertion that Chopra misuses quantum theory, Park (2000:208) sarcastically notes, "We cannot help but notice, however, that the author of *Ageless Body* shows unmistakable signs of growing old right along with rest of us." On his website *The Skeptics Dictionary*, Carroll (2003:6) asserts that the "popularity of Chopra and Ayurveda is a testament to the failure of modern life and modern medicine to satisfy deep longings for simplicity, trust, a clean and wholesome environment, something to counteract the fragmentation, alienation, and isolation that many people feel."

Perhaps prompted in part by biomedical attacks on Maharishi Ayurveda, Chopra, an Indian immigrant who has come to exemplify the American success story, has increasingly distanced himself somewhat not only from Ayurveda, and entirely from its Maharishi variant, but also from biomedicine. He apparently has discovered that New Age spirituality provides a powerful venue for promoting his entrepreneurial interests. Conversely, Weil, although apparently not as financially successful as Chopra, continues to provide an aura of respectability for the holistic health or CAM movement.

CONCLUSION

As we see in this attempt to deconstruct the two leading proponents of the holistic health/New Age movement, for the most part this movement in its present form has not lived up to such hopes. Instead, it engages in a rather limited holism, in that its focus is largely on the individual rather than on society and its institutions. In emphasizing individual responsibility for health, wellness, and spirituality, Weil and Chopra provide an alternative form of medical hegemony by reinforcing individualizing patterns in American society specifically and in the capitalist world system, given that both have an international audience. They also serve as modern exemplars of the American success story—a myth that continues to legitimize patterns of social inequality. Whereas the "worried well" found in the upper and upper-middle classes indeed often can afford to partake in the various commodities and services that Weil and Chopra promote, it is doubtful whether their advice on health and well-being bears much meaning for many working-class people and other people of modest means in the United States and around the globe.

6

Governmental and Corporate Involvement

In addition to the interest of conventional physicians, nurses, and allied health professionals in holistic medicine or CAM, various governmental and corporate bodies have expressed interest in it. Health services have become matters of public concern, particularly to third-party payers, such as government, industry, business, insurance companies, and labor.

To define and evaluate the "health care crisis" in the United States, various commissions and task forces have been formed in the past few decades and have made recommendations for health policy. Alford (1972:137) notes that "[p]redominant in all of these commissions are hospital administrators, health insurance executives, corporate executives and banks, medical school directors, and city and state public health administrators." A striking feature of these commissions is the relative absence of physicians, especially those in private practice. Salmon (1985) argues that a "class-conscious corporate directorship" has come to assume considerable power over health policy decision-making. According to Berliner and Salmon (1980:141), "Replacement of costly, high-technology medicine with cheaper, non-technological [alternative] therapies is a major redirection advocated by proliferating medical-care evaluation studies." Indeed, various corporations have expressed an interest in holistic or alternative health as a cost-saving measure.

GOVERNMENTAL INTEREST IN ALTERNATIVE MEDICINE

Perhaps the first explicit indicator of interest of the federal government in alternative medicine and holistic health was a 1979 conference sponsored by the Department of Health, Education and Welfare on "Holistic Health: A Public Policy." A congressional mandate resulting in creation of the Office of Alternative Medicine (OAM) under the umbrella of the National Institutes of Health in 1992, with an initial appropriation of $2 million, launched commitment by the federal government to exploring various dimensions of alternative medicine. The office reportedly was created "under pressure from Congress alarmed by the soaring costs of high-tech healing and the frustrating fact that so many ailments—AIDS, cancer, arthritis, back pain—have yet to yield to standard medicine" (Toufexis 1993:43). The mandate called for the "evaluation of alternative medical treatment modalities, including acupuncture and Oriental medicine, homeopathic medicine, and physical manipulation therapy" (quoted in Cohen 1998:xi).

The funding for OAM and its successor body, the National Center for Complementary and Alternative Medicine, has increased in virtually each fiscal year (FY). It grew to $3.5 million in FY 1993, $5.4 million in FY 1995, $7.4 million in FY 1996, $12 million in FY 1997, $30 million in FY 1998, and $50 million in FY 1999. Nevertheless, the OAM budget was miniscule given the fact that the annual NIH budget was set at $13.648 billion for FY 1998. Under OAM's new designation as the National Center for Complementary and Alternative Medicine, Congress appropriated $68.7 million for FY 2000, $89.2 million for FY 2001, $104.6 million for FY 2002, and $114.1 million for FY 2003 to the agency.

OAM created advisory boards, sponsored conferences, publications, and newsletters, and funded research on the efficacy of various alternative therapies. OAM sponsored its first public meeting, which featured more than eighty speakers, on July 17–18, 1992, in Bethesda, Maryland (Office of Alternative Medicine 1992). OAM sponsored a second workshop on September 14–16 in Chantilly, Virginia, with more than two hundred participants. The Chantilly conference delineated seven major "fields of alternative practice" and "alternative systems of medical practice." In May 1993, OAM sponsored a four-day conference on "Alternative Medicine, Wellness and Health Care Reform: Preparing for a Sustainable Future" in Washington, D.C. Speakers included New Ager Marilyn Ferguson, James Gordon, and David Eisenberg.

OAM had a series of directors—a pattern that reflects its rather tumul-
tuous internal politics. Joseph Jacobs, a Yale-trained pediatrician, served as
OAM's first director. Advocates of alternative medicine, including some on the
OAM Advisory Council, regarded him to be too conventional and subservient
to the larger NIH bureaucracy. Nienstedt (1998:39) argues that the OAM independent panel exhibited a "noticeable lack of alternative practitioners" and
that the OAM Advisory Council did not "question the assumptions of the biomedical research paradigm." She asserts that the focus of OAM "appears to be
on complementary medicine under the direction of biomedical methods and
personnel" (Nienstedt 1998:39).

In a similar vein, Goldstein (1999:179) maintains that "[m]any alternative
providers criticized this bias toward 'insiders' as the most flagrant form of 'cre-
dentialist' stance of OAM, which essentially froze out true alternative healers
from OAM money and insured equivocal finds about outcomes." Kligman
(1998:209) reports that for the granting period of 1993–1994, "[m]ost of the
over $1 million in grant awards [had] been to academic medical centers
throughout the country."

Maneuverings within OAM and tensions between Jacobs and various
politicians, such as Tom Harkin, resulted in Jacobs's ouster as director (Goldstein 1999:178–79). Alan Trachtenberg, a biomedical physician with training
in acupuncture and homeopathy, succeeded Jacobs as OAM director in October 1994 but served only until 1995. Wayne Jonas, a biomedical physician who
took a three-year leave from Walter Reed Army Institute of Research, replaced
Trachtenberg as director. As a medical research scientist in toxicology and im-
munology, he argued that research on alternative therapies should be "scientifically rigorous and contextually sensitive" (quoted in Goldstein 1999:179).
The OAM Advisory Council consisted of eighteen members—research scientists, health practitioners, and other interested parties, most of whom had a
biomedical orientation.

Wayne B. Jonas, OAM's third director, delineated six "functional areas" to
address the office's congressional mandate: (1) a public information and
clearinghouse area to promote public awareness and education about CAM
research; (2) the database and evaluation area to evaluate CAM studies and to
channel this information to the clearinghouse; (3) the research and development area to screen and provide technical support to CAM research; (4) the
extramural affairs area to assist with the development, review, and funding of

CAM research; (5) the intramural research training area to coordinate research training on CAM; and (6) the international and professional liaison area to facilitate cooperative CAM research and education efforts around the world and with professional bodies in the United States (*Complementary & Alternative Medicine Newsletter* 1995:1–2).

OAM funded thirteen Specialty Research Centers, eleven of which were situated at biomedical institutions. Each research site investigated the efficacy and safety of alternative therapies for various diseases or drug addictions. The biomedical research sites were located at the University of Virginia; Columbia University; the University of Maryland; the University of California–Davis; Stanford University; the University of Medicine and Dentistry, New Jersey; the University of Texas–Houston; the University of Arizona; the University of Michigan; the University of Minnesota; and Harvard University medical schools. Bastyr University—a naturopathic institution in Bothell, Washington—and the Palmer Center for Chiropractic Research in Davenport, Iowa, were the only two heterodox research sites funded by OAM. The OAM research site at Bastyr University served as the "nation's first publicly-funded natural medical clinic" (Goldstein 1999:183). In November 1996, OAM became one of ten worldwide WHO Collaborating Centers in Traditional Medicine. Other collaborating centers are located in Belgium, China, North Korea, South Korea, Italy, Japan, Romania, Sudan, and Vietnam.

Congressperson Peter Fazio (Democrat–Oregon) introduced legislation in March 1997 that called for elevating OAM into a Natural Center for Integrative Medicine with funding of nearly $200 million. Twelve other Democratic congresspersons cosponsored the bill. Passage of a modified appropriations bill in 1999 resulted in the designation of OAM as the National Center for Complementary and Alternative Medicine (NCCAM). As a center rather than an NIH office, NCCAM can directly fund research grants that have undergone an NIH peer review process. Its mission is to facilitate research and evaluation of alternative therapies and disseminate information to the general public. Stephen Straus, an M.D. and clinical researcher, became the first director of NCCAM on October 6, 1999.

In July 1999, Donna Shalala, the secretary of health and human services, appointed two naturopathic physicians to the predominantly biomedically oriented National Advisory Council for Complementary and Alternative Medicine. Many attendees at the American Association of Naturopathic

Physicians Meeting that I attended in Coeur d'Alene, Idaho, in early November 1999 were thrilled by this recent recognition of their profession. Indeed, the newly constituted National Advisory Council on Complementary and Alternative Medicine exhibited a much more "alternative" profile than did its predecessor OAM advisory body in that it also included two licensed massage therapists, a licensed acupuncturist, and a chiropractor.

NCCAM recognizes three "alternative systems of medical practice": (1) popular health care, (2) professionalized health care, and (3) community-based health care. Under the rubric of "professionalized health care," it lists traditional Oriental medicine, acupuncture, Ayurveda, homeopathic medicine, anthroposophy, and environmental medicine (National Center for Complementary and Alternative Medicine 2003b). Under that of "community-based health care practices," it includes Native American and Latin American healing systems as well as Alcoholics Anonymous. It groups CAM practices into five domains: (1) alternative medical systems, such as traditional Oriental medicine, homeopathy, and naturopathy; (2) mind–body interventions, such as hypnosis, dance, music, art therapy, prayer, and mental healing; (3) biologically based therapies, such as herbal therapies, special diet therapies, orthomolecular therapies, and laetrile and shark cartilage to treat cancer; (4) manipulative and body-based methods, such as chiropractic, osteopathic manipulation, and massage; and (5) energy therapies such as qi gong, Reiki, therapeutic touch, and bioelectromagnetic-based therapies (National Center for Complementary and Alternative Medicine 2000a:25–26).

NCCAM presently funds sixteen CAM research centers and plans to fund a Center for Frontier Medicine (see table 6.1). Of the seventeen centers, only two of them are located at alternative medical institutions: the Maharishi International University and the Consortial Center for Chiropractic Research. The Center for Natural Medicine and Prevention focuses on research on cardiovascular diseases among aging African Americans, and the Consortial Center for Chiropractic Research incorporates five chiropractic institutions, the University of Iowa, and Kansas State University. It is interesting to note that three of the research centers are situated at the University of Arizona in Tucson and two of them are situated in Portland, Oregon—an apparent indicator of the strength of CAM in these places.

NCCAM sponsors a Frontier Medicine Program for "those CAM practices for which there is no plausible biomedical explanation," such as magnet therapy,

Table 6.1.   NCCAM-Funded Research Centers

Center	Location
Center for CAM Research in Aging and Women's Health	Columbia University, New York
Center for Alternative Medicine Research on Arthritis	University of Maryland School of Medicine, Baltimore
Center for Frontier Medicine in Biofield Science	Department of Psychology, University of Arizona, Tucson
Center for Cancer Complementary Medicine	Johns Hopkins University, Baltimore, Md.
Specialized Center of Research in Hyperbaric Oxygen	University of Pennsylvania, Philadelphia
CAM Research Center for Cardiovascular Diseases	University of Michigan Taubman Health Care Center, Ann Arbor
Center for Natural Medicine and Prevention	Maharishi University of Management, Fairfield, Ia.
Consortial Center for Chiropractic Research	Palmer Center for Chiropractic Research, Davenport, Ia.
Oregon Center for Complementary and Alternative Medicine Research in Craniofacial Disorders	Center for Health Research, Kaiser Foundation Hospitals, Portland
Oregon Center for Complementary and Alternative Medicine in Neurological Disorders	Oregon Health Sciences University, Portland
Center for CAM in Neurodegenerative Diseases	Emory School of Medicine, Atlanta, Ga.
Pediatric Center for Complementary and Alternative Medicine	University of Arizona Health Science Center, Tucson
Botanical Dietary Supplements for Women's Health	University of Illinois at Chicago
Botanical Center for Age-Related Diseases	Purdue University, West Lafayette, Ind.
Center for Phytomedicine Research	University of Arizona College of Pharmacy, Tucson
Center for Dietary Supplements Research: Botanicals	University of California at Los Angeles
Exploratory Program Grant for Frontier Medicine	University of Connecticut Center on Aging, Farmington

energy healing, homeopathy, and therapeutic prayer; and the CAM Education Project, which seeks to facilitate "integration of alternative medical treatments and disciplines into conventional health care practice and delivery" (National Center for Complementary and Alternative Medicine 2000a:13–15). NCCAM admits that some CAM modalities, such as massage, may not lend themselves to double-blind trials because they are "custom-tailored to each patient's demands" (National Center for Complementary and Alternative Medicine 2000b:9).

In 2001, NCCAM created an Office of International Health Research in order to "identify promising international CAM practices and encourage their rigorous scientific assessment and development through international scientific collaborations, training of researchers, and dissemination of authoritative information to the public and professionals" and appointed John Killen, M.D., as OIHR's director in September 2003 (NCCAM Press Release, September 8, 2003). NCCAM cosponsored, with the Royal College of Physicians, a conference in London titled "Can Alternative Medicine Be Integrated into Mainstream Care?" on January 23–24, 2001. It also sponsors Distinguished Lectures in the Science of Complementary and Alternative Medicine. For example, David Spiegel, M.D., presented a lecture titled "Hypnosis and Group Support in Medical Care: Altering Perception and Reality" on May 6, 2003 (National Center for Complementary and Alternative Medicine, 2003a). In addition to NCCAM, seventeen federal public health services fund research on alternative therapies (Gesler and Gordon 1998:9).

On March 7, 2000, President Bill Clinton created the White House Commission on Complementary and Alternative Medicine Policy in response to heavy political lobbying, including by Senator Tom Harkin (Democrat–Iowa) and Senator Orrin Hatch (Republican–Utah) (Kurtz 2001:1). Stephen Groft, Ph.D., served as the executive director of the commission and stated that this new body "is charged with investigating and making recommendations on such CAM issues as access, delivery, training, and licensure, as well as development and dissemination of accurate and useful CAM information" (*Complementary & Alternative Medicine at the NIH* 2000:3). James Gordon, M.D., served as the chairperson of the commission. The commission had nineteen additional members, including eight biomedical physicians—one of whom was a licensed acupuncturist as well; Effie Poy Yew Chow, a well-known nurse, qigong grandmaster, and the president of the East West Academy of Healing Arts; another nurse; Joseph E. Pizzorno Jr., the president emeritus of Bastyr University; a dentist, a chiroprator, another acupuncturist, and five laypersons. Over eighteen months, the commission met fourteen times, heard the testimony of over seven hundred individuals, and read over a thousand written documents (White House Commission 2002b). The commission held four town hall meetings (in San Francisco, Seattle, New York City, and Minneapolis) and held ten regular meetings in Washington, D.C. In his "Chairman's Vision" statement Gordon states, "The Report's vision is holistic. It is shaped by attention to the mind, body, and spirit of each person, and to the social and ecological world in which we live" (White House Commission 2002a). In addition to summarizing the status of CAM in the United States, the commission report made twenty-two recommendations on topics such as increased funding for CAM training and research, guidelines for scientific research on CAM, the need for dialogue and collaboration between biomedicine and CAM systems, incorporation of CAM into the biomedical curriculum, the provision of training in biomedical principles and practices to CAM practitioners, and the dissemination of information on CAM to the general public.

THE INTEREST OF INSURANCE COMPANIES, HMOS, AND HOSPITALS IN ALTERNATIVE MEDICINE

A growing number of insurance companies, HMOs, and hospitals have begun to turn to alternative therapies for a variety of reasons, including consumer demand and cost-effectiveness. Since 1996, West Coast managed care organizations offering some form of CAM coverage include Group Health Cooperative of Puget Sound in Washington State, Blue Cross of Washington and Alaska, PacifiCare and Regents' Blue Cross/Blue Shield of Oregon, and Health Net in California (Milbank Memorial Fund 1998:6). The Sharp Health Plan, a southern California–based HMO with some sixteen thousand subscribers, offers its clients an eight-week wellness program designed by Deepak Chopra (Gordon 1996:261). Blue Shield of California offers a Lifepath plan that reimburses members for various alternative services, including acupuncture, chiropractic, mass therapy, somatic education (e.g., Alexander technique or Feldenkrais), and stress management (Pelletier 2000:290).

Health insurance plans in other parts of the country have also come to offer their subscribers coverage for CAM treatments. According to Goldstein (1999), in 1996:

Oxford Health Plan, which provides care to 1.4 million people in the eastern United States, announced that it would add alternative medicine to some of its health plans. The initial group assembled by Oxford included approximately one thousand chiropractors, acupuncturists, naturopathic doctors, massage therapists, and yoga instructors, with plans already underway to add practitioners of T'ai Chi and reflexology. (7)

Suburban Health Plan in Connecticut and Allina Health System in the Upper Midwest also offer coverage for CAM services (Milbank Memorial Fund 1998:7). American Western Life Insurance Company has a wellness plan that covers acupuncture, physical therapy, and spinal treatments (Patel 1998:69). Other health insurance plans providing partial or even full coverage of CAM therapies include Altercare of Washington, Alternative Health Benefit Services, Health Partners Health Plans (Arizona), and Mutual of Omaha (Weitzman 1998:135–36). Insurance companies have tended to reimburse selected CAM therapies, such as acupuncture, chiropractic, massage therapy, and nutrition, as opposed to other CAM therapies, such as herbal medicine, Ayurveda, and craniosacral manipulation.

Many states have mandated insurance reimbursements for alternative practitioners. There are state mandates for chiropractic in forty-one states, naturopathic physicians in three states, podiatrists in thirty-five states, and massage therapists in only one state (Pelletier 2000:280). Washington State requires health insurance companies to cover naturopathic care, chiropractic, acupuncture, massage therapy, and other types of licensed alternative health care. According to Snook (2001:144), "[i]n 1997, about 18% of individuals seeking chiropractic care reported having complete insurance coverage for such treatment, and another 38% reported having partial coverage." About one thousand insurance companies in the United States and Canada cover naturopathic care (Cassilith 1998:52). A few insurance companies offer their subscribers a choice between naturopathic and biomedical services. Overall, Weeks (1999:108) concludes that the extent of CAM incorporation into health insurance plans remains "extremely limited."

Furthermore, based on survey research on managed care organizations and health insurance companies, Pelletier and Astin (2002) report:

> Like conventional therapies, CAM therapies are usually covered only if treatment is medically necessary for a specific diagnosis, and reimbursement is given only for a specific diagnosis, and reimbursement is given only for a certain number of visits or dollar limit per year. Thus, whereas the popular media reports that an increasing number of insurers are offering coverage for CAM, the current status of CAM reimbursement is actually quite limited. (42)

Health maintenance organizations have increasingly been considering incorporating CAM therapies as a cost-saving mechanism and as a way to meet consumer demand. The Landmark Healthcare (2000:2) survey based on phone interviews with 114 HMO CEOs found that 67 percent of HMOs offer at least one form of CAM therapy, particularly chiropractic. HMOs offering CAM "say they do so primarily because of market, employer or consumer demand, or because of state mandates or legal requirements." A random survey of Kaiser Permanente members revealed that 15.7 percent had used CAM in the previous twelve months, that 35 percent had used it at some time, and that CAM users were more likely to be females, more educated, and more dissatisfied with their HMO (Whitlock 2001). Kaiser Permanente, the largest HMO in California with some 4.5 million members, offers in-house acupuncture benefits to its subscribers but actually provides services at a limited number of sites (Pelletier 2000:291). Health Net of California, the state's second-largest HMO, and Lifeguard Care, a Silicon Valley HMO, also offer their subscribers acupuncture benefits. Group Health Cooperative of Puget Sound, a Washington State HMO, offers subscribers chiropractic, naturopathic care, massage therapy, and home births by licensed midwives (Patton and Faass 2001).

An increasing number of hospitals have also begun to incorporate CAM "to differentiate themselves from their competition and to try to offer a full service to the community, which can include health spas, gyms, health information, preventative medicine, and lifestyle medicine" (Diamond 2001:12). The Institute for Health and Healing at the California Pacific Medical Center in San Francisco provides bodywork, meditation, yoga, tai chi, and qi gong to its patients (Mohr 2001). The North Hawaii Community Hospital employs CAM therapists in acupuncture, chiropractic, massage therapy, and naturopathic medicine (Linton, Toubman, and Faass 2001).

Natural products, including vitamins and nutritional and herbal supplements, have steadily been gaining in popularity in the United States. Marquadt and Burkink (2002) report, "Annual sales of all natural products, including food, increased from $4.64 billion in 1991 to $25 billion in 1998. Natural food sales account for $8.8 billion of this $25 billion and are expected to grow to $63 billion by 2008" (213). In 1998, echinacea, St. John's wort, ginkgo biloba, garlic, saw palmetto, Asian ginseng, goldenseal, aloe, Siberian ginseng, and valerium constituted the ten best-selling herbal supplements in the United States (Tyler 2000:4). Herbal supplements now are widely sold in supermarkets and drugstore and mass retail chains throughout the country. According to Keegan (2001:103), "In 1999, the *Nutrition Business Journal* reported that over $350 million of these [natural] products were sold directly to conventional or alternative medical practitioners, who in turn sold $700 million in products to their patients."

Recognizing the success of the natural products companies, pharmaceutical companies have become increasingly interested in marketing botanical medicine and nutritional supplements. Pharmacognosy, the study of natural drugs and their constituents, has become part and parcel of the pharmaceutical industry. An estimated 25 percent of all prescription drugs in the United States contain active elements derived from plants (Murray and Pizzorno 1999:268). American Home Products, Bayer, and Warner-Lambert expanded their vitamin business to include herbal supplements, and Wal-Mart manufactures its own line of supplements (Goldstein 2002:54). Homeopathic substances have become a $250 million per year industry. Rexall has been in the homeopathic business for some time (Diamond 2001:12). Osco/Sav-on and Rite-Aid also sell homeopathic and herbal products (Goldstein 1999:195).

The regulation of dietary supplements constitutes perhaps the greatest area of controversy in CAM regulation. The 1994 Dietary Supplement Health and Education Act spearheaded by Senator Orrin Hatch (Republican–Utah) contributed to a dramatic increase in the sale of dietary supplements from $8 billion in 1994 to $12 billion in 1997 (Stolberg 2001:42). Utah-based dietary supplement companies have annual sales in the range of $2 billion and health product companies contributed $277,000 to Hatch's campaign (Tyler 2000:51). The Federal Trade Commission maintains advertising guidelines that forbid claims that supplements can treat or prevent disease, unless the manufacturer can substantiate them. The guidelines require advertisers to disclose "qualifying information" given that misuse of supplements can cause serious side effects (Brody 2001).

As virtually anybook store indicates, books on CAM, especially those by authors such as Andrew Weil, Deepak Chopra, and Larry Dossey, have become highly popular and big business. Rees (2001:15) reports that "nearly 30 percent of all popular medical books published relate to the broad field of alternative medicine" and that more than four hundred books on CAM are published every year in the United States. Many of these titles are published by a relatively small number of publishers such as Avery, Churchill Livingstone, Ulysses, Prima, Keats, Rodale, Keningston, Element, Dorling Kindersley,

Element, and Wiley. In addition to professional CAM journals, there are a number of popular CAM magazines.

While most centers of integrative medicine are either relatively small private operations or affiliated with biomedical schools, various health care corporations and private group practices have come to offer CAM or integrative treatment. American WholeHealth provides integrative treatment, which includes family practice, internal medicine, Chinese medicine, chiropractic, and Reiki, in Boston, Denver, and Washington, D.C. (Rees 2001:13). The company describes itself as the "leading online/offline provider of integrative health solutions for consumers, medical professionals, health plans and employers" and claims a network of over twenty-five thousand CAM providers, including chiropractors, acupuncturists, massage therapists, yoga instructors, and naturopathic physicians (American WholeHealth 2003:1).

7

Creating an Authentic Holistic Health System

Impediments and Possibilities

This concluding chapter considers various impediments to the development of an authentically holistic health care system as well as various possibilities for creating such a system. With respect to the first endeavor, I consider (1) the persistence of the dominative medical system; (2) the rise of corporate medicine; (3) the opposition of the biomedical "skeptics" or "quack busters" to alternative medical systems; and (4) the overemphasis on randomized controlled trials (RCTs), or *evidenced-based medicine* as the exclusive way of determining the efficacy of CAM therapies. With respect to the second endeavor, I examine the need to develop a broader concept of holistic health and create a universal health care system in the United States and the role that critical medical anthropologists and other critical medical social scientists can play in the creation of such a system.

THE PERSISTENCE OF THE DOMINATIVE MEDICAL SYSTEM AND THE RISE OF CORPORATE MEDICINE

Despite the best efforts on the part of proponents of holistic health to develop an alternative to biomedicine, what in reality has occurred has been in large part the co-optation of alternative medicine under the rubrics of CAM and integrative medicine or integrative health care. As Cant and Sharma (1999:432–33) so aptly observe, "biomedicine is still the most powerful single health-care profession and is unlikely to cease to be so: those forms of alternative medicine that have been most successful in terms of gaining greater public recognition and legitimacy are, on the whole, those that have had the approval of a sizeable section of the medical profession." In a similar vein, Norris (1998) states:

> Despite its office at NIH, however, alternative medicine holds a marginal place in U.S. medicine, tolerated mainly because patients like it, and its lack of strong scientific credentials dooms it, so far, to the role of an optional add-on to standard biomedical therapies. . . . Alternative medicine is neither a rival capable of fully supplanting biomedicine nor a collection of optional therapies perfectly consistent with business as usual in the health care industry: It is an approach to illness that implicitly and uneasily calls into question the inadequacy of the biomedical model. (70)

Heterodox practitioners appear to have adopted several stances with respect to their relationship with conventional physicians. While some would like to cooperate with the latter, others feel that they are engaged in an entirely different endeavor and oppose the incursion of M.D.'s who have obtained brief training in CAM therapies and implement them in their practices. Whereas some proponents of alternative medicine "speak of a 'medicine of great possibilities' that can effectively reduce the growing tide of chronic illness, significantly increase life expectancy, bring about dramatic cures, and even lead humanity to a higher, more fulfilled state," others "predict the piecemeal assimilation of particular techniques into managed care settings and other large corporate providers on the basis of their ability to produce measurable, cost-effective outcomes in symptoms and client satisfaction" (Goldstein 1999:219). Despite its initial promise to provide a counterhegemonic challenge to biomedicine, the holistic health movement appears to be in the beginning stages of its transformation into CAM or integrative medicine. It has to a large extent been tamed or co-opted by biomedical physicians and schools, the federal government, and, most recently, various private corporate bodies, particularly health insurance companies, HMOs, hospitals, health corporations, and pharmaceutical companies.

While biomedicine continues to exert dominance over alternative medical systems, starting in the 1960s, this dominance began to erode as corporations and the federal government came to play a more predominant role in the creation of health policy, which in turn began to incorporate a greater tolerance for alternative medical systems, in particular osteopathic medicine (which has evolved into a variant of conventional medicine) but also chiropractic, naturopathy, and acupuncture and Oriental medicine. The growing tolerance of health insurance companies, HMOs, the federal government, and state governments toward alternative medical systems is probably more related to the perception that they are cheaper forms of health care than to the fact that they offer competing philosophies of health. As Krause (1996:47) astutely observes, "the U.S. medical profession has found its strongest opponent to be a federal government whose role has changed, allied with large American capitalist firms in pursuing cost control."

THE BIOMEDICAL "SKEPTICS" OR "QUACK BUSTERS" AND THE CALL FOR EVIDENCE-BASED MEDICINE

A lesser threat to alternative medicine but not one to be dismissed, as we saw in the discussion of Andrew Weil and Deepak Chopra, is the opposition of the biomedical skeptics, sometimes referred to as *quack busters*. The biomedical skeptics or quack busters represent an earlier era during which biomedicine, particularly in the incarnation of Morris Fishbein's (1932) campaign against "medical cults" during his stint as editor of *JAMA*, maintained a virulent stance toward alternative medical systems and therapies, particularly chiropractic. The AMA's Board of Trustees created a Committee on Quackery in November 1963 that played an important role in the decision on the part of the U.S. Department of Labor to exclude chiropractic in its *Health Careers Guide Book* (Carter 1993:40–41). Although organized biomedicine has backed off in harassing alternative practitioners since its loss of the antitrust suit filed on the part of various chiropractors, the AMA continues to house the Historical Health Fraud and Alternative Medicine Collection at its headquarters in Chicago (Hafner, Carson, and Zwicky 1992).

The National Council for Reliable Health Information (formerly the National Committee against Health Fraud) continues to function in the tradition of the AMA's now muted critique of alternative medicine (Rees 2001:12). This organization grew out of the California Council against Health Fraud and has regional chapters in various parts of the country (Carter 1993:14). William T. Jarvis, a professor of health education at Loma Linda University School of Medicine in southern California, founded the Council (Walker 1993:25). Stephen Barrett, a psychiatrist and the driving force behind the Lehigh Committee against Fraud, is another prominent member of the council. He coedited an anthology titled *The Health Robbers* (Barrett and Knight 1976), now serves as the chairperson of the Board of Quackwatch, and has asserted for a long time that heterodox medical practitioners are unscientific and fraudulent in both their theories and their applications. The council maintains task forces on acupuncture, AIDS quackery, broadcast media abuse, dietary practices, alternative cancer cures, herbal remedies, and vitamin and nutritional supplements (Walker 1993:26). The Council for Scientific Medicine created the *Scientific Journal of Alternative Medicine* (a perhaps somewhat misleading title), which is a major outlet for the writings of biomedical skeptics.

Biomedical skeptics are actually part of a larger community of skeptics who in 1976, according to anthropologist David J. Hess (1993:11), "came together under the leadership of the philosopher Paul Kurtz, then editor of the *Humanist*, the magazine of the American Humanist Association." The skeptics formed the Committee for the Scientific Investigation of Claims of the Paranormal (CSICOP), which found support among various scholars, scientists, journalists, and even magicians. CSICOP publishes the *Skeptical Inquirer: The Magazine for Science and Culture.* While the skeptics tend to be die-hard humanists and rationalists and often atheists or agnostics, politically they run the gamut from right to left, at least Old Left as opposed to New Left. Although Kurtz once defined himself as a democratic socialist, he eventually became a libertarian who is critical of the welfare state and advocates property rights and free-market capitalism (Hess 1993:161).

Conversely, Martin Gardner, a former columnist for *Scientific American*, the author of *Fads and Fallacies in the Name of Science* (1957), and later a columnist for the *Skeptical Inquirer*, identifies himself as a theist and a democratic socialist in the tradition of Norman Thomas and John Dewey. Hess (1993:163) contends that "[o]rganized skepticism emerged historically not only in the wake of the sixties and the development of the New Age movement, but also in the wake of the reactionary movements of fundamentalist Christianity and the Christian New Right, to which skeptics have directed their critical gaze as well." Kurtz played an instrumental role in the establishment of Prometheus Books, a major outlet of skeptical materials that portray a wide array of alternative medical systems and New Ageism as modern-day magic, superstition, and quackery. Prometheus has published anthologies such as *Examining Holistic Medicine* (Stalker and Glymour 1985), *Not Necessarily the New Age* (Basil 1988), and *Science Meets Alternative Medicine* (Sampson and Vaughn 2000). Christopher Wanjek (2003), an independent journalist and former in-house writer at MIT and NIH, authored one of the latest quack-busting books, titled *Bad Medicine: Misconceptions and Misuses Revealed, from Distance Learning to Vitamin O.*

James Harvey Young (1992:84), an Emory University history professor, has written several books and numerous essays denouncing "quackery," which he defines as "improper medical practice—knowingly twisted for profit." He asserts that since passage of the Food and Drug Act in 1906, the legal constraints on fraudulent medical practices have been tightened, but that the general public continues to be deceived by quacks from many quarters. Although Young's definition of quackery seems reasonable enough, he seems to assume that few biomedical physicians engage in quackery whereas many alternative practitioners, including chiropractors, health food store proprietors, and ordinary folk healers, engage in it routinely. One might argue that surgeons who knowingly perform unnecessary operations or who charge exorbitant fees for them are also quacks. In reality, quacks and charlatans are found among the practitioners of many medical systems, conventional or alternative. For example, many chiropractors attend practice-building seminars where they learn sales techniques that enable them to increase their patient loads and incomes, often without any regard for the quality of care provided to their patients (Baer 1996). Despite its counterhegemonic potential, the holistic health or CAM movement has more than its share of practitioners who have adopted the entrepreneurial aspirations of many biomedical physicians.

Occasionally, heterodox practitioners "break ranks" and criticize their profession and most of its members. Preston H. Long (2002), a chiropractor and staunch advocate of "evidenced-based" or "scientific" chiropractic, has written a scathing critique of his profession and many of his colleagues. He criticizes the propensity of many chiropractors to engage in slick practice-building techniques, overtreat back problems, perform purportedly unnecessary spinal adjustments on children, and "expand their practices to include 'aura adjustment,' nutrition therapy, aromatherapy, homeopathy, acupuncture, 'live blood' analysis, cancer treatment and even veterinary chiropractic," noting chiropractors tend to perform these procedures in order to increase their incomes (Long 2002:44). Long (2002:142) aligns himself with the National Association of Chiropractic Medicine, an organization of like-minded colleagues, and argues that chiropractors should limit their care to patients between the ages of eighteen and fifty-five who have "acute, mechanical low back pain."

The National Institute of Chiropractic Research (2003), founded in 1987 in Phoenix, raises funds for "fundamental scientific, clinical and historical research and scholarship in chiropractic," conducts research of its own, and funds research projects by outside investigators.

Both biomedical skeptics and biomedical researchers often question whether CAM therapies offer anything more than placebo effects. Increasingly CAM therapies are being subjected to the conventional randomized, double blind, placebo-controlled, clinical trials (RCTs) or the standards of *evidence-based medicine* (Riley and Berman 2002; Wilson and Mills 2002). Most of the efficacy studies of CAM therapies being funded by NCCAM appear to be of this nature. Spinal manipulation therapy, homeopathy, acupuncture, herbs, and numerous other CAM therapies have been subjected to clinical randomized trials. Furthermore, a growing number of heterodox practitioners and researchers within chiropractic, naturopathic medicine, and acupuncture and Oriental medicine have come to accept the parameters of RCTs.

Other CAM therapists and researchers, however, question the validity of RCTs as the standard for evaluating their therapeutic systems (Richardson 2002; Walach 2003). As Cohen (1998:10) observes, many heterodox practitioners "advocate an expanded epistemology of science, which includes phenomenological and experiential data." Furthermore, various therapeutic systems, such as massage, Rolfing, reflexology, guided imagery, and a wide variety of folk medicines, often stress social, psychological, and spiritual interventions more than physical ones per se (Glik 2000:196).

In contrast to their jaundiced and often ethnocentric views of alternative medical systems, most biomedical skeptics and many biomedical physicians and researchers idealize biomedicine as the only scientifically valid health care system and conventional Western science as the only legitimate form of knowledge. These parties tend to conform to Midgley's (1992:25) assertion that "science education is now so narrowly scientistic that many scientists simply do not know that there is any systematic way of thinking besides their own." Homeopathy, traditional Chinese medicine, Ayurveda, and other heterodox medical systems claim to have paradigms that operate with different epistemological premises than those present in biomedicine. In noting that attempts to anatomically find acupuncture points and meridians on the basis of physiological and biochemical differences have failed for the most part, Patel (1987) adds:

> Definitive and widely accepted proof that acupuncture channels have physical, biochemical, or electrical existence would, not doubt, go a long way towards justifying the therapeutic use of acupuncture. On the other hand, an absence of such proof could not be taken as showing that these channels do not exist in some form invisible to current technology. (671)

None other than Wayne B. Jonas (2002), a former director of the Office of Alternative Medicine, recognizes some of the epistemological difficulties involved in efficacy studies of CAM therapies. He delineates three categories of CAM topics considered in research funding: (1) integrating topics "that may be considered conventional but are of interest for, or overlap with, CAM practices," such as melatonin, vitamins, minerals, antioxidants, dietary therapies, and mind–body medicine; (2) emerging CAM topics referring to "those that involve common areas of interest for CAM and conventional medicine," such as acupuncture, herbalism, and nutritional supplements; and (3) frontier topics that "challenge our conceptual and paradigmatic assumptions about the nature of biological or scientific reality," such as homeopathy, therapeutic touch, and prayer. Jonas (2002) notes:

> In 1997, I evaluated how much of the NIH budget on CAM was being spent in each of these three categories. . . . The vast majority of funding (80 percent) was in category I . . . and less than 2 percent in category III. . . . Most research is stripped of the traditional system's assumptions about reality before the research is funded. Thus, parts of CAM systems that can be made to look biomedical are funded, but no resources are going into the investigation of basic CAM assumptions. . . . In other words, no science of CAM fundamentals is being developed, and the epistemology of CAM systems is ignored in research. (35)

Elsewhere, while not wishing to dismiss the value of evidence-based research, Linde and Jonas (1999:69) call for "new research strategies and methodologies" in the evaluation of CAM therapies. It is important to note that many biomedical procedures and techniques have not been subjected to RCTs and that aspirin and penicillin were widely used before research scientists determined how they work.

The biomedical skeptics and many biomedical practitioners and researchers fail to recognize that biomedicine and conventional science are not value-free endeavors but rather are culturally constructed and deeply embedded in larger political-economic structures that utilize them more for purposes of profit making than serving social needs (Aronowitz 1988). According to Nader (1996:273–74), "scientists [and biomedical researchers] cannot be an impartial source of knowledge in conflicts between a dispersed public and centralized large-scale organizations" but rather are compromised servants who "legitimate the vested interests of industries, utilities, banks, mining companies, and governments." Cross-cultural comparisons of conventional Western science and biomedicine and indigenous and alternative knowledge systems, including ones focused on healing, force us to reassess the universal claims that the former tend to make. For example, in their ethnosemantic examination of gastrointestinal diseases among the Tzeltal and Tzotzil Indians of Chiapas, Mexico, Berlin and Berlin (1996) argue that these Mayan peoples have a sophisticated and comprehensive comprehension of the physiology and symptomatology of gastrointestinal diseases and that they have identified a wide range of medicinal plants to treat the systems associated with these ailments. They contend that research in ethnobiology and, more specifically, ethnobotany demonstrates that the ethnobiological knowledge of indigenous and peasant peoples corresponds in many ways to basic Western scientific concepts and principles.

In contrast to the all too often hyperrelativistic stance of postmodernism, a critical anthropological perspective on science and medicine recognizes that whereas some knowledge systems may be more valid than others, ultimately they are all conditioned by social circumstances and cultural values. As Singer, Susser, and I note in our medical anthropology textbook, "The scientific method is built upon, indeed demands, open and constant critique and self-examination, . . . CMA [critical medical anthropology] brings a special concern with the political economic context in which all ideas and behaviors emerge and have impact upon the world" (Baer, Singer, and Susser 2003:53).

TOWARD AN AUTHENTICALLY HOLISTIC AND PLURALISTIC HEALTH CARE SYSTEM

Despite the fact that the notion of holistic health has in large part been eroded, perhaps critical medical anthropologists, medical sociologists, historians, health practitioners, public health people, and health activists can play a role in rejuvenating and elaborating on this concept. Critical health scholars view human health as the product of a dialectical interaction of natural, political-economic, and sociocultural forces. Disease or illness varies from society to society, in some part because of climatic or geographic conditions but in large part because of the ways productive activities, resources, and reproduction are organized or carried out. It is not just the straightforward result of a pathogen or physiological disturbance but a result of a variety of social structural conditions, such as malnutrition, social stratification, economic insecurity, alienation in the workplace, occupational risks, industrial and motor vehicle pollution, inferior housing and sanitation, and the stress that are part and parcel of the culture of consumption—all of which are ultimately rooted in the capitalist world system.

While an effort to promote an authentically holistic view of health and disease would be a monumental task, critical scholars, practitioners, and activists need to present lectures and even offer courses on the political economy of health and medicine in both CAM programs at biomedical schools and schools of alternative medicine as well as publish articles on a broader concept of holism in the growing number of CAM and integrative health care journals, which presently publish articles by holistic M.D.'s, D.O.'s, and nurses and alternative or heterodox health practitioners. Indeed, some proponents of holistic medicine or CAM already exemplify an advocacy of such a notion and are critical of the limited holism expressed by most CAM providers or conventional physicians interested in integrative medicine. In an interview with Bonnie Horrigan, Michael Lerner, the president and founder of Commonweal (a health and environmental institute in Bolinas, California) and the author of *Choices in Healing: Integrating the Best of Conventional and Complementary Approaches to Cancer* (1994), notes that while CAM has made tremendous contributions over the past three decades in terms of understanding the psychological and spiritual dimensions of health, it also exhibits some serious limitations:

> What CAM has failed to do is to ground these contributions in recognition of the social, economic, and environmental determinants of health. For a movement that prides itself on being holistic, this failure to look seriously at the economic, social, and environmental determinants of health is an extraordinary shortcoming.

Now, to be fair, we should add that mainstream medicine also fails to focus on the social, economic, and environmental determinants of health. So this is a failing of clinical medicine on both the complementary and mainstream sides. The difference is that mainstream medicine does not claim to be holistic, whereas complementary medicine does make that claim. . . . When you go to a CAM conference, you'll hear wonderful sessions on spirituality or dying or mind–body interventions. But you will virtually never hear a session on the profound stress associated with job loss and corporate downsizing. . . . You will virtually never hear a session about the more than 100 different diseases related to chemical and other environmental contaminants that contribute so much to the chronic disease burden of our time. You will never hear a session on the effect of income inequality on health outcomes. (quoted in Horrigan 2003:82)

Lerner advocates that CAM practitioners associate themselves with progressive public health and environmental advocates and implies that both conventional and CAM practitioners have in large part failed to address controversial issues for pecuniary reasons and to not risk losing patients. He is currently involved in the development of a new Collaborative on Health and the Environment, a "national partnership of individuals and organizations that share a belief in the need to prevent disease by protecting the environment" (quoted in Horrigan 2003:86).

Some time ago, Dana Ullman (1985:384–87), a staunch proponent of homeopathy with a master's of public health degree, defined *progressive health care* as "health care which is predominantly of, by and for the people it serves" and argued that "holistic health is both a friend and foe of progressive health care." He saw the holistic health movement as progressive because it incorporated insights from the human potential, Eastern philosophy/spiritualism, self-care, women's, and environmental movements but reactionary in its tendency to blame individuals for their disease, its hidden sexism through the use of "yin-yang terminology that encourages widespread stereotyping," and its tendency to stress lifestyle changes over environmental ones.

Along with the effort to foster a broader conception of holistic health, critical medical social scientists can promote the creation of a universal health care system, particularly a Canadian-style single-payer system or even a national health service, in which health providers would function as public servants (Baer, Singer, and Susser 1997; Waitzkin 2001). The creation of an authentically holistic and pluralistic medical system ultimately will have to be coupled with the demand for a universal health care system that treats health care as a human right rather than a commodity for the privileged few. Such a system would have to go beyond the Canadian single-payer system, which is neither holistic nor pluralistic (Crelin, Andersen, and Connor 1997). According to Lyng (1990), within the context of his holistic medical "countersystem,"

[n]o one medical professional group enjoys a monopoly over the right to practice medicine (a monopoly that is granted by social or legal sanction). All professional groups are granted the legal right to offer their knowledge and technique to those who need resources to attain their health care goals. Such a structure is believed to afford patients the best opportunity to attain the knowledge that is most appropriate to their own unique health care needs and to provide a truly comprehensive system of knowledge and technique. (97)

Grossinger (1995b) presents a model for a six-part North American medical system:

For clarity of illustration (alone) I will place each sphere within this system in a different region of North America. This region shall be its research center, its university, and its court of ethics. Satellite clinics and practitioners will also be spread throughout the other regions. Needless to say, all systems belong in every region. (495)

In this model, New York and the greater Northeast will function as the biomedical school, which encompasses surgery, pharmacy, conventional psychoanalysis, nutrition, and laboratory research. Toronto and the greater Midwest will serve as the base of a "school of constitutional and dietary medicine," which "will include at its heart Ayurvedic principles but will also prescribe foods and herbs from all over the world, including from Chinese recipes, American Indian formularies, African, Pacific, and Australian ethnobotanies, etc." (Grossinger 1995b:495–97). Seattle and the greater Northwest will be the site of a "college of *chi*-based medicine," which will also include yoga, acupuncture, moxibustion, Buddhist meditation, herbalism, and bodywork (497). The San Francisco Bay area will serve as the center of energy medicine, including "homeopathy, Bach flower remedies, radionics, Reiki, forms of psychic medicine, *chakra* and color therapies, massage and induction of the different sheaths of the energy body" (497). Taos, New Mexico, and the greater

Southwest will be the site of the "shamanic school of medicine," which will teach "ceremonial sand painting, visualization techniques, healing dances and chants, indigenous and Western art therapy, the dynamics of abreaction and methods for reinvoking trauma, vision questing, the uses of hallucinogens in diagnosis and treatment, and healing with feathers, drums, crystals, amulets, and stones" (497–98). West Palm Beach, Florida, and the greater Southeast would serve as the location of the "school of neo-osteopathy, which will cover all modalities of manipulation and attendant methods of psychological investigation and clearing psychosomatic blocks" and will include "independent departments representing the major somatic traditions such as Feldenkrais, Eutony, Body-Mind Centering, Rolfing, Zero Balancing, Visceral Manipulation, Aston Patterning, Chiropractic, Reichian, Acupressure, etc." (498). While many might assert that Grossinger's six-part medical system is romantic and utopian and based on the environmental notion of bioregionalism, it may be viewed as a metaphor for a pluralistic, holistic, and multicultural medical system that would incorporate the best of all existing medical and therapeutic systems.

Waitzkin (2000:204) argues that "[b]ecause of the powerful economic and political interests that dominate the health-care system, the alternative [or holistic] movement cannot succeed unless it connects itself to broader political activism as well." The creation of a universal health care system could pave the way to provide CAM therapies to working-class and poor people. Indeed, Waitzkin (2000:205) asserts that "[c]omponents of alternative medicine [may] ultimately also be useful in low-income and minority communities." Indeed, various folk medical systems, such as African American folk medicine, *curanderismo,* and Native American healing systems, could be revitalized to be included into a pluralistic, holistic, universal health care system.

Fortunately, at least a few health care centers have established CAM services for low-income populations. Lincoln Hospital, a city-funded hospital in the South Bronx, has provided acupuncture as an alternative to methadone in the treatment of heroin addiction since 1974 (Anath 2001:178–79). The Charlotte Maxwell Complementary Clinic, a cancer treatment center in Oakland, was established by a "group of volunteer acupuncturists, homeopaths, and massage therapists with a mission to provide alternative modalities of treatment to all irrespective of ability to pay" (Anath 2001:180). Finally, the King County Natural Medicine Clinic in Kent, Washington, a joint project of the Community Health Centers of King County and Bastyr University, accepts Medicare and Medicaid payments and offers services on a sliding scale according to the patient's ability to pay (Anath 2001:180–81).

Despite the fact that the plan for a managed-competition health care system failed early on in Clinton's first presidential term, growing dissatisfaction with managed care on the part of both health practitioners and patients and the failure of the existing system to provide adequate health care to a significant portion of the population has caused health care reform to reenter the public discourse, particularly as various Democratic presidential aspirants offer their health care plans to the U.S. electorate. Opposition to a universal health care system in the United States does not for the most part emanate from the public but rather from a powerful group consisting of insurance companies, pharmaceutical companies, health care corporations, some health care providers, and small businesses that provide minimal or no health care coverage for their employees.

Whereas most corporate interest and physician groups have opposed the creation of a single-payer health care system, various progressive physician groups, grassroots organizations, and legislators have favored it. Progressive medical social scientists should urge their various professional associations to join with the National Medical Association, the American Public Health Association, and the National Association of Social Workers in endorsing a single-payer system for the United States. Given their knowledge of both professionalized heterodox and folk medical systems, medical social scientists could argue in favor of including them into a universal health care plan. Rather than being divided as they were on the Clinton plan, grassroots groups, professional associations, and health activists may have a unique opportunity to rally behind a single-payer system and force it onto center stage in health care reform. As Flacks (1993:465) so aptly argues, "[t]he demand for a universal health-care program . . . has the potential to unite very diverse movement constituencies and to link these with middle-class voters."

Glossary

BODYWORK

Acupressure: A Chinese massage technique in which the meridians and meridian points are used to guide the application of finger pressure rather than the insertion of needles as in acupuncture.

Alexander technique: A technique developed by Matthias Alexander (1869–1955), a Tasmanian, that relies on visualizations and gentle touch to help the client overcome poor postural habits to promote increased comfort, flexibility, and balance. It is particularly popular with artists, musicians, dancers, architects, psychotherapists, and intellectuals.

Applied kinesiology: A therapy developed by George Goodheart, a chiropractor, in which he correlated each muscle with specific organs and reflex points in order to treat a wide variety of ailments, including allergies, headaches, chronic fatigue syndrome, environmental sensitivities, arthritis, tendonitis, hypertension, and lymphatic, endocrinal, brain, and nutritional dysfunctions.

Cranial osteopathy (or sacrocranial manipulation): A form of manipulation originally developed by William Sutherland, D.O., involving subtle manipulation of the cranial bones with the intention of improving functioning of the entire spine, including the sacrum, as well as other bodily organs.

Feldenkrais: A form of bodywork named after Moshe Feldenkrais, a Russian-born Israeli physicist, that utilizes physical movement to stimulate the nervous system, improve posture and flexibility, alleviate muscular tension and pain, and improve feeling and thought.

Hellerwork: A technique developed by Joseph Heller, an aerospace engineer and student of Ida Rolf, who incorporated concepts from physics and physiology to facilitate the release of rigid muscles in order to alleviate bodily structural misalignments and stressful emotional states.

Iridology: A form of diagnosis based on the independent work in the late nineteenth century of Ignatz von Peczely, a Hungarian physician, and N. Liljequist, a Swedish minister, who maintained that each organ of the body is represented by an area of the iris that provides a window revealing disorders in the associated organ.

Qi gong: An ancient Chinese therapeutic system entailing physical movements and breathing exercises designed to circulate *chi* and thus promote health.

Reflexology: A therapy developed by William Fitzgerald, an American who called it "zone therapy," in the early 1900s that entails manual stimulation of reflex points on the feet, ears, and hands that are believed to correspond to specific areas or organs of the body. The pressure on the reflex points is intended to relieve stress, improve blood supply, stimulate nerve transmission, and help restore balance in the body.

Rolfing or structural integration: A manipulative therapy developed by Ida Rolf (1896–1979) that entails application of deep pressure to the fascia or connective tissue supporting the musculoskeletal system in order to reorient body parts so they function more efficiently within the field of gravity. Rolf's work led to the establishment in 1972 of the Rolf Institute in Boulder, Colorado.

Shiatsu: A form of massage developed by Shizuto Masunaga in the 1950s that applies prolonged pressure and spiritual concentration to one meridian point at a time in order to alleviate a wide variety of ailments.

Visceral manipulation: A technique initially developed within osteopathic and chiropractic circles that uses touch and palpation to assess the tonicity, position, and freedom of circulating fluids of various visceral organs, including the stomach, liver, and colon.

MIND–BODY MEDICINE

Aromatherapy: The inhalation of aromatic substances and external application of scented oils for the purpose of treating a wide variety of mental and physical problems.

Bioelectromagnetic therapy: Based on the belief that electricity and magnetic fields can stimulate the body's life force, this therapy is used to treat arthritis, anxiety, depression, and symptoms of drug withdrawal and to facilitate wound healing.

Bioenergetics: A psychoanalytic approach developed by Alexander Lowen, a student of Wilhelm Reich, that seeks to release *body armours* that develop in the musculature due to traumatic emotional events. Bioenergetics entails a combination of talking and physical therapy, with the latter including kicking, beating, and breathing exercises.

Biofeedback: Procedures designed to achieve self-control of physiological processes, generally with the assistance of electromyography instrumentation that measures thermal changes and perspiration rates.

Hypnotherapy: An ancient technique involving a state of focused concentration with suspension of some consciousness. It is utilized today as a form of surgical anesthesia and recovery, to reduce pain and treat various ailments or disorders (including asthma, gastrointestinal complications, obesity, anxiety, and phobias), and to induce greater consciousness and awareness.

Meditation: A wide variety of spiritually related techniques found in many cultures that seek to encourage the student to focus attention on a single repetitive stimulus, such as a sound, breathing, or a focal point, or to observe one's thoughts in a nonjudgmental manner.

Polarity therapy: An eclectic system developed by Randolph Stone, an osteopath/chiropractor/naturopath, that seeks to merge diet, exercise, and massage or manipulation in order to release impeded energy, which is viewed as the primary cause of disease, and also enhance awareness.

Rebirthing therapy: A technique initially developed by Leonard Orr in which breathing exercises are used to release emotional traumas, including those experienced during one's birth, in order to reintegrate the body, mind, and spirit.

Reiki: A technique developed by Mikao Usui, a Japanese theologian, in the nineteenth century in which the fingers are lightly passed over body parts to stimulate the healing process.

Relaxation therapy: A wide assortment of techniques designed to induce alleviate stress and induce relaxation in the mind and body and promote a sense of wellness.

Therapeutic touch: A healing technique developed by Dolores Krieger, a nurse, in which the hands are passed over the body without direct contact in order to stimulate energy fields. Used in the treatment of pain and anxiety and in efforts to facilitate wound healing and bolster the immune system.

RELIGIOUS HEALING SYSTEMS

Christian Science: A metaphysical system developed by Mary Baker Eddy (1821–1910) that views material reality, including disease, as illusory and asserts that health can be restored by eradicating this misconception.

Pentecostalism: A Protestant sectarian healing movement that emerged in the early twentieth century among both African Americans and European Americans and that regards healing as one of the nine gifts of the Holy Spirit, along with speaking in tongues, interpretation of tongues, and so forth. Relies on praying, laying on of hands, anointing with holy oil, and the use of prayer cloths and aprons.

Scientology: An outgrowth of Dianetics, an alternative form of psychotherapy, developed by L. Ron Hubbard (1911–1986), which asserts that painful past experiences are stored in the Reactive Mind or the subconscious mind as "engrams" which prevent people from functioning to their fullest potential. It relies on various mental exercises and an E-meter (*E* for *engram*) that counselors or auditors employ in assisting clients in releasing engrams, with the ultimate purpose of becoming clear.

Seventh-Day Adventism: A religious healing sect started by Ellen G. White (1827–1915), a staunch advocate of hydropathy, cleanliness, and dietary reforms, including vegetarianism and avoidance of drugs and stimulants.

Spiritualism: A religious healing movement that first appeared in the United States during the 1840s in which mediums attempt to facilitate contact between their clients and their clients' loved ones in the spirit world. Spiritualist healers assert that some spirits, called *guides*, are willing to facilitate healing with the assistance of a medium or channel.

Unity: A variant of New Thought developed by Myrtle Fillmore (1845–1931) and her husband Charles Fillmore (1854–1948) that teaches that the human mind can exert a great deal of influence on the outcomes of events and problems, including illness, through various techniques, such as visualization and affirmation, that create a consciousness of God's omnipresence within oneself.

FOLK MEDICAL SYSTEMS

African American folk medicine: A wide ensemble of healing practices that includes *conjure* or *hoodoo* (a system of divination, magic, and witchcraft); herbalism; lay midwifery; and religious healers functioning within the context of Pentecostal (or Sanctified) and spiritual churches as well as Islamic and Judaic sects.

Chinese American folk medicine: An elaborate system that includes herbal remedies, patent medicines, and Chinese doctors who perform acupuncture and other therapies and administer herbs.

Curanderismo: A Mexican American healing system that focuses on the services of a *curandera* or *curandero* who employs both natural and supernatural healing techniques and who treats various culture-bound syndromes, such as *susto* (fright), *empacho* (the clogging of the stomach and upper intestinal tract from excessive food or the wrong kinds of food), and *mal puesto* (witchcraft).

Espiritismo: A Puerto Rican healing system that blends Native American, African, and Catholic beliefs and practices but draws primarily on the writings of Alan Kardec. It focuses on communication through mediums with a wide array of spirits who can protect the living from harm and illness.

European American folk medicine: Consists of a wide array of healing practices, including herbalism; home remedies; the use of magical charms and patent medicines; *powwowing*, in which the healer whispers prayers or biblical verses into the ear of the client, often accompanied by laying on of hands; and other healing practices.

Native American healing systems: There are as many Native American healing systems as there are Native American ethnic groups or tribes in the United States. Traditional Native American healing tends to focus on psychological, rheumatic, urinary, and gastrointestinal ailments as well as rashes, wounds, and eye irritations. Specific healing practices include sweat lodges, medicine societies among the Iroquois and the Pueblo Indians of the Southwest, singing and hand trembling among the Navajo, and peyotism (a pan-Indian religious healing system that regards peyote as a sacramental plant with healing qualities).

Santería: A syncretic Afro-Cuban religious healing system that draws on Yoruba orisha worship, the Catholic cult of the saints, and spiritism. A *santera* or *santero* can use her or his magical powers to help a client overcome evil influences, recover from an illness, secure employment, improve financial circumstances, or even subdue or destroy enemies.

Vodun: A Haitian American religious healing tradition consisting of beliefs and rituals focused on the *loa,* or African gods who have become syncretized with Catholic saints for the purpose of empowerment in this life. Male priests (*houngans*) and female priests (*mambos*) conduct ceremonies in honor of the *loa* and ancestral spirits and serve as religious healers or mediums.

References

About NCH: Welcome to the Web home of the National Center for Homeopathy. (2003). Available online: www.homeopathic.org/about.htm; accessed August 13.

Abrams, M. (1994). Alternative medicine: quackery or miracle? *Good Housekeeping*, March, pp. 99–119.

Albanese, C. L. (1993). Fisher kings and public places: The old New Age in the 1990s. *Annals of the American Academy of Political and Social Science* 527:131–43.

———. (1999a). *America: Religions and religion* (3d ed.). Belmont, Calif.: Wadsworth.

———. (1999b). The subtle energies of spirit: explorations in metaphysical and New Age spirituality. *Journal of the American Academy of Religion* 67:305–23.

———. (2000). The aura of wellness: Subtle-energy healing and New Age religion. *Religion and culture* 10:29–55.

Alford, R. (1972). The political economy of health care: Dynamics without change. *Politics and Society* 2:127–64.

Alster, Kristine Beyerman. (1989). The Holistic Health Movement. Tuscaloosa: University of Alabama Press

Alter, J. S. (1999). Heaps of health, metaphysical fitness: Ayurveda and the ontology of good health in medical anthropology. *Current Anthropology* 40 (Suppl.):S43–S58.

Alternative Medicine Herbology School Directory. (2003). Available online: www.alternativemedicinereview.com/herbal.html; accessed June 19.

American Association of Naturopathic Physicians. (n.d.). Licensing and the public interest. Leaflet. McLean, Va.: Author.

American Association of Naturopathic Physicians Quarterly Newsletter. (1986). Vol. 1(3):4.

———. (1987). Vol. 2(5):3.

American Association for Health Freedom. (2004). Available online: http://health freedom.net/about.htm, p. 1; accessed August 4.

American Botanical Council. (2003). Available online: www.herbalgram.org/ education/index.html, p. 1; accessed June 19.

American Herbalists Guild. (2003). Available online: www.americanherbalistsguild.com; accessed September 23.

American Holistic Health Association. (2003). Available online: http://ahha.org/ahhawhat.htm; accessed September 5.

American Holistic Nurses Association. (2004). Endorsed certification programs. Available online: www.ahna.org/edu/programs.html, p. 1; accessed July 22.

American Naturopathic Medical Association. (1999a). www.anma.net/anmcab.htm, p. 1; accessed November 11.

———. (1999b). Available online: www.anma.net/frontpg.htm, p. 1; accessed November 12.

———. (1999c). Available online: www.anma.net/media.htm, p. 1; accessed November 12.

American WholeHealth. (2003). Available online: www.americanwholehealth.com/ about.html, p. 1; accessed March 19.

Anath, S. (2001). Case studies in complementary and alternative medicine for the underserved. In N. Faass (Ed.), *Integrating complementary medicine into health systems* (pp. 178–85). Gaithersburg, Md.: Aspen.

Anders, V., and Lunt, J. Y. (1997). Bringing holistic nursing into the new millennium. *Alternative & Complementary Therapies* 3(1):24–28.

Anderson, R. (1991). An American clinic for traditional Chinese medicine: Comparisons to family medicine and chiropractic. *Journal of Manipulative and Physiological Therapeutics* 14(8):462–66.

———. (1997). Is chiropractic mainstream or alternative? A view from medical anthropology. *Advances in Chiropractic* 4:555–78.

Antonovsky, A. (1994). A sociological critique of the "well-being" movement. *Journal of Mind–Body Health* 10(3):3–44.

Arcury, T. A., et al. (2002). Complementary and alternative medicine use among rural older adults. *Complementary Health Practice Review* 7(3):167–85.

Armstrong, D. (1987). Theoretical tensions in biopsychosocial medicine. *Social Science and Medicine* 25:1213–18.

Aronowitz, S. (1988). *Science as power: Discourse and ideology in modern society.* Minneapolis: University of Minnesota Press.

Ashford, S., and Timms, N. (1992). *What Europe thinks: A study of Western European values.* Aldershot, U.K.: Dartmouth.

Baer, H. A. (1984). The drive for professionalization in British osteopathy. *Social Science and Medicine* 19:717–25.

———. (1987). Divergence and convergence in two systems of manual medicine: Osteopathy and chiropractic in the United States. *Medical Anthropology Quarterly* 1:176–93.

———. (1989). The American dominative medical system as a reflection of social relations in the larger society. *Social Science & Medicine* 28:1103–12.

———. (1992). The potential rejuvenation of American naturopathy as a consequence of the holistic health movement. *Medical Anthropology* 13:369–83.

———. (1996). Practice-building seminars in chiropractic: A petit bourgeois response to biomedical domination. *Medical Anthropology Quarterly* 10:29–44.

———. (2001). *Biomedicine and alternative healing systems in America: Issues of class, race, ethnicity, and gender.* Madison: University of Wisconsin Press.

Baer, H. A., Singer, M., and Susser, I. (2003). *Medical anthropology and the world system: A critical perspective.* 2nd ed. Westport, Conn.: Praeger.

Baer, L. D., and Good, C. M., Jr. (1998). The power of the state. In R. J. Gordon, B. C. Nienstedt, and W. M. Gesler (Eds.), *Alternative therapies: Expanding options in health care* (pp. 45–66). New York: Springer.

Bailey, E. J. (1991). Hypertension: An analysis of Detroit African American health care treatment patterns. *Human Organization* 50:287–96.

Bainbridge, W. S. (1997). *The sociology of religious movements.* New York: Routledge.

Baker, J. D. (1998). U.S. herbalism: A preliminary examination. Paper written for Advanced Medical Anthropology class, Arizona State University, spring semester.

Baldwin, C. M., et al. (2002). A profile of military veterans in the southwestern United States who use complementary and alternative medicine: Implications for integrated care. *Archives of Internal Medicine* 162(15):1697–1704.

Barnes, L. L. (1998). The psychologizing of Chinese healing practices in the United States. *Culture, Medicine and Psychiatry* 22:413–43.

Barnum, B. S. (1998). Rediscovering Nightingale: Back to the future. In R. J. Gordon, B. C. Nienstedt, and W. M. Gesler (Eds.), *Alternative therapies: Expanding options in health care* (pp. 177–88). New York: Springer.

Barrett, S. (2000). A few thoughts on Ayurvedic mumbo-jumbo. *Quackwatch.* Available online: http://quackwatch.com/04ConsumerEducation/chopra.html, p. 4, accessed October 1.

———. (2003). Some notes on Robert W. Bradford and his Committee of Choice in Medicine. Available online: www.quackwatch.com/04ConsumerEducation/Nonrecorg/cfem.html, p. 1; accessed September 17.

Barrett, S., and Knight, G. (Eds.). (1976). *The health robbers.* Philadelphia: Stickley.

Basil, R. (Ed.). (1988). *Not necessarily the New Age: Critical essays*. Buffalo, N.Y.: Prometheus.

Bastyr University. (1999). *Bastyr University graduate programs, 1999–2001*. Bothell, Wash.: Author.

Bauman, E., et al. (Eds.). (1981). *The holistic health lifebook: A guide to personal and planetary well-being*. Lexington, Mass.: Greene.

Becker, D. M. (2001). Public health and religion. In N. Schneiderman et al. (Eds.), *Integrating behavioral and social sciences with public health*. Washington, D.C.: American Psychological Association.

Beckford, J. A. (1984). Holistic imagery and ethics in new religious and healing movements. *Social Compass* 31:259–72.

Belasco, W. 1989. *Appetite for change: How the counterculture took on the food industry, 1966–1988*. New York: Pantheon.

Benoit, C., et al. (2001). Designing midwives: A comparison of educational models. In R. DeVries (Ed.), *Birth by design: Pregnancy, maternity care, and midwifery in North America and Europe* (pp. 139–61). New York: Routledge.

Benson, H. (1975). *The relaxation response*. New York: Avon.

Berlin, E. A., and Berlin, B. (1996). *Medical ethnobiology of the highland Maya of Chiapas, Mexico*. Princeton, N.J.: Princeton University Press.

Berliner, H., and Salmon, J. W. (1979). The holistic health movement and scientific medicine: The naked and the dead. *Socialist Review* 43:31–52.

———. (1980). The holistic alternative to scientific medicine: History and analysis. *International Journal of Health Services* 10:133–47.

Beyerman, K. B. (1989). *The holistic health movement*. Tuscaloosa: University of Alabama Press.

Bezilla, T. A. (1997). Traditional osteopathy as an integrated model of holistic medicine. *Alternative & Complementary Therapies* 3(2):140–43.

Blattner, B. (1981). *Holistic nursing*. Englewood Cliffs, N.J.: Prentice Hall.

Bliss, S. (1985). *The new holistic health handbook: Living well in a New Age*. Lexington, Mass.: Greene.

Bloch, J. P. (1998). Alternative spirituality and environmentalism. *Review of Religious Research* 40:55–73.

Bloom, H. (1992). *The American religion*. New York: Simon & Schuster.

Bloomfield, R. J. (1983). Naturopathy. In R. H. Bannerman, J. Burton, and C. Wen-Chieh (Eds.), *Traditional medicine and health care coverage: A reader for health administrators and practitioners* (pp. 116–23). Geneva: World Health Organization.

Borre, K. S., and Wilson, J. L. (1998). Paradigms and politics: Redux of homeopathy in American medicine. In R. J. Gordon, B. C. Nienstedt, and W. M. Gelser (Eds.),

Alternative therapies: Expanding options in health care (pp. 67–86). New York: Springer.

Boston Women's Health Book Collective. (1998). *Our bodies, ourselves: A book for and by women* (rev. ed.). New York: Simon & Schuster.

Bradley, R. S. (1999). Philosophy of naturopathic medicine. In J. E. Pizzorno Jr. and M. Murray (Eds.), *A textbook of natural medicine* (pp. 41–49). Orlando, Fla.: Churchill-Livingstone.

Bratman, S. (1997). *The alternative medicine sourcebook: A realistic evaluation of alternative healing methods.* Los Angeles: Lowell House.

Brennan, B. A. (1987). *Hands of light: A guide to healing through the energy field.* New York: Bantam.

———. (1993). *Light emerging: A journal of personal healing.* New York: Bantam.

Bright, M. A. (2002). Paradigm shifts. In M. A. Bright (Ed.), *Holistic health and healing* (pp. 3–30). Philadelphia: Davis.

Brody, J. E. (2001). Alternative medicine: promises and problems. In J. E. Brody and D. Grady (Ed.), *The New York Times guide to alternative health: A consumer reference* (pp. 2–6). New York: Holt.

Brown, E. R. (1979). *Rockefeller medicine men: Medicine and capitalism in America.* Berkeley: University of California Press.

Brown, Michael F. (1997). The channeling zone: American spirituality in an anxious age. Cambridge, Mass: Harvard University Press.

Bruce, S. (1996). *Religion in the modern world: From cathedrals to cults.* Oxford: Oxford University Press.

Brunk, D. (2000). Marketplace demands physicians offer more CAM. *Family Practice News,* May 1, p. 1.

Budd, S., and Sharma, U. (1994). Introduction. In S. Budd and U. Sharma (Eds.), *The healing bond: The patient–practitioner relationship and therapeutic responsibility* (pp. 1–19). London: Routledge.

Bunk, S. (1999). Is integrative medicine the future? Relman-Weil debate focuses on scientific evidence issues. *The Scientist* 13(10, May 10).

Butler, K. (1992). *A consumer's guide to "alternative medicine."* Buffalo, N.Y.: Prometheus.

Calendar. (2002). Available online: www.chopra.com/calendar.htm; accessed July 24.

California Association of Naturopathic Physicians. (n.d.). *Licensing naturopathic physicians in California.* Pamphlet. Roseville: Author.

Canfield, D., and Faass, N. (2001). Perspective: funding sources for an alternative medicine clinic. In N. Faass (Ed.), *Integrating complementary medicine into health systems* (pp. 122–25). Gaithersburg, Md.: Aspen.

Cant, S., and Sharma, U. (Eds.). (1996). *Complementary and alternative medicines.* London: Free Association.

———. (1999). *A new medical pluralism? Alternative medicine, doctors, patients, and the state.* London: Taylor & Francis.

Canyon Ranch. (2003). Available online: www.canyonranch.com; accessed November 29.

Capital University of Integrative Medicine. (2003). Available online: www.cuim.org; accessed November 29.

Caplan, R., and Gesler, W. M. (1998). Biomedical physicians practicing holistic medicine. In R. J. Gordon, B. C. Nienstedt, and W. M. Gesler (Eds.), *Alternative therapies: Expanding options in health care* (pp. 189–98). New York: Springer.

Caplan, R., Harrison, K., and Galantiono, M. L. (2003). The evolution of complementary and alternative medicine in the United States: The push and pull of holistic health care into the medical mainstream. In J. L. Carlson (Ed.), *Complementary therapies and wellness: Practice essentials for holistic health care* (pp. 9–22). Upper Saddle River, N.J.: Prentice Hall.

Carroll, R. T. (2003). Ayurvedic medicine and Deepak Chopra. *The Skeptics Dictionary.* http://Skepdic.com/ayurvedic.html; accessed March 5.

Carter, J. P. (1993). *Racketeering in medicine: The suppression of alternatives.* Norfolk, Va.: Hampton Roads.

Cassidy, C. M. (1998). Chinese medicine users in the United States, Part I: Utilization, satisfaction, medical plurality. *Journal of Alternative and Contemporary Medicine* 4(1):17–27.

———. (2002). Commentary on terminology and therapeutic principles: Challenges in classifying complementary and alternative medicine practices. *Journal of Alternative and Contemporary Medicine* 8:893–96.

Cassileth, B. R. (1998). *The alternative medicine handbook: The complete reference guide to alternative and complementary therapies.* New York: Norton.

Chamberlain, T. J., and Hall, C. A. (2000). *Realized religion: Research on the relationship between religion and health.* Philadelphia: Templeton Foundation.

Chapman-Smith, D. (1997). Advances in chiropractic around the world. *Advances in Chiropractic* 4:579–99.

Chavez, L. R. (1984). Doctors, *curanderos,* and *brujas*: Health care delivery and Mexican immigrants in San Diego. *Medical Anthropology Quarterly* 15(2):31–37.

The Choice. (2003). Available online: www.thechoicemagazine.com; accessed July 15.

Chopra, D. (1987). *Creating health.* Boston: Houghton Mifflin.

———. (1988). *Return of the rishi.* Boston: Houghton Mifflin.

———. (1989). Quantum healing. New York: Bantam Books.

———. (1991). *Perfect health.* New York: Harmony.

———. (1992). *Unconditional life: Discovering the power to fulfill your dreams.* New York: Bantam.

———. (1993a). *Ageless body, timeless mind.* New York: Harmony.

———. (1993b). *The seven spiritual laws of success.* San Rafael, Calif.: Amber-Allen.

———. (1993c). *Creating affluence: Wealth consciousness in the field of all possibilities.* New York: New World Library.

———. (1995). *Boundless energy.* New York: Harmony.

———. (1997). *The path to love.* New York: Harmony.

———. (1999a). *Everyday immortality: A concise course in spiritual transformation.* Crown.

———. (1999b). *On the shores of eternity: Poems from Tagore on death and immortality.* New York: Harmony.

———. (1999c). *Journey in the boundless.* Audio tape. Nightingale-Constant.

———. (2000). *How to know God: The soul's journey into the mystery of mysteries.* New York: Harmony.

Chopra Center. (2000). Available online: http://chopra.com/ccwbwelcome.htm; accessed October 1.

Chow, E. Poy Yew. (1984). Traditional Chinese medicine: A holistic system. In J. W. Salmon (Ed.), *Alternative medicine: Popular and policy perspectives* (pp. 114–37). New York: Tavistock.

Chowka, P. (2003a). Naturopathic licensing bill passes California State Assembly. Available online: *Natural Health Line,* www.naturalhealthline.com/newsletter/1sep03/license.htm; accessed August 15.

———. (2003b). California licenses naturopaths, and a leading ND raises questions about the future of naturopathy. Available online: *Natural Health Line,* www.naturalhealthline.com; accessed August 15.

Chryssides, G. D. (1999). *Exploring new religions.* London: Cassell.

Cimino, R., and Lattin, D. (1998). *Shopping for faith: American religion in the new millennium.* San Francisco: Jossey-Bass.

Clarkson, F. (1997). *Eternal hostility: The struggle between theocracy and democracy.* Monroe, Maine: Common Courage.

Cleary-Guida, M. B. (2001). A regional survey of health insurance coverage for complementary and alternative medicine: Current status and future ramifications. *Journal of Alternative and Complementary Medicine* 7:269–73.

Clements, W. M. (2001). The New Age sweat lodge. In E. Brady (Ed.), *Healing logics: Culture and medicine in modern health belief systems* (pp. 143–62). Logan: Utah State University Press.

Coalition for Natural Health. (2000). Licensing natural health is bad medicine. Available online: www.naturalhealth.org/license.html, p. 1; accessed January 21.

Cobb, A. K. (1981). Incorporation and change: The case of the midwife in the United States. *Medical Anthropology* 5:73–88.

Cody, G. (1999). History of naturopathic medicine. In J. E. Pizzorno Jr. and M. Murray (Eds.), *A textbook of natural medicine* (pp. 17–40). Orlando, Fla.: Churchill-Livingstone.

Cohen, M. H. (1998). *Complementary and alternative medicine: Legal boundaries and regulatory perspectives.* Baltimore: Johns Hopkins University Press.

———. (2000). *Beyond complementary medicine: Legal and ethical perspectives on health care and human evolution.* Ann Arbor: University of Michigan Press.

———. (2003). *Future medicine: ethical dilemmas, regulatory challenges, and therapeutic pathways to health care and healing in human transformation.* Ann Arbor: University of Michigan Press.

Collinge, W. (1996). *The American Holistic Health Association complete guide to alternative medicine.* New York: Time Warner.

Colorado Association of Naturopathic Physicians. (1998). Addendum to the 1997 sunrise application. Mimeographed paper. Denver: Author.

Complementary & Alternative Medicine at the NIH. 2000. Fall.

Complementary & Alternative Medicine Newsletter. 1995. Vol. 2(5):1–2.

Consumer Reports. (2000). The mainstreaming of alternative medicine. May 17–25.

Coulter, H. L. (1973). *Divided legacy: A history of the schism in medical thought,* Vol. 3: *Science and ethics in American medicine, 1800–1914.* Washington, D.C.: Wehawken.

Coulter, I. D., Hays, R. D., and Danielson, C. D. (1996). The role of the chiropractor in the changing health care system: From marginal to mainstream. *Research in the Sociology of Health Care* 13A:95–117.

Council of Colleges of Acupuncture and Oriental Medicine. (2001). Available online: www.acaom.org, p. 1; accessed September 21.

Courses on complementary medicine and alternative therapies (CAM) taught at conventional U.S. medical schools. (2002). Available online: www.healthwwweb .com/courses.html; accessed August 4, 2004.

Cox, C. (1994). *Storefront revolution: Food co-ops and the counterculture.* New Brunswick, N.J.: Rutgers University Press.

Crelin, J. K, Andersen, A. A., and Connor, J. T. H. (Eds.). (1997). *Alternative health care in Canada: Nineteenth and twentieth century perspectives.* Toronto: Canadian Scholars.

D'Antonio, M. (1992). *Heaven on earth.* New York: Crown.

Danforth, L. M. (1989). *Firewalking and religious healing: The Anasternaria of Greece and the American firewalking movement*. Princeton, N.J.: Princeton University Press.

Davis-Floyd, R. (1998a). Types of midwifery training: An anthropological overview. In J. Tritten and J. Southern (Eds.), *Paths to becoming a midwife* (pp. 119–33). Eugene, Ore.: Midwifery Today.

———. (1998b). The ups, downs and interlinkages of nurse- and direct-entry-midwifery: Status, practice and education. In J. Tritten and J. Southern (Eds.), *Paths to becoming a midwife* (pp. 67–118). Eugene, Ore.: Midwifery Today.

Davis-Floyd, R., and St. John, G. (1998). *From doctor to healer: The transformative journey*. New Brunswick, N.J.: Rutgers University Press.

Daviss, B. (2001). Reforming birth and (re)making midwifery in North America. In R. DeVries (Ed.), *Birth by design: Pregnancy, maternity care, and midwifery in North America and Europe* (pp. 70–85). New York: Routledge.

Dawson, L. L. (1998). *Comprehending cults: The sociology of new religious movements*. Toronto: Oxford University Press.

Dean, K. L. (2001). NYU's holistic nursing program: Expanding the conventional boundaries of nursing. *Alternative & Complementary Therapies* 7(3):183–87.

Deloria, P. J. (1998). *Playing Indian*. New Haven, Conn.: Yale University Press.

DeVries, R. G. (1996). *Making midwives legal: Childbirth, medicine, and the law* (2d ed.). Columbus: Ohio State University Press.

Diamond, W. J. (2001). *The clinical practice of complementary, alternative, and Western medicine*. Boca Raton, Fla.: CRC.

Diehl, D. L., et al. (1997). Use of acupuncture by American physicians. *Journal of Alternative and Complementary Medicine* 3(2):119–26.

Dosch, M. A. (1980). The Berkeley Holistic Health Center. In E. Bauman et al. (Eds.), *The holistic health handbook: A guide to personal and planetary well-being* (pp. 378–85). Lexington, Mass.: Greene.

Dossey, B. M., Keegan, L., and Guzzetta, C. E. (2000). *Holistic nursing: A handbook for practice* (3d ed.). Gaitherburg, Md.: Aspen.

Dossey, L. (1993). *Healing words: The power of prayer and the practice of medicine*. San Francisco: HarperCollins.

———. (1996). *Prayer is good medicine: How to reap the healing benefits of prayer*. San Francisco: HarperSan Francisco.

———. (1999). *Reinventing medicine: Beyond mind, body to a new era of medicine*. San Francisco: HarperCollins.

Dottinga, R. (2000). Chopra defeats sex harassment suit. *APBNews*, Associated Press, March 7.

Douglas, M. (1999). The construction of the physician: A cultural approach to medical fashions. In S. Budd and U. Sharma (Eds.), *The healing bond: The patient–practitioner relationship and therapeutic responsibility.* London: Routledge.

Dunbar, F. (1945). *Psychosomatic diagnosis.* New York: Johnson Reprint.

———. (1955). *Mind and body: Introduction to psychosomatic medicine.* New York: Random House.

Dunn, H. (1961). *High level wellness.* Arlington, Va.: Beatty.

Eck, D.L. (2001). *A new religious America: How a "Christian Country" has become the world's most religiously diverse nation.* San Francisco: HarperSan Francisco.

Eisenberg, D. M. (1995). *Encounters with qi: Exploring Chinese medicine.* New York: W. W. Norton.

Eisenberg, D. M., et al. (1993). Unconventional medicine in the United States. *New England Journal of Medicine* 328(4):246–52.

Eisenberg, D. M., et al. (1998). Trends in alternative medicine use in the United States, 1990–1997: Results of a follow-up national study. *Journal of the American Medical Association* 280(18):569–75.

Elder, N. C., Gillcrist, A., and Minz, R. (1997). Use of alternative health care by family practice patients. *Archives of Family Medicine* 6:181–84.

Engel, G. L. (1977). The need for a new medical model: A challenge for biomedicine. *Science* 196:129.

English-Lueck, J. A. (1990). *Health in the new age: A study in California holistic practices.* Englewood Cliffs, N.J.: Prentice Hall.

Farnsworth, G. R. (1999). *A history of the Northwest Naturopathic Physicians' Convention.* Self-published manuscript.

Federal Trade Commission. (2003). Available online: www.ftc.gov/us/1999/03/acafrn .htm; accessed November 29.

Ferguson, M. (1980). *The Aquarian conspiracy.* Los Angeles: Tarcher.

The fine points of acupuncture. (2003). Available online: www.thehealthpages.com/ ar-acupn.htm, p. 6; accessed July 3.

Finken, D. (1986). Naturopathy: America's homegrown alternative healing art. *Medical Self-care* (November/December):39–43.

Fishbein, M. (1932). *Medical follies.* New York: Boni & Liveright.

Flacks, R. (1993). The party's over—so what is to be done? *Social Research* 60:445–70.

Foley, L., and Faircloth, C. A. (2003). Medicine as discursive resource: Legitimation in the work narratives of midwives. *Sociology of Health & Illness* 25:165–84.

Fontaine, K. L. (2000). *Healing practices: Alternative therapies for nursing.* Upper Saddle River, N.J.: Prentice Hall.

Fox, M. (1989). *The coming of the cosmic Christ: The healing of mother earth and the birth of a global renaissance.* San Francisco: Harper & Row.

———. (1990). *Creation spirituality: Liberating gifts for the peoples of the earth.* San Francisco: HarperSan Francisco.

Fox, S. (1997). Boomer dharma: the evolution of alternative spiritual communities in modern New Mexico. In F. M. Szasz and R. W. Etulain (Eds.), *Religion in modern New Mexico* (pp. 145–70). Albuquerque: University of New Mexico Press.

Freeman, L. W. (2001a). Homeopathy: Like cures like. In L. W. Freeman and G. F. Lawlis (Eds.), *Mosby's complementary and alternative medicine: A research-based approach* (pp. 345–60). St. Louis: Mosby.

———. (2001b) Massage therapy. In L. W. Freeman and G. F. Lawlis (Eds.), *Mosby's complementary and alternative medicine: A research-based approach* (pp. 361–86). St. Louis: Mosby.

Freeman, L. W., and Lawlis, G. F. (Eds.). (2001). *Mosby's complementary and alternative medicine: A research-based approach.* St. Louis: Mosby.

Freibott, George A. (1990). The history of naturopathy or "pseudomedicalism": Naturopathy's demise. Self-published report. Priest River, Idaho.

Freidson, E. (1970). *Profession of medicine: A study of the sociology of applied knowledge.* New York: Harper & Row.

Freund, P. E. S. (1982). *The civilized body: Social domination, control, and health.* Philadelphia: Temple University Press.

Frohock, F. M. (2002). Moving lines and variable criteria: Differences/connections between allopathic and alternative medicine. *Annals, AAPSS* 583:214–31.

Fulder, S. (1996). *The handbook of alternative and complementary medicine* (3d ed.). Oxford: Oxford University Press.

Fuller, R. C. (1989). *Alternative medicine and American religious life.* New York: Oxford University Press.

———. (2001). *Spiritual, but not religious: Understanding unchurched America.* New York: Oxford University Press.

Gardner, M. (1957). *Fads and fallacies in the name of science.* New York: Dover.

Geertz, A. W. (1997). Native American religions. In J. R. Hinnells (Ed.), *A handbook of living religions* (pp. 542–45). New York: Penguin.

Gesler, W. M., and Gordon, R. J. (1998). Alternative therapies: Why now? In R. J. Gordon, B. C. Nienstedt, and W. M. Gesler (Eds.), *Alternative therapies: Expanding options in health care* (pp. 3–12). New York: Springer.

Glass-Coffin, B. (1994). Anthropology, shamanism, and the "New Age." *Chronicle of Higher Education,* July 15, p. A48.

Glik, D. C. (1986). Psychosocial wellness among spiritual healing participants. *Social Science and Medicine* 22:579–86.

———. (2000). Incorporating symbolic, experiential and social realities into effectiveness research on CAM. In M. Kelner et al. (Eds.), *Complementary and alternative medicine* (pp. 195–208). Amsterdam: Harwood Academic.

Global Directory of MT Schools, US. (2003). Available online: www.qwl.com/mtwc/educ/usa.html; accessed August 10.

Goldner, M. (1999). How alternative medicine is changing the way consumers and practitioners look at quality, planning of services, and access in the United States. *Research in Sociology of Health Care* 16:55–74.

———. (2000). Integrative medicine: Issues to consider in this emerging form of health care. *Research in the Sociology of Health Care* 17:215–36.

Goldstein, M., and Donaldson, P. (1979). Exporting professionalism: a case study of medical education. *Journal of Health and Social Behavior* 20:322.

Goldstein, M. S. (1992). *The health movement: Promoting fitness in America.* New York: Twayne.

———. (1999). *Alternative health care.* Philadelphia: Temple University Press.

———. (2002). The emerging socioeconomic and political support for alternative medicine in the United States. *The Annals of the American Academy of Political and Social Science* 586:44–62.

Goldstein, M. S., et al. (1985). Holistic doctors: Becoming a nontraditional medical practitioner. *Urban Life* 14:317–44.

———. (1987). Holistic physicians: Implications for the study of the medical profession. *Journal of Health and Social Behavior* 28:103–19.

———. (1988). Holistic physicians and family practitioners: Similarities, differences and implications for health policy. *Social Science and Medicine* 26:853–61.

Gordon, J. S. (1980). The paradigm of holistic medicine. In A. C. Hastings, J. Fadiman, and J. S. Gordon (Eds.), *Health for the whole person: The complete guide to holistic medicine* (pp. 3–24). Boulder, Colo.: Westview.

———. (1984). Holistic health centers in the United States. In J. W. Salmon (Ed.), *Alternative medicines: Popular and policy perspectives* (pp. 229–51). New York: Tavistock.

———. (1988). *Holistic medicine.* New York: Chelsea House.

———. (1996). *Manifesto for a new medicine.* Reading, Mass.: Addison-Wesley.

Greene, E. (2000). Massage therapy. In D. W. Novey (Ed.), *Clinician's complete reference to complementary/alternative medicine* (pp. 338–48). St. Louis: Mosby.

Grossinger, R. (1990). *Planet medicine.* Berkeley, Calif.: North Atlantic.

———. (1995a). *Planet medicine: Origins.* Berkeley, Calif.: North Atlantic.

———. (1995b). *Planet medicine: Modalities.* Berkeley, Calif.: North Atlantic.

Gurin, J. (1979). Homeopathy revisited. *Harvard Magazine* (November–December): 12–14.

Hadaway, C. K., Marler, P. L., and Chaves, M. (1993). What the polls don't show: A closer look at U.S. church attendance. *American Sociological Review* 58:741–52.

Hafner, A. W., Carson, J. G., and Zwicky, J. F. (Eds.). (1992). *Guide to the American Medical Association Historical Health Fraud and Alternative Medicine Collection.* Chicago: American Medical Association.

Halcon, L., et al. (2001). Incorporating alternative and complementary health practices within university-based nursing education. *Complementary Health Practice Review* 6(2):127–35.

Halpern, M. (2000). Ayurveda. In D. W. Novey (Ed.), *Clinician's complete reference to complementary/alternative medicine* (pp. 246–57). St. Louis: Mosby.

Hanegraaff, W. J. (1998). *New Age religion and Western culture: Esotericism in the mirror of secular thought.* Albany: State University of New York Press.

Harner, M. (1990). *The way of the shaman.* San Francisco: Harper & Row.

Harries-Jenkins, G. (1970). Professions in organizations. In J. Jackson (Ed.), *Professions and professionalization* (pp. 51–107). London: Cambridge University Press.

Harvard Medical School. (2003). Available online: www.hms.harvard.edu/news/releases; accessed November 29.

Hastings, A. C., Fadiman, J., and Gordon, J. S. (Eds.). (1980). *Health for the whole person: The complete guide to holistic medicine.* Boulder, Colo.: Westview.

Haynes, G. R. (1999). Continuing educational opportunities in complementary medicine. In M. S. Micozzi (Ed.), *Current review of complementary medicine* (pp. 131–38). Philadelphia: Current Medicine.

Herb Research Foundation. (2001). Available online: www.herbs.org/mission.html, p. 1; accessed September 24.

Hess, D. J. (1993). *Science in the New Age: The paranormal, its defenders and debunkers, and American culture.* Madison: University of Wisconsin Press.

———. (1999). *Evaluating alternative cancer therapies: A guide to the science and politics of an emerging medical field.* New Brunswick, N.J.: Rutgers University Press.

———. (2003). CAM cancer therapies in twentieth-century North America: The emergence and growth of a social movement. In R. D. Johnston (Ed.), *The politics of healing* (pp. 231–43). New York: Routledge.

Hoffman, D. L. (1992). *Therapeutic herbalism: A correspondence course in phytotherapy.* Sebastopol, Calif.: Hoffmann.

Homola, S. (1963). *Bonesetting, chiropractic, and cultism.* Panama City, Fla.: Critique Books.

Horrigan, B. (2002). Kenneth R. Pelletier, PhD, MD (hc): Mindbody medicine. *Alternative Therapies* 8(6):91–99.

———. (2003). Michael Lerner, PhD: Medicine and the environment. *Alternative Therapies* 9:81–88.

Hough, H. J., Dower, C., and O'Neill, E. H. (2001). *Profile of a profession: Naturopathic practice.* San Francisco: Center for the Health Professions, University of California.

Hudson, T. (2001). Building bridges between disciplines. In N. Faass (Ed.), *Integrating complementary medicine into health systems* (pp. 262–65). Gaithersburg, Md.: Aspen.

Hui, K., et al. (2002). Introducing integrative East–West medicine to medical students and residents. *Journal of Alternative and Complementary Medicine* 8:507–15.

Hunt, V. (1996). *Infinite mind: Science of the human vibrations of consciousness.* Malibu, Calif.: Malibu.

In honor of holistic medicine pioneer, Evart G. Loomis, M.D. (1910–2003). (2004). Available online: http://holisticmedicine.org/press/evartsloomis.shtml, p. 3; accessed July 26.

Inglehart, R., Basanez, M., and Moreno, A. (1998). *Human values and beliefs: A cross-cultural sourcebook.* Ann Arbor: University of Michigan Press.

Institute for Alternative Futures. (1998). *The future of complementary and alternative approaches (CAAs) in US health care.* New Orleans: Foundation for Chiropractic Education and Research.

Institute of Noetic Sciences. (2003). Available online: www.noetic.org; accessed October 11.

Introduction to Clayton College of Natural Health. (2000). Available online: www .ccnh.edu/introduction.html, p. 1; accessed July 1.

Introvigne, M. (2001). After the New Age: Is there a New Age? In M. Rothstein (Ed.), *New Age religion and globalization* (pp. 58–69). Aarhus, Denmark: Aarhus University Press.

Ivakhiv, A. J. (1997). Red rocks: "Vortexes" and the selling of Sedona. *Social Compass* 44:367–384.

———. (2001). *Claiming sacred ground: Pilgrims and politics at Glastonbury and Sedona.* Bloomington: Indiana University Press.

Ivker, R. S. (2004). Comparing holistic and conventional medicine. (2004). Available online: http://ahha.org/articles/ivker.htm, p. 1; accessed August 4.

Jacobs, J., Chapman, E. H., and Crothers, D. (1998). Patient characteristics and practice patterns of physicians using homeopathy. *Archives of Family Medicine* 7:537–40.

Jain, N., and Astin, J. A. (2001). Barriers to acceptance: An exploratory study of complementary/alternative medicine disuse. *Journal of Alternative and Complementary Medicine* 7:689–96.

Jakobsen, M. D. (1999). *Shamanism: Traditions and contemporary approaches to the mastery of spirits and healing.* New York: Berghahn.

Jensen, C. B. (1997). Common paths in medical education: The training of allopaths, osteopaths, and naturopaths. *Alternative & Complementary Therapies* 3:276–80.

Johnson, S. M., and Kurtz, M. E. (2002). Perceptions of philosophic and practice differences between US osteopathic physicians and their allopathic counterparts. *Social Science and Medicine* 55:2141–48.

Johnson, T. (2000). Complementary and alternative therapies and the question of evidence. *Advances in Mind–Body Medicine* 16:244–60.

Johnston, S. L. (2002). Native American traditional and alternative medicine. *Annals of the American Academy of Political Science and Sociology* 583:195–211.

Jonas, W., and Levin, J. S. (Eds.). (1999). *Essentials of complementary and alternative medicine.* Philadelphia: Lippincott Williams & Wilkins.

Jonas, W. B. (2002). Policy, the public, and priorities in alternative medicine research. *Annals of the American Academy of Political Science and Sociology* 583:29–43.

Kao, F. F., and McRae, G. (1990). Chinese medicine in America: The rocky road to ecumenical medicine. *Impact of Science on Society* 143:263–73.

Kaptchuk, T., and Eisenberg, D. (2001). Varieties of healing. 2: A taxonomy of unconventional healing practices. *Annals of Internal Medicine* 135(3):196–204.

Kaslof, L. J. (Ed.). (1978). *Wholistic dimensions in healing: A resource guide.* Garden City, N.Y: Doubleday.

Katz, M. (2000). Constructing the "good patient" in conventional and unconventional medical settings: Roles, relationships, and information transfer. *Health, Illness, and Use of Care: The Impact of Social Factors* 18:183–206.

Kaufman, M. (1971). *Homeopathy in America: The rise and fall of a medical heresy.* Baltimore: Johns Hopkins University Press.

Keegan, L. (2001). *Healing with complementary and alternative therapies.* Albany, N.Y.: Delmar.

Kelner, M., and Wellman, B. (2000). Introduction. In M. Kelner, B. Wellman, B. Pescosolido, and M. Saks (Eds.), *Complementary and alternative medicine* (pp. 1–24). Amsterdam: Harwood Academic Publishers.

Kirchfeld, F. and Boyle, W. (1994). *Nature doctors: Pioneers in naturopathic medicine.* Portland, Ore.: Medcina Biologica.

Kligman, E. W. (1998). Medical education: changes and responses. In R. J. Gordon, B. C. Nienstedt, and W. M. Gesler (Eds.), *Alternative therapies: Expanding options in health care* (pp. 199–218). New York: Springer.

Koenig, H. G. (1999). *The healing power of faith: Science explores medicine's last frontier.* New York: Simon & Schuster.

Kopelman, L. (1981). The holistic health movement: A survey and critique. *Journal of Medicine and Philosophy* 6:209–35.

Kotarba, J. A. (1975). American acupuncturists: The new entrepreneurs of hope. *Urban Life* 4:149–77.

Kowalak, J. P. (Ed.). (2003). *Nurse's handbook of alternative and complementary therapies* (2d ed). Philadelphia: Lippincott Williams & Wilkins.

Krause, E. A. (1977). *Power and illness: The political sociology of health and medical care.* New York: Elsevier.

———. (1996). *Death of the guilds: Professions, states, and the advance of capitalism.* New Haven, Conn.: Yale University Press.

Kreitzer, M. J., et al. (2002). Attitudes toward CAM among medical, nursing, and pharmacy faculty and students: A comparative analysis. *Alternative Therapies* 8:44–52.

Krueger, A. (2000). New Chopra trial granted because of judge's comments. *San Diego Union-Tribune,* March 16.

Kuhn, M. A. (1999). *Complementary therapies for health care providers.* Philadelphia: Lippincott Williams & Wilkins.

Kurtz, P. (2001). White House Commission on Complementary and Alternative Medicine is biased. *Skeptical Inquirer* (May).

Kyle, R. (1995). *The New Age movement in American culture.* Lanham, Md.: University Press of America.

Lambert, Y. (1996). Denominational systems and religious states in the countries of Western Europe. *Research in the Social Scientific Study of Religion* 7:127–43.

Landmark Healthcare. (1998). *The Landmark Report I.* Sacramento, Calif.: Author.

———. (2000). *The Landmark Report II.* Sacramento, Calif.: Author. Available online: http://landmarkhealthcare.com/summary.htm; accessed November 29, 2003.

Larkin, G. (1983). *Occupational monopoly and modern medicine.* London: Tavistock.

Larry Dossey, M.D. (2003). Available online: www.annonline.com/interviews/961924/biography.html; accessed November 29.

Larson, M. (1979). Professionalism: Rise and fall. *International Journal of Health Services* 9:607–27.

Lau, K. J. (2000). *New Age capitalism: Making money east of Eden.* Philadelphia: University of Pennsylvania Press.

Lawlis, G. F. (2001). Spiritual medicine. In L.W. Freeman and G. F. Lawlis (Eds.), *Mosby's complementary and alternative medicine: A research-based approach* (pp. 473–92). St. Louis: Mosby.

Lawrence, C., and Weisz, G. (1998). Medical holism: The context. In C. Lawrence and G. Weisz (Eds.), *Greater than the parts: Holism in biomedicine, 1920–1950* (pp. 1–22). New York: Oxford University Press.

Lay, M. M. (2000). *The rhetoric of midwifery: Gender, knowledge, and power.* New Brunswick, N.J.: Rutgers University Press.

Ledbetter, C. W. (1927). *The chakras: A monograph.* Wheaton, Ill.: Theosophical.

Lee, A. C. C., Berde, C. B., and Kemper, K. J. (1999). Survey of acupuncturists: Practice characteristics and pediatric care. *Western Journal of Medicine* 171:153–57.

Legan, M. S. (1987). Hydropathy, or the water-cure. In A. Wrobel (Ed.), *Pseudoscience and society in nineteenth-century America* (pp. 74–99). Lexington: University Press of Kentucky.

Legislative update, California Naturopathic Doctors Association. (2003). Available online: www.naturalmedicinenow.org/bill_info.html, p. 1; accessed November 15.

Lemley, B. (1999). Why so many doctors hate Andrew Weil. Available online: www.findarticles.com/cf_0/m1511/8_20/55248815/p1/article.jhtml.

Lerner, M. (1994). *Choices in healing: Integrating the best of conventional and complementary approaches to cancer.* Cambridge, Mass.: MIT Press.

Levin, J. S. (1994). Religion and health: Is there an association, is it valid, and is it causal? *Social Science and Medicine* 38:1475–82.

Levin, J. S., and J. Coreil. (1986). "New Age" healing in the U.S. *Social Science and Medicine* 23:889–97.

Letters to the Editor on Maharishi Ayurveda. (1991). *Journal of the American Medical Association* 266(13):1769–74.

Linde, K., and Jonas, W. B. (1999). Evaluating complementary and alternative medicine: The balance and rigor. In W. B. Jonas and J. S. Levin (Eds.), *Essentials of complementary and alternative medicine* (pp. 57–71). Philadelphia: Lippincott Williams & Wilkins.

Lindlahr, H. (1981). *Natural therapeutics. Volume II: Practice.* Saffron Walden, U.K.: Daniel.

Linton, P. E., Toubman, K. J., and Faass, N. (2001) Designing a healing center: North Hawaii Community Hospital. In N. Faass (Ed.), *Integrating complementary medicine into health systems* (pp. 424–28). Gaithersburg, Md.: Aspen.

Lisa, P. J. (1994). *The assault on medical freedom.* Norfolk, Va.: Hampton Roads.

Long, P. H. (2002). *The naked chiropractor: Insider's guide to combating quackery and winning the war against pain.* Tempe, Ariz.: Evidence-Based Health Services.

Lowenberg, J. S. (1989). *Caring and responsibility: The crossroads between holistic health practice and traditional medicine.* Philadelphia: University of Pennsylvania Press.

Lowenberg, J. S., and Davis, F. (1994). Beyond medicalisation-demedicalisation: The case of holistic health. *Sociology of Health and Illness* 16:579–99.

Luddite, L. (2002). This is anarcho-herbalism: Thoughts on health and healing for the revolution. Available online: www.swsbm.com/HOMEPAGE/Anarchoherbalism .html, pp. 2–3; accessed October 30.

Lundy, M. B., et al. (2001). Hispanic and Anglo patients' reported use of alternative medicine in the medical clinic context. *Complementary Health Practice Review* 6:205–17.

Lyng, S. (1990). *Holistic health and biomedical medicine.* Albany: State University of New York Press.

Lyons, D. B. (2000). *Planning your career in alternative medicine* (2d ed.). New York: Avery.

MacClain, C. (2000). Boost to integrative medicine: Membership group to push Weil's message. *Arizona Daily Star,* September 24. Available online: www.nimc.org/ news/articles/092400_n.asp; accessed November 15, 2001.

MacKenzie, E. R. (1998). *Healing the social body: A holistic approach to public health policy.* New York: Garland.

Maharishi Vedic Medicine. (2000). Available online: www.mum.edu/CMVM/mvm .html; accessed December 12.

Manning, R. (1976). Shamanism as a profession. In A. Bharti (Ed.), *The realm of the extra-human: Agents and audiences* (pp. 73–94). The Hague: Mouton.

Maretzki, T. (1987). The Kur in West Germany as an interface between naturopathic and allopathic ideologies. *Social Science and Medicine* 24:1061–68.

Markell, S. J. (1981). Holistically oriented politics and the Holistic Health Practitioners' Association: A model for personal and social health. In E. Bauman et al. (Eds.), *The holistic health lifebook: A guide to personal and planetary well-being* (pp. 21–25). Lexington, Mass.: Greene.

Marler, P. L., and Hadaway, C. K. (2002). "Being religious" or "being spiritual" in America: A zero-sum proposition. *Journal for the Scientific Study of Religion* 41:289–300.

Marquadt, R., and Burkink, T. (2002). Trends in natural food sales and consumer food choices. *Complementary Health Practice Review* 7:209–20.

Mattson, P. H. (1982). *Holistic health in perspective.* Palo Alto, Calif.: Mayfield.

McGoldrick, N. (1994). Un-frozen caveman doctor. Paper submitted for a course on "Medical Pluralism in North America and Europe," Department of Anthropology, University of California–Berkeley.

McKee, J. (1988). Holistic health and the critique of Western medicine. *Social Science and Medicine* 26:775–84.

McQueen, D. V. (1978). The history of science and medicine as theoretical sources for the comparative study of contemporary medical systems. *Social Science and Medicine* 12:69–74.

———. (1985). China's impact on American medicine in the seventies: A limited and preliminary inquiry. *Social Science and Medicine* 21:931–36.

Mears, D. P., and Ellison, C. G. (2000). Who buys New Age materials? Exploring sociodemographic, religious, network, and contextual correlates of New Age consumption. *Sociology of Religion* 61:289–313.

Mehl-Madrona, L. (1996). *Coyote medicine: Lessons from Native American healing.* New York: Simon & Schuster.

———. (2003). *Coyote healing: Miracles in Native medicine.* Rochester, Vt.: Bear.

Melton, J. G. (1988). A history of the New Age movement. In R. Basil (Ed.), *Not necessarily the New Age* (pp. 35–53). Buffalo, N.Y.: Prometheus.

Melton. J. G., Clark, J., and Kelly, A. A. (1991). *New Age almanac.* New York: Visible Ink.

Mertz, L. (1996). The world's oldest profession—touch therapy—and health care policy. Paper presented at the American Anthropological Association Meeting, November, San Francisco.

Meyer, D. B. (1965). *The positive thinkers.* New York: Doubleday.

Micozzi, M. S. (1996). *Fundamentals of complementary and alternative medicine.* New York: Churchill Livingstone.

——— (Ed.). (2001). *Fundamentals of complementary and alternative medicine* (2d ed.). New York: Churchill Livingstone.

———. (n.d.). Culture, anthropology, and the return of "complementary medicine." *Medical Anthropology Quarterly* 16:398–403.

Midgley, M. (1992). *Science as salvation.* New York: Routledge.

Midwives Alliance of North America. (2003). Direct-entry state laws and regulations. Available online: www.mana.org/laws.html; accessed August 4, 2004.

Milbank Memorial Fund. (1998). Enhancing the accountability of alternative medicine. Available online: www.milbank.org.

Miller, B. W. (1985). Natural healing through naturopathy. *East West Journal* (December):55–59.

Miller, J. F. (1990). "They sure do have some good medicines in here": An ethnographic account of an herb store with a cognitive analysis of illness beliefs of herb users. Unpublished paper, Department of Anthropology, Northern Arizona University, Flagstaff.

Miller, T. (1991). *The hippies and American values.* Knoxville: University of Tennessee Press.

Milton, D., and Benjamin, S. (1999). *Complementary and alternative therapies: An implementation guide.* Chicago: AHA.

Mitchell, B. B. (2002). The professionalization of acupuncture and Oriental medicine in the United States. In C. M. Cassidy (Ed.), *Contemporary Chinese Medicine and Acupuncture* (pp. 375–88). New York: Churchill Livingstone.

Moffet, H. (1996). Acupuncture and Oriental medicine update: Special report: acupuncture education: Focus on the profession. *Alternative & Complementary Therapies* 2:266–69.

Mohr, A. (2001). Mind–body medicine programs in hospital systems. In *Integrating complementary medicine into health systems* (pp. 213–15). Gaithersburg, Md.: Aspen.

Montgomery, S. I. (1993). Illness and image in holistic discourse: How alternative is alternative. *Cultural Critique* 25:65–89.

Moore, J. S. (1993). *Chiropractic in America: The history of a medical alternative.* Baltimore: Johns Hopkins University Press.

Moore, M. (1979). *Medicinal plants of the Mountain West.* Santa Fe: Museum of New Mexico Press.

———. (1989). *Medicinal plants of the desert and canyon West.* Santa Fe: Museum of New Mexico Press.

———. (1993). *Medicinal plants of the Pacific West.* Santa Fe: Red Crane.

More, T. (1997). *Care of the soul: A guide for cultivating depth and sacredness in everyday life.* San Francisco: HarperCollins.

Morgen, S. (2002). *Into our own hands: The women's health movement in the United States, 1969–1990.* New Brunswick, N.J.: Rutgers University Press.

Morton, M., and Morton, M. (1996). *Five steps to selecting the best alternative medicine: A guide to complementary and integrative health care.* Novato, Calif.: New World Library.

Moskowitz, E. S. (2001). *In therapy we trust: America's obsession with self-fulfillment.* Baltimore: Johns Hopkins University Press.

Moyers, B. (1993). *Healing and the mind.* New York: Doubleday.

Murray, T., and Pizzorno, J. E., Jr. (1999). Botanical medicine—A modern perspective. In J. E. Pizzorno Jr. and T. Murray (Eds.), *Textbook of natural medicine* (2d ed., pp. 267–85). New York: Churchill Livingstone.

Nader, L. (1996). The three-cornered constellation: Magic, science, and religion revisited. In L. Nader, *Naked science* (pp. 259–75). New York: Routledge.

National Center for Complementary and Alternative Medicine. (2000a). *Annual report to our stakeholders, 2000.* Bethesda, Md.: National Institute of Health.

———. (2000b). *Expanding horizons of healthcare: Five-year strategic plan 2001–2005.* Bethesda, Md.: National Institutes of Health.

———. (2003a). Distinguished lectures in the science of complementary and alternative medicine. Available online: http://altmed.od.nih.gov/news/lectures/upcoming.htm; accessed June 19.

———. (2003b). What is CAM? Available online: www.nccam.nih.gov/nccam/what-is-cam/fields/alternative.shtml; accessed August 27.

National Center for Homeopathy Education Directory, 2003. (2003). Available online: www.homeopathic.org/edudir03.htm; accessed August 13.

National Institute of Chiropractic Research. (2003). Available online: www.nicr.org; accessed September 23.

Natural healers. (2003). Available online: http://schools.naturalhealers.com/ewsh/html; accessed September 24.

Nauman, E. (2002). Quartz crystal therapy. In D. W. Novey (Ed.), *Clinician's complete reference to complementary/alternative medicine* (pp. 770–78). St. Louis: Mosby.

Nebelkopf. E. (1980). *The new herbalism.* Orem, Utah: BiWorld Press.

———. (1985). Roots of new herbalism. In S. Bliss (Ed.), *The new holistic health handbook: Living well in a new age* (pp. 148–55). Lexington, Mass.: Greene.

Ni, H., Simile, C., and Hardy, A. M. (2002). Utilization of complementary and alternative medicine by United States adults: Results from the 1999 National Health Interview Survey. *Medical Care* 40(4):353–58.

Nienstedt, B. C. (1998). The federal approach to alternative medicine: Co-opting, quackbusting, or complementing? In R. J. Gordon and B. C. Nienstedt (Eds.), *Alternative therapies: expanding options in health care* (pp. 27–43). New York: Springer.

Norris, D. B. (1998). *Illness and culture in the postmodern age.* Berkeley: University of California Press.

North American College of Botanical Medicine. (2003). Available online: www.swep.com/botanicalmedicine/about.htm; accessed September 24.

Novey, D. W. (Ed.). (2000). *Clinician's complete reference to complementary/alternative medicine.* St. Louis: Mosby.

Office of Alternative Medicine, National Institutes of Health. (1992). *Alternative medicine: Expanding medical horizons.* Bethesda, Md.: Author.

Ofshe, R. (1976). Synanon: The people business. In C. Y. Glock and R. N. Bellah (Eds.), *The new religious consciousness* (pp. 116–37). Berkeley: University of California Press.

Orion, L. (1995). *Never again the burning times: Paganism revived.* Prospect Heights, Ill.: Waveland.

Otto, H. A., and Knight, J. W. (1979). Wholistic healing: Basic principles and concepts. In H. A. Otto and J. W. Knight (Eds.), *Dimensions in wholistic healing: New frontiers in the treatment of the whole person* (pp. 3–27). Chicago: Nelson-Hall.

Parenti, M. (1994). *Land of idols.* New York: St. Martin's.

Park, R. L. (2000). *Voodoo science.* New York: Oxford University Press.

Patel, M. S. (1987). Problems in the evaluation of alternative medicine. *Social Science and Medicine* 25:669–78.

Patel, V. (1998). Understanding the integration of alternative modalities. In J. H. Humber and R. F. Almeder (Eds.), *Alternative medicine and ethics* (pp. 45–95). Totowa, N.J.: Humana.

Patton, L., and Faass, N. (2001). Case managed coverage in a managed care environment. In N. Faass (Ed.), *Integrating complementary medicine into health systems* (pp. 358–63). Gaithersburg, Md.: Aspen.

Pearl, D., and Schillinger, E. (1999). Acupuncture: Its use in medicine. *Western Journal of Medicine* 171:176–80.

Pelletier, K. R. (1977). *Mind as healer, mind as slayer: A holistic approach to preventing stress disorders.* New York: Dell.

———. (1978). *Toward a science of consciousness.* New York: Delacorte.

———. (1979). *Holistic medicine: From stress to optimum health.* New York: Delacorte.

———. (2000). *The best of alternative medicine: What works? What does not?* New York: Simon & Schuster.

Pelletier, K. R., and Astin, J. A. (2002). Integration and reimbursement of complementary and alternative medicine by managed care and insurance providers: 2000 update and cohort analysis. *Alternative Therapies* 8(1):38–48.

Pepper, D. (1996). *Modern environmentalism: An introduction.* London: Routledge.

Pizzorno, J. E., Jr. (1996). Naturopathic medicine. In M. S. Micozzi (Ed.), *Fundamentals of complementary and alternative medicine* (pp. 163–81). New York: Churchill Livingstone.

Pizzorno, J. E., Jr., and Snider, P. (2001). Naturopathic medicine. In M. S. Micozzi (Ed.), *Fundamentals of complementary and alternative medicine* (2d ed., pp. 159–92). New York: Churchill Livingstone.

Plant Planet. (2003). Available online: www.plant-planet.net/Voyage_Botanica.htm; accessed October 23.

Plumb, L. D. (1993). *A critique of the human potential movement.* New York: Garland.

Porter, R. (1999). Quacks: An unconscionable time dying. In S. Budd and U. Sharma (Eds.), *The healing bond: The patient–practitioner relationship and therapeutic responsibility* (pp. 63–81). London: Routledge.

Power, C. (1997). Deepak's instant karma. *Time,* October 20, pp. 53–58.

Prince, R., and Riches, D. (2000). *The New Age in Glastonbury: The construction of religious movements.* New York: Berghahn.

Rakel, D., and Weil, A. (2003). Philosophy of integrative medicine. In D. Rakel (Ed.), *Integrative medicine* (pp. 3–9). Philadelphia: Saunders.

Raschke, C. (1988). New age economics. In R. Basil (Ed.), *Not necessarily the New Age: Critical essays* (pp. 328–34). Buffalo, N.Y.: Prometheus.

Ray, P. H. (1996). *The integral culture survey: A study of the emergence of transformational values in America.* Sausalito, Calif.: Institute of Noetic Sciences.

Reddy, S. (2002). Asian medicine in America: The Ayurvedic case. *Annals of the American Academy of Political Science & Sociology* 583:97–120.

Redwood, D. (1995a). Interview with Marc Micozzi, M.D., Ph.D. *Interviews with People Who Make a Difference with Daniel Redwood, D.C.* Available online: www .healthy.net/library/interviews/redwood/micozzi.htm.

———. (1995b). Andrew Weil, M.D.—"Natural health, natural medicine." *Interviews with People Who Make a Difference with Daniel Redwood, D.C.* Available online: www.healthy.net/library/interviews/redwood/micozzi.htm.

Redwood, D., and Chopra, D. (2001). Quantum healing. Available online: www .doubleclickd.com/chopra.html; accessed January 10.

Reed, L. (1932). *The healing cults.* Chicago: University of Chicago Press.

Rees, A. M. (Ed.). (2001). *The complementary and alternative information source book.* Westport, Conn.: Oryx.

Rees, K. (1988). Water as a commodity. In R. Cooter (Ed.), *Studies in the history of alternative medicine* (pp. 28–45). New York: St. Martin's.

Reid, M. (1989). Sisterhood and professionalization: A case of the American lay midwife. In C. S. McClain (Ed.), *Women as healers: Cross-cultural perspectives* (pp. 219–41). New Brunswick, N.J.: Rutgers University Press.

Religious Movements Homepage. (2004). Available online: http://religious movements.lib.virginia.edu/nrms/noetic.html; accessed August 4.

Relman, A. S. (1996). A trip to Stonesville. *New Republic,* December 14, pp. 28–37.

Resources for the Study of Chinese Medicine, Schools and Institutes. (2001, May). Available online: www.itmonline.org/arts/acuskool.htm; accessed August 21.

Resources for the Study of Chinese Medicine—Schools of Acupuncture and Oriental Medicine. (2002, August). Available online: www.itmonline.org/arts/acuskool.htm; accessed November 29, 2003.

Richardson, J. (2002). Evidence-based, complementary medicine: Rigor, relevance, and the swamp lowlands. *Journal of Alternative and Complementary Medicine* 8:221–23.

Riley, S., and Berman, B. (2002). Complementary and alternative medicine in outcomes research. *Alternative therapies* 8(3):36–37.

Rivera, G., Jr. (1988). Hispanic folk medicine utilization in urban Colorado. *Social Science Review* 72:237–41.

Robbins, J. (1996). *Reclaiming our health: Exploding the medical myth and embracing the source of true healing.* Tiburon, Calif.: Kramer.

Rogers, N. (1998). *An alternative path: The making and remaking of Hahnemann Medical College and Hospital of Philadelphia.* New Brunswick, N.J.: Rutgers University Press.

Rooks, J. P. (1997). *Midwifery and childbirth in America.* Philadelphia: Temple University Press.

Rosch, P. J., and Kearney, H. M. (1985). Holistic medicine and technology: A modern dialectic. *Social Science and Medicine* 21:1405–09.

Rosellini, L. (2000). Alternative goes mainstream: Medical schools scramble to add courses on nontraditional therapies. *U.S. News & World Report Online.*

Rosenfeld, I. (1996). *Dr. Rosenfeld's guide to alternative medicine: What works, what doesn't – and what's right for you.* New York: Random House.

Roth, J. A., with R. R. Hanson. (1976). *Health purifiers and their enemies: A study of the natural health movement in the United States with a comparison to its counterpart in Germany.* New York: Prodist.

Rothstein, W. G. (1972). *American physicians in the nineteenth century.* Baltimore: Johns Hopkins University Press.

Ruzek, S. K. 1981. The women's self-help health movement. In P. Conrad and P. Kern (Eds.), *The sociology of health and illness: Critical perspectives* (pp. 563–70). New York: St. Martin's.

Saks, M. (2000). Medicine and complementary medicine: Challenge and change. In G. Scambler and P. Higgs (Eds.), *Modernity, medicine and health: Medical sociology towards 2000* (pp. 198–215). London: Routledge.

Sale, D. M. (1995). *Overview of legislative developments concerning alternative health care in the United States.* Kalamazoo, Mich.: Fetzer Institute.

Salmon, J. W. (1984). Defining health and reorganizing medicine. In J. W. Salmon (Ed.), *Alternative medicines: Popular and policy perspectives* (pp. 252–88). New York: Tavistock.

———. (1985). Profit and health care: Trends in corporatization and proprietization. *International Journal of Health Services* 15:395–418.

Sampson, W., and Vaughn, L. (Eds.). (2001). *Science meets alternative medicine.* Buffalo, N.Y.: Prometheus.

Sanders, P. L. (1989). *Holistic nursing practice* 3(4):38–44.

Scheff, R. (2001). The potential of integrative medicine in disease management. In *Integrating complementary medicine into health systems* (pp. 414–15). Gaithersburg, Md.: Aspen.

Schepers, R. M. J., and Hermans, H. E. G. M. (1998). The medical profession and alternative medicine in the Netherlands. *Social Science and Medicine* 48:343–51.

Schneirov, M., and Geczik, J. D. (1996). A diagnosis for our times: Alternative health's submerged networks and the transformation of identities. *Sociological Quarterly* 37:627–44.

———. (1998). Technologies of the self and the aesthetic project of alternative health. *Sociological Quarterly* 39:435–51.

Schucman, H. C. (1973). *A course in miracles.* New York: Viking.

Sebald, H. (1984). New-Age romanticism: The quest for an alternative lifestyle as a form of social change. *Humboldt Journal of Social Relations* 11(2):105–27.

Shamanic Healing Institute. (2003). Available online: http://shamanic.healing.org./location.htm; accessed October 3.

Shameless Mind. (2004). Deepak bombshell: Plagiarism suit settles. Available online: www.transcenet.org/chopra/new/plagoverview.shtml; accessed August 4.

Sharma, H. (1996). Maharishi Ayurveda. In M. S. Miccozi (Ed.), *Fundamentals of complementary and alternative medicine* (pp. 233–42). New York: Churchill Livingstone.

Sharma, H., and Clark, C. (1998). *Contemporary Ayurveda: Medicine and research in Maharishi Ayur-Veda.* New York: Churchill Livingstone.

Sharma, H. M., Triguna, B. D., and Chopra, D. (1991). Maharishi Ayur-Veda: Modern insights into ancient medicine. *Journal of the American Medical Association* 265(20):2633–37.

Sharma, U. (1992). *Complementary medicine today: Practitioners and patients.* London: Routledge.

Siegel, B. (1986). *Love, medicine and miracles.* New York: Harper & Row.

———. (1989). *Peace, love, and healing: Body/mind communication and the path to self-healing: an exploration.* New York: Harper & Row.

Sierpina, V. S. (2001). *Integrative health care: Complementary and alternative therapies for the whole person.* Philadelphia: Davis.

———. (2003). Progress notes: University of Washington School of Nursing. *Alternative Therapies* 9(2):94–95.

Simonds, W. (1992). *Women and self-help culture: Reading between the lines.* New Brunswick, N.J.: Rutgers University Press.

Skolnick, A. A. (1991). Maharishi Ayur-Veda: Guru's marketing scheme promises the world eternal "perfect health." *Journal of the American Medical Association* 266(13):1741–50.

Skrabanek, P. (1985). Acupuncture: present, past, and future. In D. Stalker and C. Glymour (Eds.), *Examining holistic medicine* (pp. 181–96). Buffalo, N.Y.: Prometheus.

Sloan, R. P., Bagiella, E., and Powell, T. (1999). Religion, spirituality, and medicine. *The Lancet* 353:664–67.

Smith-Cunnien, S. L. (1998). *A profession of one's own: organized medicine's opposition to chiropractic.* Lanham, Md.: University Press of America.

Snook, T. (2001). Considerations in the design and pricing of a complementary and alternative medicine benefit. In N. Faass (Ed.), *Integrating complementary medicine into health systems* (pp. 141–48). Gaithersburg, Md.: Aspen.

Sobel, D. S. (1979). *Ways of health: Holistic approaches to ancient and contemporary medicine.* New York: Harcourt Brace Jovanovich.

Southwest School of Botanical Medicine. (2002). Available online: www.swsbm.com, accessed October 22.

———. (2003). Available online: www.swsbm.com; accessed October 30.

Spangler, D. (1976). *Revelation: The birth of a New Age.* Elgin, Ill.: Lorian.

Spencer, J. W., and Jacobs, J. J. (Eds.). *Complementary/alternative medicine: An evidence-based approach.* St. Louis: Mosby.

Stackel, L. (1998). Are naturopaths the family docs for the 21st century? *Country Living's Healthy Living* 2(3):105–11.

Stalker, D., and Glymour, C. (Eds.). (1985). *Examining holistic medicine.* Buffalo, N.Y.: Prometheus.

Stanford Research Institute. (1960). *Chiropractic in California: A report.* Los Angeles: Haynes Foundation.

Stark, R., and Bainbridge, W. S. (1985). *The future of religion: Secularization, revival, and cult formation.* Berkeley: University of California Press.

Stolberg, S. G. (2001). Red yeast rice redux. In J. E. Brody and D. Grady (Ed.), *The New York Times guide to alternative health: A consumer reference* (pp. 39–44). New York: Holt.

Stone, D. (1976). The human potential movement. In C. Y. Glock and R. N. Bellah (Eds.), *The new religious consciousness* (pp. 93–115). Berkeley: University of California Press.

Sutcliffe, S. J. (2003). *Children of the New Age: A history of spiritual practices.* London: Routledge.

Tacey, D. (2001). *Jung and the New Age.* East Sussex, U.K.: Brunner-Routledge.

Tataryn, D. J. (2002). Paradigms of health and disease: A framework for classifying and understanding complementary and alternative medicine. *Journal of Alternative and Complementary Medicine* 8:877–92.

Taylor, E. (1999). *Shadow culture: Psychology and spirituality in America.* Washington, D.C.: Counterpoint.

———. (2000). Mind–body medicine and alternative therapies at Harvard: Is this the reintroduction of psychology into general medical practice? *Alternative Therapies* 6(6):32–34.

Thompson, C. J. (2003). Natural health discourses and the therapeutic production of consumer resistance. *Sociological Quarterly* 44:81–107.

Torgovnick, M. (1996). *Primitive passions: Men, women, and the quest for ecstasy.* Chicago: University of Chicago Press.

Toufexis, A. (1993). Dr. Jacob's alternative mission. *Time*, March 1, pp. 43–44.

Traugot, M. (1998). The Farm. In W. W. Zellner and M. Pet (Eds.), *Sects, cults, and spiritual communities: A sociological analysis.* Westport, Conn.: Praeger.

Trivieri, L., Jr., and the American Holistic Medical Association. (2001). *The American Holistic Medical Association guide to holistic health: Healing therapies for optimal wellness.* New York: Wiley.

Tyler, L. (2000). *Understanding alternative medicine: new health paths in America.* New York: Haworth Herbal Press.

Ullman, D. (1985). Holistic health: friend and foe of progressive health care. In S. Bliss (Ed.), *The new holistic health handbook: Living well in a new age* (pp. 384–87). Lexington, Mass.: Greene.

———. (1991). *Discovering homeopathy.* Berkeley, Calif.: North Atlantic Books.

University of Virginia College of Nursing. (2003). Center for the Study of Complementary and Alternative Therapies. Available online: www.nursing .Virginia.EDU/centers/alt-ther.html; accessed May 17.

U.S. Department of Education grants CNME national recognition. (2003). Available online: www.naturopathic.org/news; accessed November 15.

Van Hernal, P. J. (2001). A way out of the maze: Federal agency preexemption of state licensing and regulation of complementary and alternative practitioners. *American Journal of Law & Medicine* (Summer–Fall):1–19.

Vatel, V. (1998). Understanding the integration of alternative modalities into an emerging healthcare model in the United States. In J. H. Humber and R. F. Almeder (Eds.), *Alternative medicine and ethics* (pp. 45–95). Totowa, N.J.: Humana.

Vickers, A. (1996). Research paradigms in mainstream and complementary medicine. In E. Edzard (Ed.), *Complementary medicine: An objective appraisal* (pp. 1–30). Oxford: Butterworth-Heinemann.

Waitzkin, H. (2000). *The second sickness: Contradictions of capitalist health care.* Lanham, Md.: Rowman & Littlefield.

———. (2001). *At the frontlines: How the health care system alienates doctors and mistreats patients . . . and what we can do about it.* Lanham, Md.: Rowman & Littlefield.

Walker, M. (1993). *Dirty medicine: Science, big business, and the assault on natural health care.* London: Slingshot.

Walkley, S. (2004). When the body leads the mind: Perspectives on massage therapy in the United States. In K. Oths and S. Hinojosa (Eds.), *Bonesetters: A cross-cultural primer for manual medicine* (pp. 52–85). Walnut Creek, Calif.: AltaMira.

Wallace, A. F. C. (1956). Revitalization movements. *American Anthropologist* 58:264–81.

Walach, H. (2003). Reinventing the wheel will not make it rounder: Controlled trials of homeopathy reconsidered. *Journal of Alternative and Complementary Medicine* 9:7–13.

Wallis, R. (1985). Betwixt therapy and salvation: The changing form of the human potential movement. In R. K. Jones (Ed.), *Sickness and sectarianism: Exploratory studies in medical and religious sectarianism* (pp. 23–49). Brookfield, Vt.: Gower.

Wanjek, C. (2003). *Bad medicine: Misconceptions and misuses revealed, from distance healing to vitamin O.* New York: Wiley.

Wardwell, W. I. (1972). Orthodoxy and heterodoxy in medical practice. *Social Science and Medicine* 6:759–63.

———. (1982). Chiropractors: challengers of medical domination. In J. A. Roth (Ed.), *Research in the sociology of health care.* Vol. 2: *Changing structure of health service occupations* (pp. 207–50). Greenwich, Conn.: JAI.

———. (1992). *Chiropractic: History and evolution of a new practice.* St. Louis: Mosby–Year Book.

Weeks, J. (1999). Insurance coverage for alternative therapies. In M. Micozzi (Ed.), *Current review of complementary medicine* (pp. 107–19). Philadelphia: Current Medicine.

———. (2001). Major trends in the integration of complementary and alternative medicine. In N. Faass (Ed.), *Integrating complementary medicine into health systems* (pp. 4–11). Gaithersburg, Md.: Aspen.

Weil, A. (1980). *The marriage of the sun and moon.* Boston: Houghton Mifflin.

———. (1986). *The natural mind.* Boston: Houghton Mifflin. (Originally published in 1972.)

———. (1995a). *Health and healing.* Boston: Houghton Mifflin. (Originally published in 1983.)

———. (1995b). *Spontaneous healing.* New York: Fawcett.

———. (1996). Foreword. In *Coyote medicine* by L. Mehl-Madrona. New York: Fireside.

———. (1997a) *Eight weeks to optimum health.* New York: Knopf.

———. (1997b). *Your top health concerns.* New York: Ivy.

———. (2000). *Eating well for optimum health.* New York: Knopf.

Weil, A., and Rosen, W. (1983). *Chocolate to morphine: Understanding mind-active drugs.* Boston: Houghton Mifflin.

Weil, A., and Toms, M. (1997). *Roots of healing.* Carlsbad, Calif.: Hay House.

Weitzman, S.M. (1998). Insurance coverage for complementary and alternative medicine. In J. H. Humber and R. F. Almeder (Eds.), *Alternative medicine and ethics* (pp. 127–61). Totowa, N.J.: Humana.

Welcome to Hallmark Naturopath College. (2000). Available online: www .cd-marketing.com/school/index.html; accessed July 1.

Wendel, P. (1951). *Standardized naturopathy: The science and art of natural healing.* Brooklyn, N.Y.: Author.

Westbrook University. (1999). Available online: www.westbrooku.edu/conathea.html, p. 2; accessed June 6.

Westbrook University—A world leader in distance education. (1999). Available online: www.westbrooku.edu/import.htm, p. 3; accessed June 6.

Westbrook University—Registration and tuition cost for degree programs. (1999). Available online: www.westbrooku.edu/tuition.htm, p. 2; accessed June 6.

Westley, F. R. (1983). Ritual as psychic bridge building: Narcissism, healing and the human potential movement. *Journal of Psychoanalytic Anthropology* 6:179–200.

Wetzel, M., et al. (2003). Complementary and alternative therapies: Implications for medical education. *Annals of Internal Medicine* 138:191–96.

What is CCAOM? (2001). Council of Colleges of Acupuncture and Oriental Medicine. Available online: www.CCAOM.org/what_is.htm; accessed September 21.

Wheeler, T. J. (1997). Deepak Chopra and Maharishi Ayurvedic medicine. Available online: www.hcrc.org/contrib/Wheeler/Chopra.html; accessed March 5, 2003.

White House Commission on Complementary and Alternative Medicine. (2002a). Available online: www.whccamp.hhs.gov; accessed December 15.

———. (2002b). *Final report of the White House Commission on Complementary and Alternative Medicine.* Washington, D.C.: U.S. Department of Health and Human Services.

White, M., and Skipper, J. K. (1971). The chiropractic physician: A study of career contingencies. *Journal of Health and Social Behavior* 12:300–6.

Whitlock, E. P. (2001). Use of complementary and alternative medical services by HMO members, 1995–1996. *Complementary Health Practice Review* 7(2):85–98.

Whitman, W. W. (1999). Licensure laws seek to restrict freedoms for naturopaths. Available online: www.anma.net/hereinam.htm, p. 1; accessed November 12.

Whorton, J. C. (1986). Drugless healing in the 1920s: The therapeutic cult of sanipractic. *Pharmacy History* 28:14–25.

———. (2002). *Nature cures: The history of alternative medicine.* New York: Oxford University Press.

Wiese, G., and Ferguson, A. (1985). Historical directory of chiropractic schools and colleges. *Research Forum* 1(3):79–94.

Wild, P. B. (1978). Social origins and ideology of chiropractors: An empirical study of the socialization of the chiropractic student. *Sociological Symposium* 22:33–51.

Wilson, K., and Mills, E. J. (2002). Introducing evidence-based complementary and alternative medicine: Answering the challenge. *Journal of Alternative and Complementary Medicine* 8:103–5.

Williams, P. W. (2002). *America's religions: From their origins to the twenty-first century.* Urbana: University of Illinois Press.

Wolpe, P. R. (1985). The maintenance of professional authority: Acupuncture and the American physician. *Social Problems* 32:409–24.

———. (1994). The dynamics of heresy in a profession. *Social Science and Medicine* 9:1133–48.

———. (1999). Alternative medicine and the AMA. In R. B. Baker (Ed.), *The American medical ethics revolution: How the AMA's code of ethics has transformed physicians' relationships to patients, professionals, and society* (pp. 218–39). Baltimore: Johns Hopkins University Press.

———. (2002). Medical culture and CAM culture: Science and ritual in the academic medical center. In D. Callahan (Ed.), *The role of complementary and alternative medicine: Accommodating pluralism* (pp. 163–71). Washington, D.C.: Georgetown University Press.

York, M. (1995). *The emerging network: A sociology of New Age and neo-pagan movements.* Lanham, Md.: Rowman & Littlefield.

Yoshida, M. (2002). A theoretical model of biomedical professionals' legitimization of alternative therapies. *Complementary Health Practice Review* 7:187–208.

Young, J. H. (1992). *American health quackery: Collected essays.* Princeton, N.J.: Princeton University Press.

Zeff, J. (1996). The future of naturopathic medicine. *The Best of Naturopathic Medicine* 1:59–61.

Zimmerman, M. E. (1994). *Contesting earth's future: Radical ecology and postmodernity.* Berkeley: University of California Press.

Index

About the Author

Hans A. Baer is a visiting senior lecturer in anthropology at the Australian National University and a professor of anthropology at the University of Arkansas at Little Rock. His areas of research interest include critical medical anthropology; medical pluralism in the United States, United Kingdom, and Australia; Mormonism; African American religion; postrevolutionary societies; and sociopolitical life in East Germany. Baer has published eleven books, including *Medical Anthropology and the World System* (with Merrill Singer and Ida Susser), *Biomedicine and Alternative Healing Systems in America*, *Critical Medical Anthropology* (with Merrill Singer), and *Encounters with Biomedicine*. He is serving his second term on the editorial board of *Medical Anthropological Quarterly*.